THE MAIN ISSUES IN BIOETHICS
(Revised)

D0591384

The Main Issues in Bioethics (Revised)

Andrew C. Varga

PAULIST PRESS
New York/Ramsey

Library of Congress
Catalog Card Number: 80–82084

ISBN: 0-8091-2327-4

Published by Paulist Press
545 Island Road, Ramsey, N.J. 07446

Printed and bound in the
United States of America

Contents

v

Preface

Ethics is the study of the rightness or wrongness of human conduct. The general ethical principles gained by this study can be applied to particular areas of human activity. This procedure results in the formation of the different disciplines of specialized ethics, for example, social ethics, political ethics, medical ethics, business ethics, media ethics, etc. *Bioethics* studies the morality of human conduct in the area of the life (*bios* means life in Greek) sciences. Although ethics has been examining human conduct in this area for a long time, bioethics as a special ethical discipline emerged only recently. The rapid growth of knowledge in the life sciences created a great number of ethical problems that called for special study. Bioethics includes medical ethics but it goes beyond the customary ethical problems of medicine because it also examines the various ethical problems of the life sciences which are not primarily medical.

All applications of general ethical principles to particular fields presuppose a cooperation between ethicians and experts in a particular area. In other words, these studies are interdisciplinary. Bioethics, therefore, is an interdisciplinary enterprise.

The rapid progress in the life sciences has stimulated the publication of many books concerned with the bioethical problems. Most of them are monographs and anthologies of articles; there are relatively few which survey all the major problems of bioethics and discuss them in a systematic way. This is only natural when a branch of science experiences an unexpectedly rapid growth.

This book intends to respond to a need for a systematic approach to the major questions of bioethics. Its aim is not only to point out moral questions but also to give answers to them in a consistent manner. The first chapter deals with the criteria of morality that must be used in the analysis of bioethical questions. Without first establishing a sound ethical norm one cannot attempt to give rationally con-

1

sistent answers to bioethical issues. It is not expected that everybody will agree with the natural law approach this work follows. Nevertheless, it is hoped that the reasons presented are worthy of everybody's serious consideration no matter what ethical system one espouses.

A one-volume book cannot exhaustively deal with all the issues of bioethics. The purpose of this work is to discuss all the major bioethical problems concisely and systematically. It is written in a language that students in colleges and professional schools and generally educated persons can easily understand.

Having established the criterion of morality in the first chapter, the bioethical questions are discussed in the sequence of human life: birth, the control of birth, population, the quality of life, reproductive technology, improving human life through genetic engineering and various forms of medical intervention, preserving or restoring mental and physical health and finally facing death. The first part of each chapter provides the relevant scientific background and reports on new developments; the second part analyzes and answers the ethical questions.

Thanks are due to many persons who have encouraged and helped me in writing this book. I want to thank especially Fr. Joseph Murray, S.J., of the Biology Department of Fordham University, for drawing the illustration of gene-splicing; Fr. Martin Hegyi, S.J., of the same department at Fordham University, for advising me on biological matters; and particularly, Dr. Bernard B. Gilligan, of Fordham University, for his expert help and great patience in reading and correcting the final draft of the manuscript.

Preface to the Second Edition

In recent years, the pace of development in the field of bioethics has accelerated. As the first edition of *The Main Issues in Bioethics* was sold out in two and a half years, a new edition has become necessary, one that is not simply a reprint of the first but one that brings the book up-to-date. This new revised edition reports on the many important changes that have taken place in the meantime. In addition, changes have been introduced in the book that make it easy to use as a college text. Questions for review and discussion have been added at the end of each chapter, illustrations have been inserted where they are helpful, and the chapters have been broken up by subtitles. The first chapter, dealing with general moral principles, has not been changed except for a typographical arrangement making for easier readability. Students who desire more detailed treatment of these principles are advised to read my book *On Being Human: Principles of Ethics* (Paulist Press, 1978).

I wish to thank my friends who encouraged and helped me in working on this revised edition. I want to thank especially Dr. Bernard B. Gilligan, of Fordham University, who was kind enough to read the final draft of the manuscript and advised me on corrections, as well as Fr. Andrew Szebenyi, S.J., of the Biology Department of LeMoyne College, and Fr. Martin A. Hegyi, S.J., of the Biology Department of Fordham University, for the fine illustrations they have prepared for this edition.

1 Moral Principles and the Life Sciences

Recent developments in the life sciences have created many unusual situations in which people in a great variety of roles have to make decisions concerning the morality of alternative courses of action. Before considering the moral quality of the different choices that will be discussed in the following chapters, it is necessary for us to have a clear understanding of what morality is and of what moral good or evil means. Whether moral decisions take place in customary or unusual circumstances, we must be guided by valid ethical principles. Otherwise our moral discernment will lack any solid basis and the opposing opinions will fail to motivate a logical assent.

This introductory chapter on the moral principles to be applied in the life sciences must be limited to the fundamental problems of ethics. The reader who wants a more detailed treatment of these principles is advised to study some of the works that deal exclusively with the basic questions of ethics.[1]

The Good

What is meant by calling something morally good or morally bad? We use words to signify reality. Various languages agree to use different words to stand for a specific reality so that we can communicate with one another. Words are symbols that are substituted for reality, for example, a horse, a tree, the moon, the sun, etc. Now, the term good also stands for a reality. This reality, however, is not perceived as easily as a tree or a horse. Truth, justice, beauty, goodness are terms that express realities that definitely mean something for us. We may have very strong convictions about these realities and yet we find it difficult to describe them clearly. Philosophers try to determine clearly the reality behind these words. Throughout history they have given us a number of definitions of these terms. Some of them are opposed to each other, but in the case of moral goodness many agree on certain common factors that are proposed as essential elements of it. A brief survey of the most important views on the subject will be given here in the hope that a comparison of different moral systems will help us to find the one that is convincing.

The Natural Good

What is the reality denoted by the term moral good? Before answering this question, it will be helpful for us to examine *the most general meaning of the term good*. When the farmer states that the rain is good, he is relating the goodness of the rain to the growth of his crop. Too much rain would be bad because it would cause the plants to rot. The skier considers abundant snowfall good because it enables him to go skiing. The driver of a car, however, will hold it bad because it makes his commuting to his job more difficult. Moderate physical exercise is judged good because it contributes to our health. Too much physical exertion, on the other hand, may be bad because it weakens our health. We can conclude that in these instances good means any action or any object that contributes to the attainment of some desirable goal. This goal can be self-chosen as skiing, or given by nature, as health or the growth of a plant. This consideration indicates that goodness is based on and constituted by a special relationship.

One can explore further, however, the meaning of the term good. The farmer may call his crop good, and this without reference to his monetary gain or winning a prize. His crop is good when it grows to the fullness of its capacity, when it "fulfills" its nature. A car is judged good when all its parts are in order and are functioning properly according to plan. The crop and the car are considered in themselves, in terms of whether they are complete and have attained the fullness of their nature or design. One could say that their actual reality is being compared with their ideal nature and is being judged as to whether it has come close to it or has reached it. This kind of good is called *natural good*.

The Moral Good

In ethics we are interested in the goodness of man, and not in the goodness of plants or machines. The term moral good is used for the specifically human good. A good man is a person who is good in his humanity and not just in some skill, for instance, in sport or surgery. A great sportsman is not necessarily a good man. There is also general agreement that we are not born morally good or bad but grow up to be good or bad persons by performing good or bad acts. A specifically human act differs from the actions of animals by the fact that it is done deliberately, that is, with freedom of choice and with the knowledge of the object of the act. The result of a free and conscious act is responsibility; the act is imputed to the free agent. A court will acquit an accused person if it is proved that he was not a free and knowing agent concerning a particular violation of law.

The question remains: if we become good persons by performing goods acts, *what is the particular quality of the human act that makes it good or bad?* We have seen above that objects or actions are considered good, in general, if they contribute to the growth of a being, helping it to achieve the totality of its being. We are not born complete persons but as incomplete human beings with a number of characteristic potentialities. We can then try to achieve the ideal perfection of humanity as we grow up. Some actions are considered to increase our humanity; other actions, on the contrary, are seen as diverting us from becoming well-balanced, perfect persons. Courtesy and truthfulness, for example, help us to get along with others in the kind of social cooperation that is necessary for our growth as human beings. Lack of self-control, antisocial behavior, lying, living by thievery, on the other hand, degrade us in our humanity.

The central issue for ethical judgment is to find a criterion by which to determine what actions contribute to the achievement of the fullness of our humanity, what actions make us more of a human being or, in other words, what kind of actions are morally good. Ethical theories, developed throughout the centuries, are distinguished from one another by the criterion of morality they explicitly or implicitly profess. These criteria in some way always refer in turn to a theory of what man is in his humanity. We turn now to a consideration of the main ethical criteria proposed by different philosophers that are relevant to our search for a valid standard of morality.

Morality and Emotions

Many people judge the goodness or badness of actions by their likes or dislikes. Their emotions and feelings determine what they consider good or bad. A philosophically sophisticated variety of this approach was proposed by Alfred Jules Ayer (born in 1910) in his *Emotive Theory*. Morality according to this theory would be subjective, as it would depend on the varying feelings and emotions of the acting person. A moral statement has no rational basis because it is simply an expression of an emotional reaction. Charles L. Stevenson (born in 1908) holds, however, that the emotional content of moral judgments is not entirely irrational. We can find some reasons for our likes and dislikes, and thus our moral judgments have an objective foundation.

It seems to me that a purely emotional reaction as the basis of moral judgment cannot be a satisfactory criterion of morality. Emotional attitudes do not make an act good or bad. If this were true, the gangster, the rapist and the thief could claim that they are performing good acts. If it is maintained, as Stevenson does, that our moral reactions, our likes and dislikes, have a rational basis, this rational foundation still has to be shown in order to arrive at a valid criterion of morality. It seems that this search would lead us to the objective wants and needs of human nature. As a result, the view that subjective emotional reaction is the basis of moral judgments must be discarded.

Intuitionism

The *intuitionist* theory of ethics holds that the morally good or bad act can be recognized by all normally developed persons. It is claimed that we have an intellectual insight into the goodness or badness of an act but we cannot give reasons why an act is good or bad. Good is a simple concept that cannot be broken into component parts. Ethical systems that define the good in terms of something else commit the *"naturalistic fallacy,"* as *George Edward Moore* (1873–1958) stated. According to him, these systems confuse ethical facts with natural facts as they identify the good with either pleasure or the useful or self-fulfillment. They do not explain, however, what makes pleasure or self-fulfillment good. They only define the good objects. They do not define the predicate "good" itself. The intuitionists hold that the good cannot be defined, but that it still can be known, just as we cannot define the color yellow and yet we know what yellow is.

The intuitionist theory may be attractive for its directness and simplicity, but it leaves many problems unsolved. Whose intuition is correct and should be followed when there are conflicting opinions? Can we be trained to exclude the influence of selfishness, public opinion and other extraneous factors in trying to have a genuine intuition of the good without any distortion? The basic assumption of intuitionism is that things can be defined only by analysis of their component elements. Many realities, however, are the result of relations and can be defined and known by their relations to other things. Justice, faithfulness and goodness are determined by relations and are the effect of certain relations. The goodness of the human act, too, can be determined by its dynamic relation to the growth of a human being in his humanity. This relation is a peculiar reality and can explain the goodness of the act.

Moral Positivism

Moral positivism is a widely held theory that morality is not determined by the nature of an act but by extrinsic factors. Morality is made and not discovered. This doctrine has a long history. One of its formulations is the *social-contract theory*. In order to live in peace and security, individuals leave it to public authority to determine what actions should be prescribed and what actions should be forbidden. Individuals enter into a contract, as it were, with the government to obey its orders in exchange for peace, order and security. The origin of good and evil can be traced back in some way to such a social contract. Morality is made by this positive factor which is extrinsic to the nature of the act. The fact that something is prescribed or forbidden makes it good or bad. In the religious field this positivist theory holds that certain actions are good because God commands them and other actions are bad because God forbids them. In this theory God would be arbitrarily free to determine what actions should be good and what actions should be bad. Lying would be bad because

God prohibits it and not because the nature of a lie is such that it contradicts man's drive for truth and need for social cooperation.

The Power of the State

According to positivism, the power of the state to enforce laws has become the basis and origin of morality. In the international field, too, might makes right. Whatever a stronger nation is able to acquire becomes its legal and moral possession.

Today many individuals give a slightly different formulation of moral positivism when they state that morality is determined by the "way of life" of a certain society or nation, by public opinion, by the will of the majority. As the way of life and public opinion change, so does morality. What the majority does becomes the standard of morality. Premarital sex, for instance, was considered morally bad not so long ago, but the "attitude" and opinion of the majority has changed, and so premarital sex becomes morally acceptable. Ultimately, social customs and "mores" determine what is right or wrong.

Challenge to Moral Positivism

The ethical doctrine of moral positivism, under various names, was widely accepted by many individuals and international organs until World War II occurred. The great changes caused by the war produced a gradual transformation of opinion concerning the basic tenets of moral positivism. Many individuals challenged the right of governments to legislate in an arbitrary way and rejected even the validity of the majority decisions of parliaments if they conflicted with basic human rights. They affirmed that slavery is morally bad even if a majority can enforce it; depriving a minority of its basic human and civil rights is evil even if the majority can uphold discrimination by military and police power. Reform movements that spread all over the world after the war emphasized that governments have no right to pass laws that are contrary to a fundamental law of humanity, because that law is more basic than man-made statutes and is alone the original determining force of right and wrong. Morality, then, is discovered by studying the fundamental needs and existential goals of man. In these respects we are all equal, and no man-made law can validly contradict our natural ends and prevent us from working for the fulfillment of our existential goals. The task of legislation is to help the implementation of this fundamental law. No positive law may be arbitrary, as no parliament could pass laws approving murder, lying and theft without destroying the very foundation of a nation. In other words, morality is natural rather than conventional.

In the post-war period many persons, both young and old, joined movements or adopted attitudes that rejected the tenets of moral positivism with almost a revolutionary fervor. Paradoxically, however, the same persons are sometimes swayed by shifting public opinion and fads in their own moral lives. Thus while moral positivism has lost its influence in many areas of human enterprise, it still prevails in the moral life of many individuals.

Legislation and Moral Positivism

Moral positivism holds that morality is made by factors that are extrinsic to the act, but the followers of this theory are forced to abandon their basic thesis when it comes to practical applications. Legislators, for instance, have to examine the *nature* of a proposed act from the viewpoint of its intrinsic ability to promote human well-being. They are compelled to look for the good in the nature of the act. Even public opinion is based on either a correct or a mistaken understanding that certain actions and practices are apt by their nature to promote or hinder the well-being of man, whatever they may consider that well-being to be.

Hedonism

There are a number of ethical theories, however, that explicitly designate some intrinsic aspect of a human act as the criterion of its moral goodness or badness. *Hedonism* is one of these theories. As an ethical system it goes back to ancient Greece. *Aristippus* (ca. 435–ca. 356 B.C.) and his followers are believed to have held that an act is good when it is capable of producing sense pleasure (*hedone* in Greek), which they identified with happiness. According to the hedonists, happiness is undoubtedly the goal of man, and it is logical to hold that the goodness of an act is determined by its intrinsic property, i.e., pleasure, that takes us closer to the end of man. The good is a means for the fulfillment of man in happiness. Actions that produce pain and disturb our happiness are considered morally bad. Seeking sense pleasure immoderately, however, may cause pain and boredom. The wise man knows how to exercise sufficient self-control so that he will not become a slave of pleasure, which would be a painful experience.

Epicurus (314–270 B.C.), like Aristippus, identified the goal of man with pleasure. But he emphasized rational pleasures that are more enduring than sense pleasures. Rational pleasure consists in peace of mind, friendship and harmonious living with one's fellow human beings. Acts that have the ability to increase our tranquility of soul or intellectual pleasure are morally good and should be sought. Acts that disturb our peace of mind are bad and should be avoided.

Utilitarianism

Modern *utilitarianism* is the further development and refinement of the hedonistic ethical theory. Its main exponents were *Jeremy Bentham* (1748–1832) and *John Stuart Mill* (1806–1873). Utilitarianism accepts as self-evident that all men act to gain pleasure or to avoid pain. Pleasure is identified with happiness, and the goal of human acts is to achieve the greatest possible happiness. The task of ethics is to find out what kind of acts increase our happiness. The actions that increase our happiness are morally good and obligatory by the very nature of man, who necessarily seeks happiness. Acts are judged good or bad according to their consequences of producing happiness or pain. Bentham called the property of the act that produces happiness "utility." Hence the theory is named utilitarianism.

Bentham held that all pleasures can be measured quantitatively. The different kinds of pleasures can be reduced to units of pleasure, and thus it is possible to calculate the greatness of happiness. The task of ethics is to help us choose those actions that produce the greatest happiness. Men are basically selfish, but they are compelled to consider the happiness of other persons too because they need the cooperation of their fellow human beings for their own happiness. Thus the morally good act is that which produces the greatest happiness of the greatest number of people.

Mill accepted the basic principles of Bentham's utilitarianism but rejected the opinion that all pleasures can be measured quantitatively. Pleasures differ qualitatively, and we should strive to have pleasures that befit rational human beings rather than animals. He also emphasized the social character of happiness more than did Bentham. The goal of moral actions is not just one's own happiness but the greatest happiness of all members of society.

Act Utilitarianism and Rule Utilitarianism

Act utilitarianism and *rule utilitarianism* are further refinements of the utilitarian theory. *Act utilitarianism* considers the ability of individual acts to promote the greatest happiness of individuals or the greatest happiness of the greatest number of people. *Rule utilitarianism*, on the other hand, deals with universal laws and tries to establish rules that are capable of promoting the greatest happiness of the greatest number of people. The rule-utilitarian insists that laws are universally binding and no exceptions are allowed because exceptions would ultimately disturb the social order. Even the person who tried to increase his own happiness by the exception would be hurt by the weakening of the social order.

Utilitarianism is professed by many persons either in its sophisticated, philosophical form or, more frequently, as a practical guide in moral decisions. It is attractive to hold that any action is good that contributes to the happiness of everybody or at least of the greatest possible number of people. What could be wrong with that?

Evaluation of Utilitarianism

There are a number of problems with the utilitarian ethical theory. One could question even the starting point. Is it true that all our conscious and deliberate actions seek pleasure? Are pleasure and good the same thing? If we necessarily seek pleasure in some way and pleasure is equated with good, all our actions would be good. It seems, however, that pleasure and good cannot simply be identified. In addition, Bentham's theory that all pleasures, even rational pleasures, can be quantitatively measured has been abandoned by modern utilitarians. Nevertheless, they affirm that we can calculate in some way how much our actions can contribute to the happiness of people, and we are obliged to choose that way of action which produces the best results. The rule-utilitarians will especially insist that it is a rational procedure to examine possible ways of action and determine those rules which promote the greatest well-being and happiness of the greatest number of people.

Justice and Utilitarianism

Rules, however, that aim at producing the greatest well-being of the greatest number of people may neglect or even violate the interests and happiness of a minority or even a sizable part of society. The utilitarians' answer to this objection is that such a rule would not be moral because it would violate the just and equitable distribution of goods. But this answer contradicts the moral criterion of utilitarianism because it appeals to a more fundamental standard, namely justice.

Happiness and Utilitarianism

Utilitarians will emphasize that people in general can estimate what actions promote happiness and are, therefore, morally good. There are a number of suppositions here. It is presupposed that everybody knows what happiness or the well-being of man is, and that everybody understands it the same way. If every individual could propose his own interpretation as a valid criterion of morality, we would end up with a chaotic and totally subjective moral system. The utilitarians are obviously against such a system. Rule-utilitarianism intends to eliminate exactly this subjective interpretation of morality. It follows from this analysis that the utilitarians tacitly presuppose that all human beings become happy the same way and have the same interests; somehow we all know what happiness and the best interests of men are. But it seems that the best interests of men are not always served by pleasant acts; Mill himself admitted that it is "better to be a human being dissatisfied than a pig satisfied." The tacit presupposition of the utilitarians is that we have some idea of the universal character of human nature and we know how this nature can be fulfilled. Thus it seems that the utilitarians go beyond their explicitly advocated norm of pleasure or satisfaction, for they implicitly appeal to human nature as the standard of morality.

Natural-Law Ethics

Many ethical theories turn directly to human nature as the criterion of morality. The common element of these theories is the position that we are born incomplete human beings but that we have specific potentialities which enable us to bring our nature closer to its fulfillment or completion and thus become good persons. Hence these systems are called *self-realization theories*. The moral good for the individual consists in actions that bring him as close to the ideal of human nature as possible. We are obliged by our very nature to build the genuinely human in us and avoid actions that are "dehumanizing." We have a number of potentialities that are the exclusive characteristics of human beings. Ethics has the task to study and clarify these characteristics in order to determine what is genuinely human and hence morally good.

Plato (ca. 429–347 B.C.) assumed that there is a world of "ideal forms" which are the perfect archetypes of every species of being. All things on earth participate in the ideal forms by resembling them more or less closely. There exists also an archetype or ideal form of man. Our intellect connects us somehow with this ideal form and indicates to us how we have to approach the perfect nature of man. The morally good life consists in developing our nature so that it resembles more and more the ideal form of man.

Aristotle (384–322 B.C.) rejected Plato's theory of a concretely existing world of ideal forms. According to him, universal ideas or essences of things do not exist separately but they are realized in every

concretely existing being. The essence of a being is a real principle
that makes a being what it is. The essence or nature of a being is the
cause and source of its activities. All beings can be classified according to their specific essence or nature: we recognize beings according
to their specific natures. We cannot see or touch the natures of
things, but we can conclude to their existence from their activities.
We perceive the growth and specific activities of different kinds of
beings, and we know that there must be an energy, a cause that explains these operations. The effects must have a cause. An acorn always grows into an oak tree, an apple tree bears apples and not
cherries. Aristotle called the source of the specific activities of beings
substantial form. Modern science is based on the assumption that the
dynamic nature of things explains their operations, actions and reactions. Scientific research tries, in its own way, to penetrate the
mysteries of the nature of things: what it is that makes gold gold and
uranium uranium, can we change the basic nature of things, can we
produce new kinds of beings by reaching down to the center of beings
and manipulating their properties?

Aristotle held that human beings have a specific nature as all
beings do. The great difference between us and other kinds of beings
is that we have intellect and free will, while other beings are driven
by blind forces and instincts. Man is free in many of his activities and
can freely act according to his rational nature or go against it; he can
act in a human or in an inhuman way. The morally good act is that
which freely builds the genuinely human in us and brings us closer
to our self-realization. Acts that are in conformity with our nature
are the morally good acts.

This theory, refined and further explained by other philosophers, has become known as *natural-law ethics or teleological ethics*
(from the Greek word *telos* which means goal). It is an ethic that aims
at bringing man closer to his goal or fulfillment.

Human Nature

In the concrete application of this theory a great deal will depend
on our understanding of what man really is. One frequently hears
the objection that human nature is so complex that it is difficult to

know it well enough to use it as a practical guide in determining the morality of actions. One can admit that man is a complex being. Nevertheless, we can safely state that we know enough about our nature to take it as a practical criterion; its main existential drives and goals are the object of our direct experience. Nothing is closer to us than our own nature. We know our needs, the requirements for decent human living without much philosophical reflection. We experience that our individual material and intellectual needs are greater than our individual power to satisfy them. This experience leads us to the acceptance of the moral necessity of social cooperation, the recognition of the exigency of mutual trust and truthfulness, the acknowledgment of parental and legitimate civil authority. We understand that we have to respect the life and bodily integrity of our fellow men, to be faithful in marriage, to keep promises and agreements, to respect the rightful property of others. Throughout history the human race has had a remarkable agreement about the basic principles of morality and the requirements of justice. It seems that men always have had a natural insight into the main characteristics of human nature and what it really means to be human, that is, to act in conformity with our nature and thus lead a morally good life. Non-free beings must act according to their nature and, consequently, the question of responsibility and morality does not apply to them. Man, being free, can act in conformity with his nature or can go against it; he can conduct himself as a social being or can act antisocially. Our dynamic nature, striving for the fullness of human life, makes us understand that we ought to act in a human way. In other words, we grasp the moral imperative to do the good and avoid the evil.

Human Nature and the Life Sciences

Some critics might remark that human nature may be a practical criterion in the simple and obvious moral questions of our lives but that it cannot be used for moral decisions related to the intricate new developments of science. It is willingly admitted that the task is not easy. Full clarity is not always easily obtained and can be gained only after lengthy study and research. This fact explains the tentative and sometimes contradictory answers of even experienced ethicians. Nonetheless, human nature can be our guiding principle in these cases, too, as we try to find the truly human way of action and the requirement of humanness in these particular instances. All branches of the human sciences can assist us in our effort to discover what truly human conduct is. The terms "humanizing" and "dehumanizing" are frequently used in recent literature in this regard. Discerning what is humanizing or dehumanizing will not always be a simple and easy task, since dynamic human nature cannot be measured physically or placed under a microscope. Notwithstanding the laboriousness of the task, it seems that this is the best way to clarify moral problems and arrive at a judgment of what is in conformity with our humanness, what befits human beings and, consequently, is the right way to act.

Throughout this work human nature will be used as the criterion when the morality of certain actions or practices has to be determined. A critical analysis of the various aspects of our humanness will be undertaken concerning the more obscure factors of our nature to see what course of action contributes to the building of the genuinely human in us. The totality of our nature has to be taken into consideration, however, because man is more than just his bodily or biological functions. In this regard all the various human sciences contribute to our understanding of what man is. With the advance of these sciences our knowledge of human nature increases and, consequently, our ethical judgments will improve, too.

The Golden Rule and Human Nature

The *Golden Rule*, "Treat others as you would like to be treated by them," is often recommended as the best and most practical criterion of morality. Most religions incorporate this as a basic precept among their moral principles. The Golden Rule is certainly a convenient practical guide in our daily moral decisions. It presupposes, however, that we all have the same nature, the same needs and desires. Otherwise the principle could not be applied and could hurt those whose tastes and wishes might be different from ours. Thus the Golden Rule basically appeals to a uniform human nature as the objective norm of morality. It also indicates the belief that we can easily recognize the major constitutive elements of human nature, as we have direct experience of our existential drives and goals.

Situation Ethics

Finally we should mention the theory of *situation ethics* that has become fashionable since World War II. Its clearest and most explicit form is based on the existentialist philosophy of *Jean Paul Sartre.* He took a stand against essentialist philosophy and held that our nature is not given to us by a great designer, God, because he does not exist. There is no fixed human nature that would bind us to a certain way of action. What man makes of himself depends entirely on his free actions. Man creates values freely according to his varying circumstances and situations. Morality is, then, subjective and changeable. The morally good act is the one that is freely performed and takes into consideration the actual situation.

If such a theory were accepted without any restrictions, it is obvious that no order could be maintained in society and no organized state could function. This objection forced Sartre to admit that a "universal situation of man" has to be taken into consideration before everything else and that this must be the basis of other decisions. The universal situation of man is that he must work in order to live; that he necessarily lives among other human beings; that he is necessarily in this world; and he is mortal. With these restrictions, however, Sartre actually returned to human nature as the basis of objective morality and implicitly admitted what he explicitly had denied.

The Role of Conscience

Before concluding this brief survey of the criteria of morality, we have to mention the role of *conscience* in forming a moral judgment. Many persons simply state that they follow their conscience when they are faced with a moral decision and do not turn to any of the elaborate criteria mentioned above. It is a generally accepted prin ciple that the good person lives according to his conscience. The principal moral law obliges us to listen to the "voice of conscience" and live according to our honest conviction.

What Is Conscience?

Few moralists would argue about this. This position, however, becomes more complex when we begin to consider the meaning of conscience and the "voice of conscience." Conscience is not a mysterious entity within us. It is our intellect passing judgment on the rightness or wrongness of an action. "My conscience tells me" means that I judge this or that action to be good or bad. The formulation of a judgment, however, always presupposes some criteria according to which we come to our conclusions. As most people are taught from childhood by their parents, the school system, their church and public opinion what actions are good or bad, the "voice of conscience," that is, the formation of a moral judgment, comes quickly and easily in the customary cases of everyday life. A number of ethical principles are readily available in our memory and we quickly apply them to concrete and particular cases almost without any reflection. When we are faced with the possibility of taking a towel from a hotel room, for instance, our "conscience tells us" that stealing is wrong and this particular action would be a theft and that consequently it would be wrong to take the towel.

Conscience and the Norm of Morality

It seems that this analysis of conscience throws us back again to the problem of the criterion of morality. Why do we judge certain actions good or bad? Were we taught correctly in our childhood as to the morality of certain actions? Moral maturity means that we examine the ethical principles we were given in the early years of our life, questioning whether they are correct or not. If we find them justified, we will follow them in the future on the basis of our own intellectual conviction and not because of the force of external authority. The process of examining our previously learned moral principles is nothing else but the application of our criterion of morality to the different problems of human life.

The Rules of Conscience

It follows from the nature of conscience that the main law of moral living obliges us to live according to our honest conviction or, in other words, to follow our certain conscience. The certitude of conscience means that we have no reasonable ground to fear that our judgment as to the morality of an act is incorrect. This does not exclude possible mistakes, but this is the only human way to prepare for action. We are obliged to seek truth honestly and with good will. Any error that might then occur would be due to our fallible, finite reasoning ability. The error would not be deliberately and freely willed and thus what may be an objectively evil act would not come under our responsibility.

Ethicians call conscience the subjective norm of morality, in opposition to other criteria, which are called objective norms. It seems obvious that the inescapable drive of our intellect to discover the truth obliges us to bring our conscience into conformity with objective truth as much as is humanly possible. Ultimately, however, it is always the acting human being who knows whether he is acting in good faith and following his sincere conviction or is just lining up false reasons for his conduct. We are judged by our own conscience.

When we discuss various ethical questions in the following chapters, we do not exclude the possibility that somebody can honestly disagree with our conclusion and thus can perform in good faith an act which we think is morally objectionable. The purpose of these ethical analyses is not to condemn persons who follow their honest convictions, but rather to examine the correctness of the reasons upon which moral judgments rest.

Means and Ends

How can we go about the task of comparing the criterion of morality with our acts in order to arrive at an ethical judgment? A human act is a complex entity. It is customary to distinguish in it the object, the motive, the circumstances and the foreseen or unforeseen consequences. Works dealing with the basic principles of ethics explain the procedure of comparing these elements of the act with the norm of morality. "The end does not justify the means" is a principle that is often quoted in connection with this procedure. It means that a good motive does not change the basic wrongness of an act. We are not allowed to murder innocent persons or to skyjack an airplane to call the attention of the world to the violation of human rights in our native country. A good intention does not justify the performance of an act that by its object is inhuman, that is, morally wrong.

The Principle of Double Effect

In judging the morality of an act that has foreseen bad consequences, the *principle of double effect* may be helpful in some cases. The rules of this principle have been developed by moralists who generally followed the natural-law tradition. The phrase "double effect" signifies that the act in question has two effects, one good and the other bad. According to the rules of this principle, an act that has foreseen good and bad consequences may be performed under the following conditions:

(1) the act to be performed is good or at least indifferent by its object;

(2) the good and evil effects follow immediately from the act, i.e., the good effect is not obtained by means of the evil effect;

(3) one only intends the good effect and merely tolerates the bad effect;

(4) there is a proportion between the good and bad effects, i.e., the good must outweigh the bad or, at least, must be equal to it.

The following diagram may be useful in the analysis of a case:

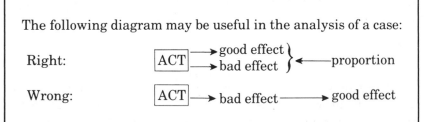

An oft-mentioned example is a surgical operation on the cancerous uterus of a pregnant woman. The operation has two results, the saving of the woman's life and the death of the fetus. Both are caused immediately by the surgery, since the death of the fetus is not the means by which the mother's life is saved; it is the operation that saves her. Only the good effect is intended; death of the fetus is not the purpose of the operation. There is proportion between the effects, as life is here compared with life.

One has to be careful about the use of the principle of double effect, however, because it cannot easily be applied to every moral dilemma. The application of the criterion of morality to concrete cases requires a careful analysis, and sometimes a prolonged study of an act's consequences is needed.

We turn now to the consideration of the main ethical issues in the life sciences.

QUESTIONS FOR REVIEW AND DISCUSSION

1. What do words, as symbols, stand for? How would you describe the reality that is expressed by the word "good"?

2. What is the difference between natural and moral good?

3. Explain the concept of standard or criterion in general and as it is referred to morally.

4. Is morality constituted by factors extrinsic to human acts or is it discovered in the nature of an act?

5. Explain the following statement: The moral good is fundamentally determined by the objective reality of human nature, and not by emotions, pleasure, utility or the arbitrary decisions of governments. Do you agree or disagree with this statement? Why?

6. By what arguments can you validate the principle of double effect?

Note

1. A concise discussion of basic ethical principles can be found in my *On Being Human: Principles of Ethics*. New York: Paulist Press, 1978.

2   Population and Moral Responsibility

According to the United States Bureau of Census, the estimated population of the world in mid-June of 1983 was 4,721,887,000 people.

Demographers who study the trends of population growth, relying on certain facts of history, try to give us an account of how the world population has grown to this number. The Old Testament mentions two censuses (Numbers 1:2; 1 Chronicles 21). There were real estate and agricultural censuses taken in Babylonia, and population censuses also were conducted in ancient Persia, China and Egypt. Rome counted its citizens every five years, and censuses were taken every fourteen years in the whole of the Roman Empire. Such a census is described in the New Testament (Luke 2:1–7). It seems that the counting of people for various purposes continued in the Roman Empire until its collapse. Many of the census documents written on papyri have been well preserved in the dry dust-heaps of Egypt. Taking these and other documents and historical facts into account, demographers estimate that there were about

- 250 million people in the world at the time of the birth of Christ

- 400 million in 1492, the time of the discovery of America

- 850 million in 1776, the year of the Declaration of Independence

- 1 billion in 1830, at the beginning of the Industrial Revolution

- 1.55 billion in 1900

- 2 billion in 1930

- 2.5 billion in 1950

- 3 billion in 1960

- 4 billion in 1975

- 4.41 billion in 1980

- 4.72 billion in 1983

Population Growth

The annual rate of growth, the difference between the number of births and the number of deaths, at the dawn of history must have been very low. It took about sixteen hundred years to double the estimated 250 million people at the time of the birth of Christ. But it took only one hundred years, from 1830 to 1930, to double the world's population from 1 billion to 2 billion. Then it took only thirty years to add one more billion by 1960, and only fifteen years to add another billion by 1975. It is projected that it will take twelve years to add the fifth billion by 1987, and only eleven years to add the sixth billion by 1998.

As can be seen, the rate of growth has gradually increased in the last 150 years, rapidly accelerating after World War II until it reached almost 2% in the 1960's. Two percent annual growth means the doubling of the world population every thirty-five years. If the annual rate of growth is constant the size of the actual population can be calculated by applying the formula of compound interest.

World population figures given by demographers are not the result of actual count but are scientific estimates. This fact explains the variations of population data one finds in demographic publications. There is, however, an agreement among experts that the growth of world population has slowed somewhat during the last eight years, but it still stands at about 1.8%. If this rate of growth is kept stable, the world population will double in thirty-eight years.

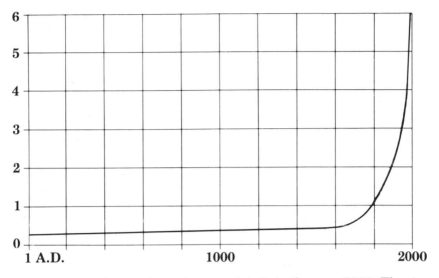

Growth through time from the year 1 A.D. to the year 2000. The size of the population is measured in billions.

The United States Bureau of Census reported that according to their estimate the world population was growing at 1.8% in 1982 and the world population had increased in absolute number by 82 million. This means that the world adds about 224,000 people, the size of a fairly large city, to its population every day. The Population Reference Bureau calculates that the world population will be 6.13 billion in the year 2000 and 7.81 billion in 2020.

Projecting the growth of the world population is a difficult task as the absolute number of population is the result of the varying factors of birth rate and death rate. Demographers, assuming that the world fertility rate will be reduced, give projections that are based on either a slow or a rapid rate of fertility reduction. On the assumption of a slow fertility decline, the world population would stabilize at about 15 billion people by the twenty-second century. In the case of a rapid fertility reduction, the world population could stabilize at about 8 billion during the twenty-first century.[1]

The sudden growth of population in modern times is attributed to decreasing infant mortality and increasing life expectancy, both of which are the result of better hygiene, improved medical care and the eradication of contagious diseases. At the dawn of history, the

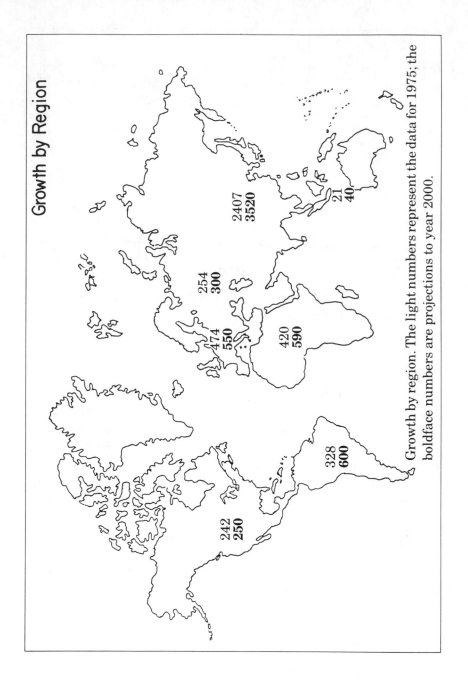

Growth by Region

2407
3520

254
300

474
550

420
590

21
40

242
250

328
600

Growth by region. The light numbers represent the data for 1975; the boldface numbers are projections to year 2000.

population of mankind grew very slowly, at times probably even decreasing because of adverse climatic conditions and diseases. If there had been one hundred people ten thousand years ago and the annual rate of growth had been 1%, that is, if the population had doubled every seventy years, the world population would be expressed today by a number consisting of forty-six digits (288 and 43 zeros), rather than the ten digits of 4,720,000,000 representing the present population. Since mankind is considerably older than ten thousand years, we must conclude that the rate of growth must have been just a small fraction of 1% at the beginning and then remained very low until recent times.[2]

It has been calculated that about 50 billion humans have lived so far on this planet. If this estimate is true, then about 9.44% of everyone who ever lived are alive now.[3]

It is important to note that the growth of population is uneven in the world. While the growth rate in the advanced nations is well below the world average, developing countries grow at a much higher rate than the average. Some examples of population data, rate of growth and population doubling time at the present rate:[4]

Region or Country	Population in mid-1983 in millions	Rate of growth in %	Doubling time in years
World	4,721	1.8	39
More developed	1,158	0.6	118
Less developed	3,563	2.1	32
U.S.	234.2	0.7	95
Europe	489	0.4	199
Western Europe	155	0.2	436
USSR	272	0.8	83
Asia	2,730	1.9	36
China	1,023.3	1.5	46
Middle South Asia	1,011	2.3	30
India	730	2.1	33
Latin America	390	2.3	30

It is estimated that the 3,563 million population of the less developed countries will grow to 4,860 million by the year 2000. The more developed countries, however, will grow from 1,158 million to only 1,273 million.

According to the projection of experts, the underdeveloped countries will absorb 90% of the growth of the world's population. This may mean that there will be a widening economic gap between the rich and poor nations because the developing nations would have to double their economic output in the next twenty-five years just to stay even with the growth of their population. To improve their standard of living, they would have to more than double their present economic output, a goal they can hardly achieve. By the end of the century hundreds of millions of new jobs will have to be created in the developing nations for an increased labor force to ease the scourge of unemployment and to encourage further economic development.

Population and Natural Resources

Scarcity of food and natural resources is the obvious consequence of the rapid growth of population. Some resources, such as agricultural products, are renewable. Oil, minerals and many raw materials of industrial products, on the other hand, are not renewable and their limited supplies sooner or later will be exhausted.

Hunger

There has always been some degree of hunger or starvation somewhere on the earth in the history of mankind. But in our days the scarcity of food affects a larger number of people than ever before, and hunger is fairly widespread in spite of all the improvements in agricultural methods.

According to a Newsletter of *Bread for the World*,[5] "One of every eight people on earth is hungry most of the time. Up to 40 percent of the population in many countries is malnourished. Sixteen percent of all the world's children are malnourished. . . ."

Few of the developing nations can sufficiently provide for their growing populations; hence a large segment of their people is locked in the vicious circle of mental and physical underdevelopment and dire poverty. According to medical evidence, infants deprived of sufficient, balanced nutrition will never grow to their full mental capacity, and thus poor nations will lack the most important power for their development, that is, the mental ability and energy of their people.

Food Production

Worldwide per-capita food production has increased after World War II, but most of the increase took place in developed countries. Several third world nations have substantially raised the rate of their food production, but this gain has been offset by the fast growth of their population, so that the per-capita increase of food has been only minimal. Paradoxically, affluence in the world at large and within the confines of individual nations also adds to the problem of food scarcity. The developed nations consume between twelve hundred and nineteen hundred pounds of grain per person. Most of it is eaten indirectly in the form of eggs, milk products and meat. In Liberia and Haiti, however, the per-capita consumption is less than two hundred pounds, in India less than four hundred pounds of grain, most of it consumed directly in the form of bread, rice and cereals. It is obvious that food consumption is not distributed evenly, so that the poor who cannot buy sufficient food are reduced to starvation. The more affluent a country is, the more its agricultural products are converted into better quality food. One pound of beef is produced by as many as ten pounds of grain. The wealthier a country is, the more it can afford either to convert grain into higher-quality food or to buy grain from other countries, as is the case with Europe, the U.S.S.R. and the oil-producing nations. The result is, of course, that the poor and hungry nations of the world cannot afford to compete with the wealthier nations and import enough grain to improve the diet of their people.

Renewable and Non-Renewable Resources

The rapid growth of population also causes scarcities of other renewable and non-renewable resources. Over 1 billion people use wood for fuel, cooking and heating, and this excessive consumption of wood leads to deforestation, upsetting the ecological balance. The scarcity of firewood forces many people in poor countries to burn dried cow dung for fuel. But cow dung is used in these countries for fertilizer and thus another shortage develops that adversely affects food production. The problem of energy shortage is well known. No industrial or agricultural growth is possible without energy. The cost of energy, however, is steadily increasing as reserves are depleted. Since petrochemicals are the basis of fertilizers, poor nations are less and less capable of buying the much needed fertilizers to improve their agricultural production. According to United Nations statistics, the consumption of energy is growing three times as fast as the population. Also the consumption of minerals is growing much faster than the population and, in spite of some recycling of minerals, the accessible reserves are being depleted. More and more land is used for residential purposes and roads, so the available acreage for agriculture keeps steadily shrinking.

As can be seen, the problems are interconnected, and economic growth, which is the source of the improvement of man's life on earth, is greatly affected by the growth of population. The standard of living was very low thousands of years ago, of course, when the earth had a much smaller population, but today there is a stronger causal relationship between population growth and the rise in the standard of living than there was in the past.

Education

One of the sources of economic growth is an educated population: the farmer, the industrial worker, the manager—all of whom learn their trade and employ the best scientific methods of production and organization. Persons who are unable to read or barely go beyond the level of the three R's cannot be easily taught to improve their productivity or plan and organize their own lives with foresight and prudence. It seems that certain developing nations are fighting a losing battle with illiteracy and the attempt at upgrading their educational systems. They cannot build enough schools and train teachers in sufficient numbers to educate everybody at even the elementary level. In Latin America a fairly large percentage of the population is still illiterate, and the situation in Africa and Asia is even worse. Any development of their educational systems is more than offset by the yearly addition of large numbers of children to the growing population. It is true that centuries ago the education of the population was very low everywhere compared to present-day standards, but after the scientific revolution that precipitated the industrial revolution, much greater knowledge and more advanced education are needed to make possible a steady economic growth. The world economy today could not provide even the bare minimum for the more than 4 billion people on the globe without scientific methods of production.

The *Overseas Development Council* estimated in 1981 that the literacy rate in developing countries was 52%. In some developing countries children are simply abandoned when their parents cannot provide for them. It is estimated that in Latin America alone there are 40 million "children of the street." There is little government action to help these youngsters who live at the margin of society. A study done by the Catholic University of Sao Paolo found that 80% of the prison population was made up of former street children.[6]

According to UNICEF (United Nations International Children's Emergency Fund), in 1982 in the less developed countries 74% of the boys and 54% of the girls of school age were enrolled in primary schools. Will the developing nations be able to make progress in educating their children so that they can contribute to their economic growth as skilled labor? Can they do this without lowering the growth rate of their population?

As the population increases, new jobs have to be created for those who reach adulthood and enter the job market. Unemployment and underemployment are a great problem even in advanced nations, but in developing countries they are an ever-worsening predicament that seems to defy solution. The International Labor Office (I.L.O.) projects that in Latin America the labor force will increase by 96 million by the end of this century. How many of these people will find jobs? It is estimated that in many third world countries the number of the new entrants into the job market is twice as large as the number of the new jobs that are being created. It has been calculated that it takes an investment of over $50,000 to create a new job in the United States. It costs less in developing countries, but since their gross national product is much lower than that of the rich countries, they are less able to invest even a smaller amount in the development of their industry to create new jobs. We need not dwell on the misery and frustration unemployment causes.

Another consequence of the rapid growth of population is urbanization. In itself, urbanization should lead to better education and improved cultural conditions. But the migration of unemployed, unskilled people to cities in the hope of finding work produces crowded living conditions, poor housing, crime and the frustrations of the unwanted who live at the margin of humanity. Thus the cities, which used to be fountains of civilization and places of improved living conditions, swallow up the millions of the desperate newcomers and offer them little hope for a better future.

The Green Revolution

Human ingenuity and science have solved many emerging problems of mankind in the past, and one would like to believe that further development in agriculture and industry will successfully increase the production of food and other necessities so that the needs of a growing population can be satisfied at an acceptable level. The example of the so-called *Green Revolution* is frequently mentioned in this regard. Dr. Norman E. Borlaug, an Iowa farmer and plant pathologist, won the Nobel Peace Prize in 1970 for his work in developing high-yield varieties of grains, especially wheat and rice, thus helping poor nations to increase their agricultural output. Dr. Borlaug, former Director of the Rockefeller Foundation's wheat-breeding program in Mexico, and his team achieved encouraging breakthroughs in plant breeding and are credited with considerably increasing agricultural production in developing countries and saving many millions of people from starvation during the past two decades. Unfortunately, the gains in food production have been wiped out by the rapid growth of population in those nations, and it is doubtful that technology can continue indefinitely to increase crop yields to keep up with population growth. Furthermore, the high-yield seeds need more fertilizer, insecticides, water, irrigation and energy just when the production of all these necessary ingredients of the Green Revolution are becoming more expensive to produce. As competition for fertilizer intensifies, it will be the poor nations that will not be able to afford to pay the high price of fertilizer and energy.

The International Maize and Wheat Improvement Center (CIMMYT) in Mexico now directs its research activities to raising yields in marginal production environments. Dr. Borlaug doubts that "significant production benefits will soon be forthcoming from the use of genetic engineering techniques with higher plants" and is of the opinion that it is urgent to continue conventional plant breeding research to maintain the gains achieved by the Green Revolution.[7]

Limits to Growth?

All these facts drive us to the conclusion that we live on a finite planet with limited carrying capacity. This conclusion was elaborately and forcefully presented in *The Limits to Growth*,[8] a report for the Club of Rome's project on the predicament of mankind. Published in 1972, its message was that our finite planet cannot support the present rates of economic and population growth beyond the year 2100 even if science and technology improve productivity. The book produced lively controversy and was criticized by many scientists and economists as overly pessimistic.[9] *Mankind at the Turning Point*, the second report to the Club of Rome,[10] is less pessimistic. The authors substitute the idea of "organic growth" for the previous proposal of "no growth" as the solution of saving the world economic order from total collapse.

The problem of producing food and other necessities for the growing population of the planet cannot be ignored by governments and all those who are involved in national and international economic planning. As a result of the almost universal concern about the so-called "population explosion," the United Nations declared 1974 "World Population Year." It called upon all member states to investigate the question during the year and to try to work out a plan for action to be discussed at the world conference on population that was to be held in Bucharest. The two-week-long population conference recommended that "countries which consider that their present or expected rates of population growth hamper their goals of promoting human welfare . . . consider adopting population policies within the framework of socio-economic development which are consistent with basic human rights and national goals and values."[11]

The Global Reports

In 1977 President Carter authorized a three-year study to project global population, natural resources and environmental trends. The 800-page study is entitled *The Global 2000 Report to the President* by the Council on Environmental Quality and the U.S. Department of State.[12] The Report does not intend to foretell what will certainly happen, but it predicts the consequences of present trends. These are some of the predictions:

For every two persons in the world there will be three persons in the year 2000. World food production between 1970 and 2000 will increase by 90% but most of the increase will occur in developed nations. Per capita consumption will improve little in the developing countries and in some it will even decline. The real price of food will double.

Deforestation will continue in developing countries. About 40% of their forests will be gone by the year 2000. At the same time serious deterioration of agricultural soil will occur worldwide. Water shortages will be more acute and the cost of developing new water supplies will increase. Coal, oil and gas will not be exhausted, but their uneven distribution will be a source of international tensions. Arable land will increase only by 4%. The gap between the richest and the poorest nations will have increased by the year 2000.

The picture presented by The Global 2000 Report is rather gloomy. Many similar comprehensive studies agree with the government report in its predictions.[13] The reports all agree, however, that the problems are solvable if we do not delay planning to correct the trends that are endangering the world economically and environmentally. Nevertheless they see extremely difficult times ahead.

There are, however, a number of scientists who disagree with the overly pessimistic view of the global reports and foresee a bright future and relative abundance for mankind. Herman Kahn, who died in July 1983 and was chairman of the Hudson Institute, in his *The Next 200 Years*[14] foresees that the world population will stabilize at about 15 billion people 200 years from now and the gross world product (GWP) will be some $300 trillion or $20,000 per capita. The GWP will not be distributed equally but everyone will be a great deal better off than now. There will be sufficient consumer commodities and food for all and only relative poverty will remain. In other words, the rich will be richer but the poor also will get richer. Technological development, economic growth and industrialization will solve most of our present problems.

Julian Simon, professor of Business Administration and Economics at the University of Illinois,[15] also presents an optimistic view in his *The Ultimate Resource*. In the short run all resources are limited, but in the long run the human intellect will solve such problems. As the population size grows, additional people will bring useful knowledge to our existing stock of scientific data that will help the economic development of the world to provide for the whole human race.

At his death, Herman Kahn left behind a partially completed book that he co-authored with Julian Simon. The book, *Global 2000 Revised*, which will probably appear in 1984, takes issue with the assumptions and methodology of *Global 2000* published by the Carter Administration. The book, even though only in manuscript form, has drawn a great deal of attention because of its attempt to refute the conclusions of *Global 2000*.[16]

Amidst the gloomy reports, the voice of a minority is being raised that questions the accuracy of the statistics on food and resources and maintains that the ills of the world have been vastly exaggerated. There are not enough reliable data about world hunger and other problems and the estimates cannot be supported by hard evidence, they argue.[17]

While the pessimism-optimism controversy continues, a consensus has developed that the difficulties and problems of the world are real but something can and must be done before it is too late. The rate of population growth has been so high in the post-war period that even the optimistic analysts of the earth's supply of natural resources and of the increased needs of a growing population are in agreement that *one* of the elements of the solution is the reduction of the rate of fertility. *Responsible parenthood* is the term that is frequently used in reference to the duty of married couples to bring their personal rights of procreation into conformity with the demands of the common good and the good of their own offspring. Before we consider the meaning of responsible parenthood in concrete situations, we must turn our attention to the morality of the means by which fertility in marriage may be regulated. This is the problem of contraception or, using a more general term, of birth control.

Contraception

The morality of birth control, or more appropriately contraception, is concerned with the rightness or wrongness of the use of various methods by which conception can be prevented in the marital act. The instruments that obstruct the union of the sperm and ovum can be chemical or physical. Conception can also be prevented by the sterilization of one or both spouses, by withdrawal before ejaculation, or by limiting intercourse to the infertile period of the wife's menstrual cycle.

History of Birth Control

Historical documents attest that various birth control methods were in use in ancient times in the Mediterranean world. Genesis 38:8–10 describes the most simple form of birth control. " . . . when he [Onan] had intercourse with his brother's widow, he let the semen spill on the ground, so that there would be no children for his brother. What he did displeased the Lord and the Lord killed him." It has to be noted here that, according to Scripture scholars, God did not punish Onan because of the sin of birth control but rather for the violation of the Jewish law that obliged him to have intercourse with his childless brother's widow so that his brother might have descendants to continue his name.[18]

Ancient Greek and Latin sources that contain contraceptive information do not express any opinion about the morality of the practice. Stoic philosophers, however, held that sexual organs should be used exclusively for their biological purpose which, in their opinion, was procreation. To use sex differently, that is, exclusively for the sake of pleasure and love, went against its purpose and was consequently wrong. The Church Fathers accepted the Stoic view and taught that intercourse is permitted only in marriage and only for the purpose of procreation. Their doctrine became prevalent in Christianity, and the Church maintained for centuries that the conjugal act is procreative by its very nature and that it is morally good only when it is performed with the intention of having children. Hence intercourse during pregnancy, for example, was considered immoral. Sterile persons were permitted to have intercourse if they did it with the hope of having children and trust in God to bless their marital union with offspring. Official declarations of the Catholic Church until the time of the Second Vatican Council maintained that the primary end of the conjugal act is procreation and that the expression of love is only a secondary or subordinate goal. Vatican Council II, however, speaks of the great value of conjugal love, declaring that "this love is uniquely expressed and perfected through the marital act,"[19] and abandons the traditional listing of primary and secondary ends of marriage. Pope Paul VI, nevertheless, in his encyclical *Humanae Vitae*, On the Transmission of Human Life, issued on July 25, 1968, maintains the traditional doctrine that contraception is against the nature of the conjugal act and, therefore, morally evil. Only the rhythm method of birth regulation is considered morally permissible. The rhythm method means the restriction of marital relations to the infertile period of the wife in her menstrual cycle. It is judged admissible because it does not violate the natural laws of the generative process.

Birth control became a widespread practice in Europe in the nineteenth century when, as a result of the industrial revolution and economic development, large families became a burden rather than the economic asset they used to be in the feudal, agricultural era. Fertility greatly declined in the industrial countries in the twentieth century, and ethicians, turning their attention to this phenomenon, began to consider the question on the basis of a newly acquired knowledge of human sexuality. Moralists, especially of the Protestant churches, did not think that contraceptive practices were immoral if the spouses did this for the purpose of responsible parenthood. This book cannot deal with the documents of the various Christian churches concerning contraception. We can only examine the ethical arguments concerning birth control so that the reader can weigh them and arrive at his own well-reasoned conclusion.

The discovery of the sterile period in the menstrual cycle injected a new consideration into the ethical evaluation of acts that deliberately exclude procreation from the conjugal act. The works of the Japanese Kyusaku Ogino, in 1924, and of Hermann Knaus, an Austrian physician, presented evidence that a woman is infertile for a considerable time during the menstrual cycle. This fact seems to prove that not every conjugal act is procreative by its very nature. In other words, the biological nature of human sexuality itself separates the unitive and procreative aspects of the conjugal act. In the twenty-eight day cycle, only about six days are fertile and twenty-two days are infertile. If we assume that normal sexuality continues after menopause until about the age of sixty-six, only one day out of seven is fertile during the sexually active life of a woman. If morality is discovered in the biological nature of sexuality, the purpose of sex, it seems, is much more intercourse for the sake of love than for conception.

Morality of Contraception

Ethical arguments, then, concern the question of how human nature, and especially the nature of the conjugal act, has to be understood as the norm of morality. Utilitarians have no difficulty in justifying contraception as morally permissible or even obligatory. The controversy about contraception is really between two groups of moralists, both following natural-law ethics. Both sides agree that human nature is the criterion of morality, but they differ in their interpretation of human nature in regard to human sexuality. One theory, developing during the nineteenth century by Neo-Scholasticism, considers the natural law in an "essentialist" framework. According to this theory, the natural order designed by God is a reality preceding man, and any interference with this order is forbidden. The other theory follows the idea of the natural law held by St. Thomas Aquinas, according to which the natural law is found in the human intellect (*recta ratio*, right reason) as it participates in the divine law. The human reason is bound by the laws of the created world, but it is through reason that man discovers and understands his nature and goal. His reason weighs the value of his life and establishes a rational order out of conflicting values. Thus the values of the person and the family that concern the totality of man's unique nature are judged superior to the biological laws of sexuality that regard only a part of man's nature.

Reasons against Contraception

Pope Paul VI appointed a commission to study the question and advise him in this matter. The majority of the group took the position that contraception does not conflict with human nature and the natural law if it is practiced to promote responsible parenthood. The minority of the group, however, argued for the opposite position and the Pope followed their advice as he maintained in his encyclical, *Humanae Vitae*, that couples must respect the "biological laws which are part of the human person,"[20] and hence no artificial intervention to suppress the procreative power of the conjugal act is morally licit. He declared that it would be against God's will to go beyond the plan of God clearly indicated in the biological process, the biological laws of procreation and rhythm, because man does not have "unlimited power over his own body, and this applies especially to procreative powers, since such powers by nature are concerned with propagating life."[21] The use of the infertile period or the rhythm method is licit because it does not interfere with the biological processes of human nature.

Reasons for Contraception

Opponents of this interpretation of human nature and natural law point out that man has a certain dominion over his body and that biological laws should not be identified with morality. Man is more than the sum total of biological processes. He is spirit in matter, a unique being, neither pure spirit nor pure matter. Through his reason he can appraise the importance of values that refer to his whole being and not just to his body. Human sexuality differs from animal sexuality, and the use of the generative faculties must take into consideration the good of the whole family, the parents and children together, and even the good of the larger social body. One may interfere with biological laws for the well-being of the person because man is a rational being and as such is under the guidance of his intellect and not of his instincts. By virtue of his rational nature, man is obliged to search for the good of his total being, to which the biological laws are subordinated. This group argues that furthermore the use of the rhythm method, allowed by the encyclical, deliberately eliminates conception and is thus morally equivalent to other means of contraception. One cannot truthfully state that the conjugal act performed during the sterile period remains "open to the transmission of life" and does not purposefully prevent conception.

Government and Population Control

Governments are set up by the people for the defense of their individual rights and for the promotion of the common good. This means the establishment of an order in which individuals and families, through the cooperation of society and their individual efforts, can attain the fulfillment of their humanity. As we have seen, the fast rate of population growth in the developing countries greatly diminishes the ability of their governments to create an order in which all members of these nations could properly be fed, clothed, sheltered and educated so that they can lead a life worthy of rational human beings. Since the rapid growth of population adversely affects the well-being of most people in the developing countries, it is obvious that their governments have a duty to influence the fertility rate to bring it to a level compatible with the common good. The question is what ethical means a government may use to control population in attempting to solve the conflict between individual self-determination and the right of society to act for the common good.

India, whose emergence from one of the world's most serious conditions of underdevelopment is constantly being blocked by its population growth, proposed compulsory sterilization in 1976. Since its population is increasing by more than 1 million a month, and fewer than 45% of couples use conventional birth control devices, Indira Gandhi's government argued that legislation was necessary to make sterilization compulsory for couples who had a certain number of children. Civil servants were ordered to limit their families or face penalties. Prime Minister Indira Gandhi said that "some personal rights have to be kept in abeyance for the human rights of the nation, the right to live, the right to progress."[22] In the opinion of the government, the situation was comparable to a state of war, and in such a grave emergency the personal rights of individuals had to be sacrificed for the sake of the good of the entire nation.

Mrs. Gandhi was accused of forcing men to undergo sterilization during the emergency rule she imposed on India from 1975 to 1977. She said that the charges against her were exaggerated and nobody was really forced to undergo sterilization. Her party, nevertheless, was defeated in parliamentary elections in 1977 and the government that followed hers toned down the campaign for birth control.

In a new election, Mrs. Gandhi has become prime minister again and she is vigorously promoting a national birth control program for which she can give good reasons. Although India has greatly increased wheat and rice production, so that in normal monsoon years it can feed itself however meagerly, the yearly 2.1% population growth absorbs a great deal of its economic growth, leaving few resources for the improvement of the quality of life.

India's population in mid-1983 was 730 million, which will grow to 966 million by 2000, if its population control methods are not further improved or more widely used. The Indian government distributes subsidized birth control pills and condoms and promotes sterilization of both men and women. Women who come to medical camps for a quick surgery, closing their Fallopian tubes, receive $22, and men who subject themselves to vasectomies are given $15. Other birth control devices are also distributed to women but the emphasis is on sterilization. A group of "concerned citizens" pointed out that 290 million people in India "earn less than $6 a month and their miseries are growing." Reviewing the welfare of the Indian people, Mrs. Gandhi declared that her government is "totally committed" to voluntary birth control.[23]

China's population policy is even more forceful than that of India. In 1979 the government announced a plan of not permitting the population to grow larger than 1.2 billion. The goal is ultimately to reduce the population to 700 million by the year 2080. Recently the limit of two children per family has been replaced by the "one couple one child" policy. Couples are urged to "volunteer" to have only one child. "Mass voluntarism," however, is not enough to achieve this goal, and rewards and penalties are being used in many areas of the country. Certificates are awarded entitling couples to free medical care and school tuition for their only child. There are also direct payments, preferential treatment in housing and other rewards for having only one child. Couples who break their pledge by having a second child must return all payments, and those who have a third child will have their monthly wages reduced by ten percent or more. Birth planning cadres "mobilize" men and women to undergo sterilization or procure abortion when an unplanned pregnancy would mean the addition of a second child to the family. The one child family is not an official law yet, but it is a national policy that is being carried out through various administrative measures.[24]

Morality and Forced Birth Control

Can compulsory sterilization or other forced birth control methods ethically be justified to control population growth? This is a case of conflict between individual rights and the demands of the common good, and one first has to investigate whether the public interest can be promoted without the limitation of individual rights. The common good would suffer if individual rights are curtailed without necessity, for the protection of individual rights is part of the common good. Curtailment of individual freedoms, as in the case of military conscription, is justified only in an emergency, when the survival of a nation is in danger. It seems that the grave population problem of India and of other third world countries can be alleviated without resorting to compulsion. There are less stringent methods that have not been either tried yet or adequately put into practice. Well-conducted educational campaigns and incentives that respect the freedom and voluntary cooperation of people have had good results in several developing nations. The art of government is to persuade people, to treat them as rational beings and thus obtain their necessary cooperation for the common good. A government should not turn to coercion when the citizens' cooperation for the assurance of the common good can be obtained by their free consent.

The Right To Have Children

To marry and have children is a basic human right. The free exercise of this right is necessary for the fulfillment of human nature for most people. Since governments are instituted to defend the rights of the individuals and promote the common good, they have a serious duty to enable their citizens to exercise this right responsibly in a way that is compatible with the common good. It seems evident, however, that the problem of poverty and the promotion of the material welfare of the population in developing countries cannot be solved by population control alone. To achieve a human acceptable standard of living, economic production has to be greatly increased in the third world. As many studies have found, the desire to have a large family frequently springs from an economic motivation. In poor nations children are a kind of social security for poor parents since they cannot count on anybody else but their children to look after them in their old age or when they are ill. The history of Europe and the industrialized countries generally indicates that family size decreases when the economic security of the parents increases. Obviously, it takes more than one generation to reduce the fertility rate this way, and poor nations, unfortunately, cannot afford to wait several generations. These countries are running out of time. They are locked in a vicious circle as their population growth greatly impedes or slows down their economic development under present circumstances. This fact brings us to the problem of international responsibility concerning development in the third world and its connection with population control.

World Population Year

An increasing international concern that population growth is exhausting the natural resources of the planet and threatens world stability prompted the United Nations to proclaim 1974 *World Population Year*, as was mentioned before. Member states were invited to consider their demographic problems and prepare a population plan of action to be discussed at the world population conference held in Bucharest, Rumania, in the second half of August 1974.

The population plan of action that was adopted by the delegates of 135 nations at the end of the conference made several recommendations. Countries which considered that their population growth hindered the program of human welfare of their citizens were invited to adopt population policies "which are consistent with basic human rights and national goals and values."[25] Developed nations were asked to recognize the fact that their per capita use of the natural resources of the world is much higher than that of the developing countries, and they were urged to adopt "appropriate policies in population, consumption and investment, bearing in mind the need for fundamental improvement in international equity."[26]

It was agreed in Bucharest that the promotion of social justice, more equitable distribution of land, income, health and social services tended to reduce fertility levels. Also, the full integration of women into the economic, social and cultural life of the nation and the promotion of the education of both sexes at all levels were seen as having a restraining effect on fertility. The introduction of social security and old-age benefits were indicated as means to eliminate the necessity of having many children in poor families as a social security for old age.

Countries which have found that birth rates adversely affected the promotion of human welfare were invited to set quantitative goals and initiate policies that would make the attainment of these goals possible by 1985. The sovereignty of each country was to be respected, however, and no international body was to interfere with the planning and execution of population policies of any country. It was recommended, nevertheless, that the United Nations monitor population trends and the policies contained in the plan of action, reviewing them every two years, beginning in 1977. A more comprehensive review and evaluation of the plan of action was to take place every five years by the United Nations specialized agencies.

Feeding the Hungry

The world population conference did not develop any concrete plans concerning world food supplies and the sharing of the wealth of advanced nations with the third world. The problem of developing plans for emergency cases of starvation and for helping developing nations to produce more food was discussed by the United Nations World Conference on Food in Rome, in November 1974 at the headquarters of the United Nations Food and Agricultural Organization (F.A.O.). The conference adopted twenty-two resolutions that can be grouped around three goals the international community should strive to achieve. (a) There should be direct assistance by food and funds where it is needed. (b) An international food reserve system should be set up that could provide emergency supplies and, just as importantly, could stabilize prices on the international food market. (c) Agricultural production should be improved in countries with food deficits.

The third goal, a long-term approach, is the most important initiative for attempting to solve the chronic food shortages in the third world countries. These countries were invited to develop their economies in a balanced way so that industrial development would not be favored over agricultural development. The International Fund for

Agricultural Development (I.F.A.D.) has assumed the task of helping developing nations in the improvement of their agriculture. Western industrialized nations and OPEC countries pledged the initial 1 billion dollars that was needed to begin the operation.

International Responsibility

Considering the ethical question of international justice, we must note that the treasures and resources of the earth were given to the whole human race to satisfy its natural needs. International distributive justice imposes an obligation upon the whole human race to help feed the hungry. This question, however, cannot be solved just by charity, by merely donating more food to the hungry. Helping the needy within one particular nation is not a question of charity either, but a matter of distributive and social justice, involving a complex reorganization and constant adjustment of the national economy to ever changing situations. Charity and donations cannot solve the problem on the global level either because, first of all, living constantly on the charity of others degrades human dignity and, secondly, one has to deal with the economic and technical difficulties of increased food production and worldwide distribution by the advanced nations. There is an old saying: "Do not give a fish to a hungry man but give him fishing gear and teach him how to catch fish." If you give food to hungry people, they will eat for a few days, but if you teach them how to produce their own food and help them to develop their agriculture, they will be kept from starvation for the rest of their lives. Both the advanced and the developing nations are morally obliged to do their share in solving the world's food problem.

Lifeboat Ethics

The ethical problem of international help in feeding the hungry is sharpened by the contentions of so-called *lifeboat ethics* and the ethics of *triage*. Garrett Hardin[27] argues that governments, having the responsibility to assure the survival and well-being of their citizens, must also have the right to limit the number of children to be born. Otherwise, we cannot avoid the "tragedy of the commons," that is, outstripping of the carrying capacity of the land. Lifeboat ethics compares the rich nations to a well-maintained and well-stocked lifeboat. The poor nations are in crowded and ill-provisioned boats or are swimming in the water after the lifeboat hoping to be picked up. Lifeboat ethics contends that there is not enough room for everybody to be saved, and that if the advanced nations try to be generous with the poor nations, disaster cannot be avoided because all will sink. It is a lesser evil to let some or even many drown than to jeopardize the safety of all.

The French word *triage* means sorting. It was the practice in World War I to separate the wounded soldiers into three groups. One group consisted of those who were most likely to die no matter how much treatment they received. The second group would recover even if untreated because their wounds were slight, while the third group was made up of those who could be saved if treated immediately. Since medical supplies and medical personnel were limited, the logical decision was made to treat only the third group. The policy of *triage* is applied by some to the international food situation. Many countries cannot adequately provide food for their own population. The few countries that have a food surplus should decide which nations are salvageable and should be given food, which can survive without help since they are capable of improving their agriculture, and which are hopeless and consequently should be abandoned. Those who control surplus supplies will have the awesome duty to decide who shall be fed and who shall starve. The point of the argument is that we have to choose between two evils: starvation of a considerable part of mankind or the danger of bringing ruin to the whole human race. It is not so much nuclear devastation that threatens the world but overpopulation and famine.

In *evaluating lifeboat and triage ethics*, the obvious questions to ask are whether their promoters correctly state the facts, whether the disjunction is correct, so that we have no other alternatives. It seems that the allegory of the lifeboat does not correctly describe the actual situation. There are no separate boats for the rich and for the poor nations. We all are in the same boat, rich and poor, as we are interdependent. Advanced nations use up a considerably larger portion of the world's natural resources than the poor nations, so the question of distributive justice cannot be overlooked. Who owns the natural resources of the planet? The energy crisis sheds some light on this problem. But even if we accept the allegories of lifeboat and *triage*, we have to conclude that their disjunctions are not valid because there are alternative solutions.[28] During the 1960's worldwide food production rose by 2.8% a year while population increased by about 2%. In the 1970's food production slowed to an increase of 2.4% yearly; world population growth slowed to about 1.8%. This does not mean, however, that there is no food problem in the world. It just indicates that the world is not approaching universal famine. Nobody denies the complexity of increasing food production to a level that would be sufficient to feed everybody adequately, but it seems that we are not in the desperate situation that would oblige us to let a large part of the world population starve in order to save others from famine.[29]

Responsible Parenthood

The size of the population has not yet outstripped the natural resources of the earth necessary for the well-being of all the people living today. Nevertheless, even the experts who do not think that doomsday is at hand are convinced that the rate of population growth must be reduced because the planet and its resources are limited. Tragedy cannot be avoided unless the proportion between the increase of population and the availability of natural resources is brought into balance.

Procreation has always been a responsible human activity. The idea of responsible parenthood, however, has taken on added significance in these years of extraordinary population growth. We have to examine, then, what sort of moral duties this responsibility involves in the contemporary context. One can consider procreation and the size of the family in regard to a particular conjugal society, in relation to the larger community of a nation, or, even going beyond one's nation, in reference to the well-being of the whole human race.

Marriage and procreation are natural rights of every competent adult. No right is unlimited, however, for it may come into conflict with the rights of others, or with the duties that are the result of the very exercise of rights. Procreation carries with it the ensuing duty to care for the physical and mental upbringing of children. It would not be a morally responsible act, then, to have a greater number of children than a couple can provide for. Children are not the product of society, and it is not the duty of society to take over the role of parents. The principle of subsidiarity means that society has to come to the help of individuals either in particular accidental cases of need or in the fulfilling of duties that surpass the power of individuals or lesser groups, for example, in organizing schools for the education of children. The physical, mental and moral care of children is the duty and right of the parents; consequently, the state would violate the primary rights of the parents to educate their children if, for example, it took the children away from them and placed them in institutions.

Criteria of Responsible Parenthood

It follows from the previous consideration that the first criterion of responsible parenthood is the ability of the parents to care for their children; they should not have more children than they can provide for. But there may be other factors that also have to be taken into consideration. The growth of population in a particular country may be so rapid that economic development cannot keep pace with the needs of a growing population. In this case the couples have to look beyond their own conjugal society and weigh the consequences a large family may have on the common good and the possibility of providing for other children. Some couples may be economically, physically and psychologically capable of looking after a large number of children, but their buying power may prevent poorer couples from acquiring the necessary food, clothing and shelter that are in short supply. One is obliged to abstain from an act when it can be clearly foreseen that the consequences of the act would hurt others. In a country, however, where the national economy can sufficiently provide for the population and the growth rate is in balance with economic growth, to have a greater than average number of children in a family would not be an irresponsible act as long as the couple are capable of bringing them up decently. The couple have the right to decide how many children they want to have as long as they can adequately fulfill their parental duties and their decision does not harm the common good.

Someone could reason, however, that it is irresponsible to have a large family even if the couple can provide for the children and the country in which they live has no population problem. The reason is that each person in a developed nation uses up ten times the amount of food and natural resources that people in the third world do. Since the world has become a "global village," in that all nations are interdependent, every person, the argument continues, is obliged to consider the effects of his actions and avoid those that hurt others in the village.

The catchy phrase and the theatrical allegory of "global village" probably is being carried too far in this context, because one cannot prove that an occasional larger-than-average family in an advanced nation will perceptibly hurt others in the world and will deprive growing children of food and other natural resources. International distributive and social justice is achieved by mutual governmental actions and trade rather than by the scattered actions of a small number of families.

Responsibility for the Future

Is the present generation of mankind obliged to be concerned about the problems of future generations, the size of the population in the twenty-first century, the amount of required energy, food and natural resources necessary for their well-being? One could say that we have enough problems of our own, that we should not worry about preserving the natural resources of the planet for the billions of people who will come after us. We should rather try to satisfy our immense immediate needs by using the resources of the earth. "What has posterity ever done for me?" one might ask. We are not obliged to reciprocate for what we have not received. A narrowly utilitarian view could argue that we should not deprive ourselves of things that could increase our happiness; let future generations solve their own problems. There are also some religiously motivated persons who insist, especially in regard to population control, that if God gives life, he will also provide the necessary means to support it. Consequently, they say, we should not worry too much about the future but trust in divine providence.

These and similar opinions are the expression of poor ethics and poor theology. God entrusted the earth to the care of man and gave him an intellect to work out plans of how to use the finite resources of a finite planet. It is bad ethics to deny responsibility for the future effects of our actions. If I place a powerful time bomb in the basement of a skyscraper to go off years later, possibly after my death, I perform a morally evil act because I am responsible for the bad consequences of my act even if they occur after my death. Many actions that certain individuals or whole industries perform today may have far-reaching consequences later. Dumping chemicals in rivers or carelessly burying them in the soil, destroying forests, polluting the air, or other actions that tend to destroy our environment may endanger the lives of people coming after us. According to sound ethical principles, deliberate omissions are also responsible decisions. Negligence concerning the well-being of present or future generations may harm a great number of people, and if we foresee the bad consequences of our negligence, these will be imputed to us. There has been so much written and said about ecology in these days that it is difficult to be ignorant of the consequences of our actions or omissions in this regard. The problems of population growth and of the provision of all the necessities for a decent life for all peoples concern the future, and that future is being shaped today by our actions or omissions.

Questions for Review and Discussion

1. What are the causes of the accelerated population growth in this century and especially after World War II?

2. How is the total growth of population distributed in the world?

3. What are the economic and educational consequences of the "population explosion" in the third world?

4. How do you evaluate the pessimistic and the optimistic projections of the consequences of the rapid growth of population?

5. Can science solve the problems of food, energy and natural resources if the population continues to increase at the present rate?

6. Does overpopulation increase unemployment or, on the contrary, will it help to eliminate it because it will add many talents to the intellectual pool of mankind, ultimately bringing about the solution of all existing problems?

7. Is the reduction of the present fertility rate *one* necessary element for the solution of many economic problems in developing nations?

8. How do you evaluate the arguments for the rightness or wrongness of contraception?

9. Do governments have a duty to promote the well-being of their citizens by controlling population growth?

10. What are the ethically justifiable methods that governments may use in controlling population growth? Can compulsory sterilization be justified?

11. What is your evaluation of "lifeboat ethics"?

12. Are rich nations morally obliged to send food to hungry nations? What is the best form of international aid?

13. Explain the concept of responsible parenthood. The size of a family can be considered in relation to an individual couple, to a nation or to the whole human race. What are the ethical principles that govern these relationships?

14. Is the present generation obliged to conserve natural resources for future generations? How do you prove such a duty?

Notes

    1. *Population Handbook*. Washington, D.C.: Population Reference Bureau, 1978, p. 48.
    2. If the population increases exponentially, that is, if the increase

each year is equal to a constant percentage of the population of the previous year, this growth can be expressed by the formula of compound interest.

3. Cf. *The New York Times*, Oct. 6, 1983, p. C 1.

4. Cf. U.S. Bureau of the Census and Population Reference Bureau.

5. Stephen Coats, Issue Analyst, "Hunger, Scarcity and U.S. Foreign Policy." May 1981, p. 3.

6. Warren Hoge, "UNICEF Does What It Can To Help Latin America's 40 Million Abandoned Children." *The New York Times*, Sept. 11, 1983, p. E 8.

7. Norman E. Borlaug, "Contribution of Conventional Plant Breeding to Food Production." *Science*, February 11, 1983, pp. 689–693.

8. Donella H. Medows *et al.*, *The Limits to Growth*. New York: Universe Books, 1972.

9. H.S.D. Cole *et al.*, eds., *Models of Doom*. New York: Universe Books, 1973.

10. Mihajilo Mesarovic and Eduard Pestel, *Mankind at the Turning Point*. New York: Reader's Digest Press, 1974.

11. *The New York Times*, August 31, 1974.

12. The Global 2000 Report to the President by the Council on Environmental Quality and the U.S. Department of State. Washington, D.C.: Government Printing Office (Volume 1: The Summary Report, Stock No. 041–011–00037–8; Volume 2: The Technical Report, Stock No. 041–001–00038–6; Volume 3: The Government's Global Model, Stock No. 041–011–00051–3), 1980.

13. See the following books:

Global Future: Time To Act by the Council on Environmental Quality and the U.S. Department of State. Washington, D.C.: Government Printing Office, 1981.

Interfutures: Facing the Future by the Organisation for Economic Cooperation and Development. Paris, France: OECD (2, rue Andre-Pascal, 75775 Paris Cedex 16, France), 1979.

North-South: A Program for Survival. Report of the Independent Commission on International Development Issues. Cambridge, Massachusetts: The MIT Press, 1980.

World Development Report 1982 by the World Bank. New York: Oxford University Press, 1982. (This is also available directly from the World Bank, 1818 H Street, N.W., Washington, D.C. 20433.)

14. Herman Kahn, William Brown, and Leon Martel, *The Next 200 Years: A Scenario for America and the World*. New York: William Morrow and Company, Inc., 1976.

15. Julian L. Simon, *The Ultimate Resource*. Princeton University Press, 1981.

16. "Simon and Kahn versus *Global 2000*." *Science*, July 22, 1983, p. 341.

17. Cf. Ann Crittenden, "Food and Hunger Statistics Questioned," *The New York Times*, Oct. 5, 1981, p. A 1.

18. For the history of contraception see John T. Noonan, Jr., *Contraception*. Cambridge: Harvard University Press, 1965.

19. Walter M. Abbott, S.J., ed., *The Documents of Vatican II*. New York: America Press, 1966, p. 253. "Gaudium et Spes."

20. *Humanae Vitae*, n. 10.

21. *Ibid.*, n. 13.

22. *The New York Times*, March 19, 1976.

23. *The New York Times*, March 7, 1982, p. 6.

24. H. Yuan Tien, "China: Demographic Billionaire." *Population Bulletin*, April 1983, pp. 31–34.

25. *The New York Times*, August 31, 1974.

26. *Ibid.*

27. Garrett Hardin, *Exploring the New Ethics for Survival: The Voyage of the Spaceship "Beagle."* New York: Viking Press, 1968, 1972. Also, by the same author, "Living on a Lifeboat." *BioScience*, October 1974, pp. 561–568.

28. James W. Howe and John W. Sewall, "Let's Sink the Lifeboat Ethics." *Worldview*, October 1975, pp. 13–18.

29. *The New York Times*, July 16, 1978.

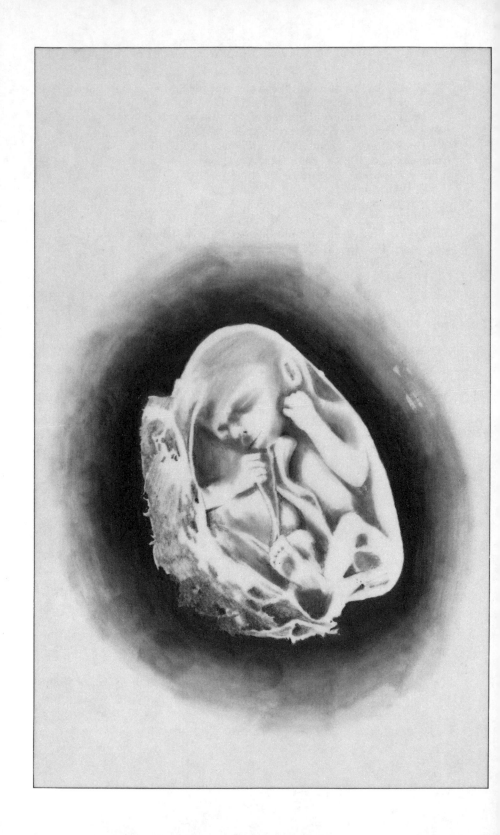

3 Abortion

Brief History of Abortion

From ancient times to the present, abortion has been used as a method of birth control. It achieves birth control not by preventing conception, but by killing the already conceived life. Attitudes concerning its morality varied widely in ancient cultures. Plato and Aristotle approved of it for the prevention of excess population in the small Greek city-states. Aristotle, however, was against abortion after "quickening" of the fetus. The Sumerian, Assyrian, Hammurabi and Persian codes, ranging from 2000 to 600 B.C., prohibited abortion and imposed very harsh punishments on those who caused the death of an unborn child. The Hippocratic oath, attributed to Hippocrates (460?–377? B.C.), contains a pledge not to give a treatment to a woman to cause abortion. Since infanticide was morally and legally accepted in ancient Rome, abortion was considered even less objectionable there. It was punishable, however, when it was procured without the father's consent. The permissive attitude of Rome changed when the population began to decline during the second century A.D. Imperial Rome then passed strict anti-abortion laws to stop the moral decay and strengthen the nation. Jewish and Christian attitudes have been unanimously against abortion, and so was Western secular legislation of the Christian era until recent times.

After World War II, despite restrictive laws and harsh punishments imposed on violators, a fairly large number of illegal abortions were performed in the United States and many other parts of the world. This fact was one of the reasons used by the advocates of abortion to influence legislators and courts to lift the prohibition against it. Permissive laws passed by about two-thirds of the world's nations during the last decade now make it possible for pregnant women to have an abortion almost on demand. In the United States, the Supreme Court's *Roe v. Wade* (Texas) and *Doe v. Bolton* (Georgia) decisions, on January 22, 1973, legalized abortion. For the first trimester the abortion decision is "left to the medical judgment of the pregnant woman's attending physician"; for the second trimester, a state "may, if it chooses, regulate the abortion procedure in ways that are reasonably related to maternal health"; for the last stage to viability the state "may, if it chooses, regulate, and even proscribe, abortion except where it is necessary . . . for the preservation of the life or health of the mother." The term health, however, is interpreted so broadly by the Court that it includes "all factors—physical, emotional, psychological, familial, and the woman's age—relevant to the well-being of the patient" as judged by any physician. "In its official report on the Hatch Amendment, published in 1982, the U.S. Senate Judiciary Committee concluded: 'The committee observes that no significant legal barriers of any kind whatsoever exist today in the United States for a woman to obtain an abortion for any reason during any stage of her pregnancy.' "[1]

It is estimated that about 1.5 million abortions are being performed annually in the U.S. alone. According to a recent estimate of the Population Crisis Committee, about 40 million abortions are performed annually worldwide, that is, about one in four pregnancies ends in abortion. Other estimates, however, are substantially higher than this. As a birth control method, abortion takes third place behind voluntary sterilization (about 100 million) and oral contraceptives (about 55 million). About two-thirds of the world's population live in countries where abortion is legal on request or under certain conditions. The rate in the United States is estimated at 417 abortions per 1,000 births. Rates in Europe are generally higher. Patterns of abortion vary widely. "In the U.S., for example, 74 percent of women who procured an abortion in 1978 were unmarried and 57 percent were childless. In Mexico by contrast, according to a 1979 study, 95 percent of women seeking an abortion were married and had more than three children."[2]

Legality and Morality of Abortion

The Supreme Court ruling made abortion legal but it could not change the morality of abortion by its majority decision. Only a moral positivist would hold that whatever the Supreme Court or public authority approves becomes, by this very fact, morally good and permissible. But just as slavery, segregation and discrimination against certain groups of people cannot be made morally acceptable by a court decision, so abortion also cannot be made good if it is morally objectionable by its nature. Our task is now to examine the nature of abortion from this point of view. A woman procuring an abortion in the U.S. does not face a prison sentence, but she and the operating surgeon must answer the question in their consciences as to whether they are performing a morally objectionable act.

The issue of abortion has understandably aroused strong emotions in both pro-abortionist and anti-abortionist camps. If the 1.5 million legal abortions performed annually in the U.S. are the deliberate killing of that many human beings, the question cannot be dismissed as unimportant. But a debate influenced by strong emotions can easily degenerate into name-calling. It is necessary, then, to clarify the ethical questions involved in abortion and offer the type of rational answers that can be seriously considered by all persons of good will.

The Beginning of Human Life

When does human life begin? This is the central issue of the abortion controversy. The question is sometimes formulated: Is the fetus a person?

Let us consider first the question of personhood and whether the use of this term clarifies the central issue of the beginning of human life or just makes it more ambiguous. What is a person? We usually equate a person with a human being, that is, with an individual being who has the *capacity* for rational self-consciousness and self-determination. Some restrict the use of the term person to those individuals who actually have already manifested the development of the capacity of self-consciousness to a lesser or greater degree. The Supreme Court argued that "the word 'person,' as used in the Fourteenth Amendment, does not include the unborn." The various stages of development suggested as the starting points of personhood can be arbitrary, however, and proposed according to the purpose one wants to achieve by a particular definition. Thus slaves originally were not considered persons in every regard; in some countries, even up to the present time, women were not legally considered persons with the full rights due to persons.

Is there any objective criterion for saying that a fetus, a slave or a woman is not a person in the complete sense? A fetus is obviously not a fully developed person. But when does a human being become a person? At the end of the second trimester in the womb or at birth? Or even later, when he learns the three R's and can earn a living? One could assign a number of arbitrary conditions and argue for the correctness of each but with little objective evidence.

It seems to me that the use of the term person only clouds the main issue because the definition of person can be arbitrary depending on the goal for which that definition was constructed. It would seem advisable, then, to exclude this term from our consideration and to direct our analysis to the central issue of when *human life* begins.

It might be objected that the answer to this question is equally arbitrary, for that, too, depends on the purpose for which one is attempting to use that particular definition of human life. This can be true. Nevertheless, arbitrariness can be better eliminated here because there are certain objective facts that can serve as a starting point for our analysis.

Embryology and Human Life

Modern genetics and embryology give us a rather accurate and detailed account of the development of human life. It begins with the union of ovum and sperm and continues to grow to viability and the birth of a child. The continuous and uninterrupted development of the *conceptus* into a newborn child suggests that human life is present from the moment of conception. Some hold, however, that certain stages can be pointed out in this growth, one or another of which could be taken as the beginning of human life. One of these suggested stages would be the implantation of the fertilized egg in the uterine wall that occurs about six to seven days after fertilization. Catholic theologians of the past held that ensoulment or animation, that is, the infusion of the spiritual soul into the embryo, occurs when the matter is sufficiently organized to sustain the spiritual soul or substantial form of man. No contemporary theologian or philosopher of the Aristotelian tradition is willing to indicate any specific degree of development or any point in time when the ensoulment or hominization takes place, but some do not exclude the possibility that it does not happen at the moment of fertilization. Most contemporary philosophers of the Aristotelian tradition, however, hold that the substantial form of man, that is, "humanness," is present from conception because only the presence of a specifically human cause can explain the human effects of the orderly teleological growth of the *conceptus* into a fully developed child who is undoubtedly a human being.

In its latest document on abortion,[3] the Catholic Church does not take a stand concerning the time the spiritual soul is infused into the *conceptus*. This question is left open, as is clearly stated in footnote 19 of the *Declaration on Procured Abortion* made by the Sacred Congregation for the Doctrine of Faith. The *Declaration* insists, however, that even if the *spiritual* soul is infused later than at the time of fertilization, *human* life is present from the time of conception. Furthermore, even if there were some doubt as to the humanity of the *conceptus*, we are prohibited from endangering the life of a being that is possibly already man with a spiritual soul. One has to follow the safer course in this case, for one is not allowed to perform an action that might kill a person. The question of the beginning of human life is not a scientific, but a philosophical and ethical one, the *Declaration* insists.

Beginning of Brain Waves

Some hold that human life begins when the brain starts functioning and brain waves can be observed. The reason for this position is the widely held opinion that death is the cessation of the electric activity of the brain. The electric waves of the brain can be measured by the electroencephalogram (EEG). A flat EEG reading means that the brain is not functioning anymore and the person is dead. It would be logical, they argue, to count the beginning of human life from the moment the brain starts functioning since brain activity is the basis of rational human life. The difficulty with this position is that brain death indicates the end of human life as we know it, the dead brain having no capacity to revive itself. But the developing embryo has the natural capacity to bring on the functioning of the brain. The two stages of human life are, then, entirely different from the point of view of brain functioning. The embryo contains the natural capacity to develop all the human activities: perceiving, reasoning, willing and relating to others. Death means the end of natural growth, the cessation of these abilities.

Quickening

Another opinion held that "quickening," that is, the noticeable movements of the fetus in the womb, is the starting point of human life. This moment can be easily determined because it is perceived by the mother. Aristotle and some legal traditions permitted abortion only before quickening. The perception of a living being in the mother's womb is certainly an important time for the woman who is "with child," but it is difficult to argue convincingly that the fetus is not human until its movement and growth can be felt. What is the particular effect of this movement on the humanity of the fetus? How can the movement indicate the transformation of the non-human fetus into a human being? If it is only a sign of a cause that produces this transformation, what is this cause that suddenly appears and brings into existence a human being?

Viability

Viability is another dividing line that some maintain is what distinguishes the non-human fetus from the human. This opinion seems to be the basis of the Supreme Court decision of 1973 ruling that states can prohibit the killing of the fetus in the last stage of development. The reasoning is that at this point the fetus could survive outside the womb and thus already has an independent human life. It would seem that the previous difficulties have to be faced by the followers of this opinion, too. How does viability transform *the nature* of the fetus so that the non-human being then turns into a human being? Is viability not just an extrinsic criterion imposed upon the fetus by some members of society who simply declare that the fetus will be accepted at that moment as a human being? In addition, the time of viability cannot be determined precisely, and this fact would create great practical problems for those who hold this opinion.

Birth

Finally, some would consider humanity to be present only after birth, when the child has become biologically independent of his mother. But the independence of a newborn baby is very tenuous. It is not convincing to argue that this kind of independence turns the allegedly non-human viable fetus into a human being.

A Philosophical Question

It seems to me that science can give us valuable data about the development of a human being from conception until birth and beyond, but all the scientific information cannot pinpoint the time at which the developing fetus should be considered a human being. The question is primarily a philosophical and not a scientific one. Are we not, then, thrown back into a dilemma based on the arbitrary opinions of the philosophers? There are certainly many contradictory opinions in philosophy, and one can wonder whether one philosopher's opinion is better than another's.

Cause and Effect

The task of philosophy is to clarify concepts and to offer reasons for the understanding of the great questions of human life to which scientific data cannot give us the answers. One factor that somehow can clarify the question of the humanity of the fetus is the connection of specific effects with specific causes. The union of ovum and sperm results in a specific being with a specific energy that produces activities in the embryo which finally issue in a fully developed child, a human being. From the activities of a being we can conclude to its nature; from the effects we can conclude to the presence of an appropriate cause. The effects and operations of the cause in this case are human, so the cause must be human, too. If it were not human, it could not produce the effects that are human. Aristotle called the source of the growth and specific operations of a being its substantial form. Today we call this mysterious center of beings their nature, that which explains to us why they act in a specific way and produce specific effects characteristic of their species. Going backward from the birth of the child, we cannot find any break in the continuous development of the being just born that would make it a different individual being before birth. There is a personal identity in that being. It is the same being from the fertilized ovum to birth and adulthood. It is different from any other being. It seems that human life is a continuous development and growth from conception until death.

It could be objected that the development and activities of the early embryo can be explained by a vegetative or animal nature. Human nature, as the cause of specifically human activities, replaces the vegetative or animal nature later, according to this theory. The followers of Aristotelian hylomorphism, St. Thomas Aquinas among them, accept this position as reasonable. But this theory has to explain satisfactorily the uninterrupted, continuous development of the embryo that is not broken up into three detectable and separate stages. A fertilized ovum genetically differs from the initial stage of a specific plant or animal. Its nature and specificity does not change during its growth toward a specific being we call man. We should not unnecessarily assume the existence of multiple causes or beings when one cause or being can explain the phenomenon satisfactorily.

Twinning and Recombination

The facts of occasional twinning and recombination are sometimes brought up as an objection against the previous argument. Twinning is the division of one fertilized ovum into two separately developing embryos. The result is identical twins. According to some embryologists[4] twinning may occur until about the fourteenth day after fertilization. Recombination is the joining of the two independently developing cell-groups into one so that ultimately there will be only one fetus instead of twins. Recombination, too, can occur until about the beginning of the third week after fertilization. According to some, the facts of twinning and recombination prove that a fertilized ovum cannot be a human person because individual incommunicability is the essential note of personhood. A zygote that can become two persons or two zygotes that can combine into one are not irrevocably individuals and thus cannot be considered human persons. Although zygotes contain forty-six chromosomes and human genes and thus are human in a certain way, they are not irrevocably individual human persons.

The objection carries some weight. Twinning and recombination, however, can be understood in such a way that the validity of the argument for the presence of a human individual from the moment of fertilization is not destroyed. Before twinning, there was certainly one organism, an initial developing being. This being continues on its own individual existence. But in addition to this being, there is another individual, distinct being whose origin has to be explained. Some biologists think that the origin of this second being can be explained by some form of asexual reproduction.

It has been observed that life at an early stage of development sometimes reproduces by asexual fission. In this explanation recombination, too, could be understood as one of the original beings continuing its development and existence while the other ceases to exist. In both cases, one definite cause and source of the activities and development of a human individual is there from the beginning.

The philosophical argument for the presence of a human vital principle from the time of fertilization may not force the assent of even the philosophically educated person. Nonetheless, it has enough weight to establish at least the probability of the presence of a human individual from conception. This probability in turn substantiates the duty not to expose the developing fetus to danger or deliberately to kill it, because we are obliged to choose the safer course and to avoid harming a being that is possibly or probably human.

Conflicting Values in Abortion

After having discussed the central issue of abortion, that is, the humanity of the fetus, we have to consider the arguments that are usually offered for the justification of abortion. All the arguments compare the value of the developing human life with some other value. It is reasoned that in the case of conflicting moral values, when only one value can be safeguarded, the logical and moral choice is to favor the greater value.

The Life of the Mother

In some cases, the *life of the mother* can be in danger if a pregnancy continues. One such instance is that of an ectopic pregnancy. This occurs when the fertilized ovum does not descend into the womb but becomes implanted in the fallopian tube and begins to develop there. The embryo has no chance to grow to viability in the tube, and in the course of its growth it will cause a rupture with bleeding, endangering the life of the mother. In the present state of medicine, only surgical removal of the fetus can save the mother's life. Here we have an instance of one human life opposed to another human life. Only the mother's life can be saved. It would be unreasonable not to remove the embryo and let both human lives perish. The moral law is rational and never obliges us to do something that goes against sound reason.

Advances in obstetrics have eliminated many dramatic cases in which there was a clear conflict between the life of the mother and that of the fetus. Cesarean operations have become a routine procedure when difficult birth is foreseen. These have greatly reduced the dilemma of being forced to choose between two lives. Nevertheless, if there are cases when sound medicine cannot save both lives, the ethical principle remains valid, namely, it is better to save one life than let both human beings die.

The clear conflict of maternal and fetal lives, however, is not the controversial issue of the abortion debate. Most abortions are performed not to save the life of the mother but to obtain some other human value that is opposed in some way to pregnancy.

The Health of the Mother

In the case of *therapeutic abortion* the life of the fetus is opposed to the health of the pregnant woman. The advocates of such an abortion attempt to justify it by affirming that the pregnant mother's physical health is more valuable than the life of the fetus; the greater value is chosen, they say. But there are some problems with this sort of justification. First, human life is more valuable than physical health. Then, the question remains as to whether the abortion is necessary to restore health. Modern methods of medicine can deal with most complications of pregnancy. Illnesses that are not connected with pregnancy are not cured by abortion, and if pregnancy would intensify the illness, remedies can be applied until the fetus reaches viability. It is not argued that there are no cases when the health of the mother would not suffer because of pregnancy or that health is not a great value, but it is being maintained that the life of the fetus is a greater value than physical health and that remedies should be applied to cure the mother's illness in place of an abortion.

Mental health that comes into conflict with the life of the fetus offers even less convincing reasons for abortion. Normal pregnancy of a married woman is not a disease and, in itself, does not cause mental illness. Psychological problems that are somehow occasioned by pregnancy or its accompanying circumstances can be treated, just as any other psychological problem, without resorting to abortion. There are alternative solutions to abortion, and in order to preserve the human life of the fetus, one is obliged to use a therapy that does not endanger human life.

Rape, Incest

A woman whose pregnancy is caused by *rape or incest* is the victim of cruel and inhuman violence. Her mental anguish and psychological suffering is the direct result of a pregnancy forced upon her against her will. Statutory rape is the legal term for an illicit intercourse with a consenting woman who is under the legal age for free consent, but it will help the clarity of our moral evaluation if we limit our consideration to rape and incest that are forced upon a woman against her will. It is argued that in these tragic cases the great value of the mental health of a woman who becomes pregnant as a result of rape or incest can be best safe-guarded by abortion. It is also said that a pregnancy caused by rape or incest is the result of a grave injustice and that the victim should not be obliged to carry the fetus to viability. This would keep reminding her for nine months of the violence committed against her and would just increase her mental anguish.

It is reasoned that the value of the woman's mental health is greater than the value of the life of the fetus. In addition, it is maintained that the fetus is an aggressor against the woman's integrity and personal life; it is only just and morally defensible to repel an aggressor even by killing him if that is the only way to defend personal and human values. It is concluded, then, that abortion is justified in these cases.

In discussing the criminal cases of rape and incest, we must avoid even the appearance of insensitivity to the serious plight and suffering of the victims. Once a woman has been violated, it does not help her if we plead for greater police protection and safety in the streets. It is assumed that victims of rape should receive immediate medical treatment to prevent conception. But if pregnancy nevertheless occurs, we must deal with the assessment of the opposing values, the life of the fetus and the mental and physical sufferings of the woman if she carries the fetus to term.

To clarify the issue, we have to state that the fetus is not an aggressor. The aggressor is the rapist and the fetus is an innocent victim just as much as the mother. It may not be killed, therefore, on the ground of its being an aggressor. Also, if we compare the human life of the fetus with the expected psychological relief of the woman through abortion, human life objectively has to be placed higher on the scale of values than the values a woman could obtain by abortion. In these tragic cases alternative ways must be used to help the victims of rape. These include psychological, religious and social help, and preparation for adoption if the victims do not want to keep the child. It is well known that society has not always been solicitous enough about the victims of rape. In recent years, however, the situation has improved. The police, courts and hospitals treat rape victims with much greater understanding and sensitivity, so that women are not pushed by their shock into procuring an abortion as the only way to alleviate their suffering. There are now more than 700 centers in the nation helping rape victims.

Eugenic Abortion

Another argument for abortion is offered by the advocates of *eugenic abortion*: it is better for a child not to be born than to lead a life burdened with crippling genetic disorders. Abortion is recommended in cases where certain defects are discovered in the developing fetus. Defects can be produced by various causes. Viral infections can cause crippling defects. Exposure to rubella, for instance, especially during the first trimester of pregnancy, can cause deafness, cataract, mental retardation and several kinds of deformities. The use of certain drugs during pregnancy can also cause defects. Thalidomide, the German tranquilizer, was a tragic example. According to recent findings, even alcohol and tobacco smoking can harm the developing fetus. Many abnormalities, however, are due to genetic defects, that is, to faulty genes inherited from one or both parents. Irregular distribution of chromosomes also produces defects. One of the most common examples of this kind of abnormality is Down's syndrome. Amniocentesis and other tests can discover about seventy inherited disorders in the fetus. Amniocentesis involves the analysis of a small amount of the amniotic fluid that surrounds the fetus in the uterus and contains some fetal cells. The fluid is obtained through the insertion of a hollow needle into the uterus.

For amniocentesis to work the woman must wait until at least the sixteenth week of pregnancy before the fluid is taken from the uterus. For the result, she must then wait another two or three weeks. A new technique for obtaining and testing fetal cells for genetic defects has been recently tested in the United States and Europe. It is called Chorionic Villi Sampling (CVS). The test can be done during the first three months of pregnancy and its results can be evaluated overnight. It is a painless procedure and the risks are probably the same as those of amniocentesis, which are about one in 200 women suffering some infection or some other complication that may lead to miscarriage.[5]

It is argued that eugenic abortion is primarily for the sake of the child and only secondarily for the sake of the mother or both parents. Recent rulings of the New York Court of Appeals (1978) and of the New Jersey Supreme Court (1979) hold physicians liable for abnormal births if the doctor fails to advise the patient that she may give birth to an abnormal child. If the doctor's negligence deprives a woman of her legal right to an abortion, he may be required to pay damages for the "wrongful birth." These and similar court rulings in other states will increase the incidence of eugenic abortions. Some eugenicists even would make it obligatory to destroy seriously defective life before birth. As it stands now, eugenic abortion is legal in most countries but not obligatory.

The morality of eugenic abortion has to be judged again by comparing the opposing values. The comparison is difficult here because one of the values is really a disvalue, that is, the ending of life before it can truly develop. One could perhaps speak of an absence of suffering caused by genetic defects and of an avoidance of burdens placed on parents and society in having to care for the defective child. The value of the defective child's life should be compared with these advantages. Eugenic abortion is not for the sake of the patient, the defective child, because it does not cure the disease but simply destroys the patient. We all wish we could prevent or cure genetic defects, but this desire does not entitle us to destroy incipient life. It seems that many defective children who are allowed to be born enjoy life according to their capacities. A number of them have become useful members of society. Our social nature imposes a duty upon us and the whole society to look after the less fortunate members of the human family. That many persons understand this obligation of our common humanity is indicated by the fact that the number of couples adopting victims of genetic defects recently has been growing rapidly.[6]

Unmarried Women and Abortion

According to a report of the National Center for Disease Control, most women requesting abortion, at least in the United States, are young and unmarried. The reasons for these requests are obvious. These women do not want to be burdened with the undesired results of their premarital sexual activities. Abortion is being used in these cases as a method of birth control. The growing number of teenage pregnancies and abortions has rightly aroused a general concern. Even pro-abortionists agree that abortion is the least desirable method of birth control. It causes psychological scars in most young women and weakens their ability to form a lasting and stable relationship in marriage.

Professors Melvin Zelnik and John F. Kantner at the Johns Hopkins School of Hygiene and Public Health have been conducting periodic research on premarital teenage sexual activity and pregnancy.

According to their latest finding, some 50% of U.S. teenage women (aged 15–19) in metropolitan areas had premarital sexual activity in 1979 as against 30% in 1971 and 43% in 1976. In spite of the availability of contraceptives, premarital pregnancy among teenagers almost doubled during the past decade. Young women are less likely to legitimize pregnancy through marriage than in the past and they are more likely to terminate pregnancy through abortion. During the same survey years abortions procured by these young women rose from 23% to 33% and then to 37% of all premarital pregnancies.[7]

Abortions are obviously not the solution to this problem. Pragmatic school authorities have come to the conclusion that more contraceptive information and services will prevent pregnancies and abortions. But several years of sex education have not achieved this goal. Exactly the opposite has happened: the proportion of teenage pregnancies nearly doubled and the absolute number more than doubled between 1971 and 1979, according to data published by the Planned Parenthood Federation of America. According to the National Center for Health Statistics, "A majority of black babies, 55 percent in 1979 as opposed to 38 percent in 1970, were born out of wedlock. But the percentage increase for whites is even more pronounced; the number of illegitimate babies rose from 4.7 percent in 1970 to 9.4 percent in 1979."[8]

More sex education is needed, but it should be a real education, and not just biological information about male and female sexuality and contraceptives. Sex education should emphasize the values of family, respect for persons, the meaning of true love, which is not just sexual attraction, and especially the responsibility for the consequences of one's actions. In other words, young people should be taught to grow up morally, to become responsible persons who can understand that proper and responsible sexual activity should take place between two loving, mature persons joined in a stable marriage.

Abortion as a birth control method, whether outside or within marriage, cannot be justified. The killing of unwanted innocent human beings is here compared with the social and economic problems their birth causes. We have to conclude that killing innocent human beings is a greater evil than the very real social and economic ills of unwed motherhood or unwanted parenthood. The alternative solutions have to come from two directions: (a) prevention of extramarital pregnancies through moral education for responsible sexual conduct; (b) psychological, social and material help for unwed expectant mothers to give birth to their children. If they do not want to give up their children for adoption, they should be assisted in bringing them up. They should be especially helped to be sexually mature and responsible in their future life.

The role of adoption should not be overlooked as an alternative to abortion. There are many childless couples who would be happy to adopt children. In recent years, however, it has been true that there are not enough children available for adoption because of the high number of abortions.

The most frequent cases of abortion, as we have seen, are not the tragic dilemmas of life or death of the mother or the child, but those of premarital pregnancies. Since many pro-abortionists are also concerned about this situation, there should be cooperation, at least in this area, between anti-abortionists and pro-abortionists to reduce the number of premarital pregnancies and thus prevent a great number of abortions. Abortion certainly has to be judged to be the worst method of birth control.

QUESTIONS FOR REVIEW AND DISCUSSION

1. How did the ancient world judge the morality of abortion?

2. Can the Supreme Court make actions right which are morally wrong by their nature or vice versa? What is the difference between legality and morality?

3. When does human life begin? Can embryology decide the question? Does philosophy, applying the principle of causality, complement biology on this question?

4. Is there a difference between personhood and "humanness"?

5. How do you evaluate the morality of saving the mother's life by abortion when, without it, both mother and child would die?

6. What are the human values pro-abortionists intend to defend through abortion? How do you evaluate these values as opposed to the life of the fetus?

7. How do you evaluate the social and ethical problems of abortion procured by unmarried young women?

Notes

1. Quoted in Douglas Johnson, Letters to the Editor, *The New York Times*, January 5, 1983.

2. "World Abortion Trends Detailed." *Intercom.*, September/October 1982, p. 13.

3. Sacra Congregatio pro Doctrina Fidei, "Declaratio de abortu procurato." *Acta Apostolicae Sedis*, 1974, pp. 730–747.

4. James J. Diamond, M.D., "Abortion, Animation and Biological Hominization." *Theological Studies*, June 1975, pp. 305–342.

5. "New Tests for Birth Defects." *Science News*, August 20, 1983, p. 116.

6. Lesley Oelsner, "More Couples Adopting Victims of Genetic Defects." *The New York Times*, March 8, 1979.

7. *Intercom.*, November/December 1981, p. 7.

8. *Intercom.*, November/December 1981, p. 11.

4 Eugenics and the Quality of Life

Certain facts about heredity have been known from ancient times. It has been observed that children resemble their parents and grandparents, that certain typical traits are transmitted from generation to generation. Man learned to improve crops and domestic animals by cross-fertilization and by selecting good specimens for reproduction. *Francis Galton* is considered the father of the modern movement to improve the human stock by the application of the laws of heredity. He coined the term *eugenic*, which means well-born. Eugenics as a movement is based on the science of *eugenics*, which investigates the methods by which the genetic make-up of human beings can be improved.

Galton's ideas are described in his book, *Hereditary Genius: An Inquiry into Its Laws and Consequences* (London, 1869). A cousin of Charles Darwin, he applied the principle of the survival of the fittest to the human race as it existed in his time. He and his followers claimed that natural selection did not work any more for human beings because charitable institutions and governments protected the feeble, the sickly, the unfit, who survive to propagate their kind. This leads to the decay of the human race and to all kinds of social ills that plague society. The decline has to be stopped by preventing the propagation of the degenerate, the feebleminded, the drunkard, the criminal, that is, all the undesirable elements of society. This should be done through government intervention, by forbidding marriages between inferior persons, by separating them from society or by forcibly sterilizing them. The superior races, especially the North European type, have to be encouraged and helped to propagate their own kind and thus improve the human stock. Real charity means to help the strong rather than the weak and thus hasten the demise of the "inferior" races. Genetically defective human beings and "inferior" races cannot achieve a quality of life that would make life worth living for them.

Negative and Positive Eugenics

Two kinds of eugenics can be distinguished according to the goal each proposes: *negative and positive eugenics*.

Negative eugenics tries to weed out genetic defects. Its main methods are sterilization or institutionalization of the defective, whereby they are prevented from transmitting genetic defects and breeding inferior human beings. At the beginning of the movement, forced sterilization was proposed as preferable and less expensive. Modern eugenicists, however, would rather use information and persuasion than force. The means they want to apply is genetic screening, whereby people can find out whether they carry defective genes, allowing them to decide to abstain from procreation in order to prevent the birth of defective children.

Positive eugenics, on the other hand, tries to breed in desirable traits and produce people of "higher quality." This could be achieved in various ways. Semen and ova of "superior" human beings could be used for artificial insemination or inovulation; artificially produced or separated genes for superior traits could be introduced into the genetic material; in a less futuristic way, "superior" human beings simply could be encouraged to get married and have children.

History of the Eugenic Movement

The eugenic movement quickly spread from England to continental Europe, the United States and Japan. Two phases have to be distinguished in the development of the movement. The dividing line between the two stages is more or less the end of World War II. The ideas of the first stage were based on a rather deficient knowledge of heredity. The simple observation that certain traits are transmitted from parents to children was the basis of a generalized formula of the early geneticists according to which bad character traits and all kinds of faults were said to be inherited. The rediscovery, in 1900, of

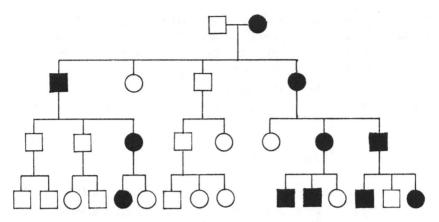

Dominant inheritance. All the shaded individuals (circles for female and squares for male) have the dominant gene.

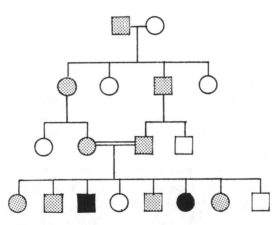

Recessive inheritance. The lightly shaded individuals are carriers of a single recessive gene. The last generation was produced by consanguineous marriage where both parents were carriers. There are many carriers among the offspring and some, being homozygous for the recessive gene, will show the disorder.

the heredity laws of Gregor Mendel seemed to furnish a scientific basis to the eugenics movement. The pioneering and now well-known experiments of Mendel with pea plants demonstrated that inherited characteristics are carried by certain discrete units, which he called elements, now known as *genes*. Geneticists believed that most of our traits are determined by single genes. When the German biologist August Weismann proved that acquired characteristics are not transmitted by heredity, the obvious conclusion for eugenicists was that social reforms cannot improve the condition of the human race; it can be ameliorated only by selective breeding, that is, by preventing inferior individuals from procreating and producing their kind.

Modern Biology and Eugenics

The second phase of the eugenic movement began with the rapid development of microbiology and molecular genetics after the Second World War. New discoveries showed that the transmission of human traits and genetic defects basically follows the Mendelian laws of inheritance, but that it is not due to one single gene acting independently. It is known that the physical bases of heredity are the chromosomes that carry more than fifty thousand genes and perhaps as many as one hundred thousand. The nucleus of every human cell contains forty-six chromosomes, each half inherited from each parent. Chromosome analysis, called karyotype, can identify certain hereditary defects and can detect certain abnormalities, such as an extra chromosome. The replication of chromosome twenty-one, for instance, is the cause of Down's syndrome or mongolism. Locating or "mapping" the genes on the chromosomes is progressing at an amazing speed, despite the painstaking procedure it involves. Some 800 genes have already been located. Scientists hope that by the end of the century the approximately 100,000 genes will be mapped and catalogued.

Defective Genes

A large number of genetically inherited defects have been classified. Tay-Sachs disease, cystic fibrosis, hemophilia, sickle-cell anemia, and phenylketonuria (PKU) are some of the more serious diseases caused by defective genes. The goal of the present-day eugenics movement is the prevention of congenital diseases by *genetic screening* and *genetic counseling*. Future parents can be told what kind of recessive or dominant genes they carry that might cause ge-

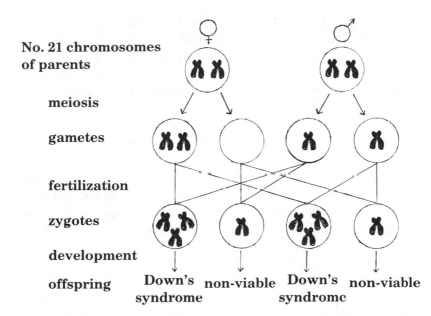

No. 21 chromosomes of parents

meiosis

gametes

fertilization

zygotes

development

offspring   Down's   non-viable   Down's   non-viable
                 syndrome   syndrome

Down's syndrome results when No. 21 chromosomes fail to separate (non-disjunction) during meiosis, giving rise to an ovum with two No. 21 chromosomes. When this ovum is fertilized, the zygote contains three No. 21 chromosomes (trisomy).

Down's syndrome also results from translocation (not illustrated here) when a third No. 21 chromosome, or most of it, comes attached to a larger chromosome, usually No. 15.

netic disease in their children. Prospective parents can calculate the probability of having a defective child if they decide to have a family.

Compulsory Sterilization

The early eugenicists, turned political activists, succeeded in pushing through legislation for compulsory sterilization of idiots, imbeciles and the feebleminded who today would be called mentally retarded. Feeblemindedness was considered to be the cause of criminal behavior, sexual aberrations and other anti-social conduct. Two reasons were given for mandatory sterilization. First, since mental retardation is inherited (as the eugenicists believed), the common good demands the prevention of the birth of defective offspring who are a burden to society. Second, mentally retarded parents cannot fulfill the basic duties of parenthood, i.e., the education of their children, and therefore they should not be allowed to reproduce.

The Courts and Sterilization

In the United States there are still twenty-one states that permit sterilization of mental defectives. Some allow the sterilization of habitual criminals, epileptics and syphilitic persons. Seventy thousand Americans have been sterilized by court orders since 1907.[1]

The constitutionality of compulsory sterilization laws was challenged in the courts, but in 1925, in the case of *Buck v. Bell*, the U.S. Supreme Court upheld the validity of these laws. The plaintiff, Carrie Buck, an eighteen-year-old imbecile white woman, was confined in the Virginia State Colony for Epileptics and the Feebleminded. She was the daughter of a feebleminded mother in the same institution and had given birth to an illegitimate daughter, who, in the opinion of a nurse, was also an imbecile. The Virginia State Department of Health ordered Carrie to be sterilized, as the newly enacted Virginia law permitted. Carrie resisted the order and brought a suit against J.H. Bell, the superintendent of the State Colony. The order was upheld by the Supreme Court. Chief Justice Holmes gave the following reasoning in his summation of the case: "We have seen more than once that the public welfare may call upon the best citizens for their lives. It would be strange if we could not call upon those who already sap the strength of the state for these lesser sacrifices, often not felt to be such by those concerned, in order to prevent our being swamped with incompetence. It is better for the world if instead of waiting to execute degenerate offspring for crime, or let them starve from imbecility, society can prevent those who are manifestly unfit from continuing their kind. The principle that sustains compulsory vaccination is broad enough to cover cutting the fallopian tubes. Three generations of imbeciles are enough."

Soon after Adolf Hitler came to power in Germany, the Third Reich prepared a new law for compulsory sterilization of the unfit. This Heredity Health Law came into force in 1933. It was the beginning of a large-scale eugenics program in Nazi Germany. The cruel application of the law and the great number of the victims of the racial policies of Nazi Germany contributed to the lessening of enthusiasm for eugenics in the United States after World War II. Laws that are still in force are not carried out with the same vigor as before. Nevertheless, some states still enforce some provisions of the law, so that the ethico-legal problems of eugenics have become even more manifest as the ideas of eugenics are based more and more on the new developments in genetics.

Morality of Eugenic Sterilization

The ethical questions involved in eugenic sterilization can be grouped around three goals:

(a) compulsory sterilization for the sake of society;
(b) sterilization as punishment for criminal sexual behavior;
(c) voluntary eugenic sterilization for the sake of retarded persons in order to prevent their being sexually abused.

(a) *Sterilization for the Sake of Society*
Most existing eugenic laws in the United States offer the good of society as justification for compulsory sterilization. The argument proposes that the individual, at least in some cases, can be obliged to do certain things for the good of the whole society. Draft laws and compulsory immunization laws are cited as examples. As members of society, we are obliged to cooperate with others to protect and promote the common good, in which we all participate in some way. This cooperation becomes especially crucial when some great evil threatens the good of all, for example, a military aggression or the spread of contagious diseases. Eugenic sterilization, however, is not necessary for the prevention of any great evil threatening society. Persons with a low I.Q. or those who are physically defective, or alcoholics, can have very healthy and bright offspring, as many such cases have been recorded in history. Criminal behavior is not transmitted by genes to the offspring. The state does not have a right over the bodies of innocent citizens. Societies and governments are formed to protect the rights of the individuals and not to take them away.

Some persons may be so retarded that they could be unable to fulfill the duties of married life and take care of children. But sterilization would not help these persons; it would not improve their mental abilities. So there is no justification for violating their physical integrity. Since they cannot understand and fulfill the duties of marriage, they are not competent to conclude a marriage contract. Such persons have to be institutionalized if their families cannot take care of them. This is a much more humane and a better way to help the unfortunate members of society than sterilization, which would not be of any benefit to them.

(b) *Sterilization as Punishment*

Sometimes it is argued that sterilization may be imposed on criminals for sexual offenses as a punishment. If capital punishment or hard labor may be justified, the reasoning goes, the lesser punishment of sterilization should not involve any moral difficulties. But it can be objected to this argument that it belongs to the nature of punishment that it be contrary to a person's wishes, for instance, the loss of freedom in jail, that it be painful in some way and that it bring some disadvantage to the person who is punished. Hardly any of these properties of punishment is realized in sterilization. The sexual deviate would probably welcome sterilization because he could engage more freely in sexual activities without fear of causing pregnancy. Sterilization performed by a surgeon is a minor operation and it is not painful. More and more societies are abandoning capital and corporal punishment as inhuman and not proper in an advanced civilized society. There is no justification for introducing sterilization now as a form of corporal punishment, especially considering the fact that it lacks any of the essential properties of real punishment and that it would not deter a prospective criminal. Sex criminals can be punished in more fitting ways.

(c) *Sterilization for Preventing Sexual Abuse*

Recently, some parents and guardians of retarded young women have asked hospitals to sterilize their charges to prevent sexual abuse and rape of these incompetent persons. There is an attempt to get their consent to the operation. They are given as much information and as many reasons for the operation as these persons can understand. It is argued that guardians can give proxy consent if these retarded women are legally and morally incompetent to give their own consent.

Hospitals, as a rule, refuse to perform this kind of operation without a court order. It seems that the pendulum has swung back from a 1925 Supreme Court decision to the other extreme. Although the *Buck v. Bell* Supreme Court decision has never been directly revoked, there was a Supreme Court decision in 1942 which, in a different context, maintained that the right to procreate was a basic constitutional right and stated that sterilization forever deprived a person of this right.[2] Mindful of this decision, hospitals refuse to sterilize young women even at the request of their legal guardians without a court order.

Recently, in the case of Lee Ann Grady, a nineteen year old retarded woman, the New Jersey Supreme Court ruled that the courts, and not the parents, must decide whether the sterilization of a mentally retarded person would be in the subject's best interest, and whether the person was incapable of participating in the decision.[3] The court held that reproductive capacity is a personal right and the courts, as protectors of individual rights, must make the decision whether the curtailment of this personal right by a surgical intervention serves the best interest of the person involved.

Although the reasons listed under (a) are generally valid, it seems that in this and similar cases a special circumstance adds weight to the arguments proposed to justify sterilization, that is, to take away a capacity which the person could not legally and morally use. Parents and institutions agree that it is much better not to institutionalize the mentally retarded when they can live with their families, so that they may have a greater freedom of movement and preserve some degree of human dignity. The promoters of this opinion argue that precluding pregnancy of a retarded woman through sterilization does not violate her right since, in any case, she may not use this right, for she is incapable of understanding and responsibly exercising the right of reproduction. The courts, however, must consider "the possibility of pregnancy . . . the likelihood of sexual activity; inability of the person to understand contraception; feasibility of a less drastic means of contraception; possibility of postponing sterilization . . . ."[4] It seems that even those who favor sterilization of the retarded want to restrict it only to those cases in which it would appear that less drastic methods to prevent a possible or probable extramarital pregnancy are not feasible.

Genetic Screening

As was mentioned previously, contemporary eugenicists rely mostly on genetic screening and genetic counseling to achieve the goals of the eugenic movement.

Genetic screening refers to various procedures by which inherited abnormalities can be discovered. The procedures can be applied at various stages of a person's existence. It can be prenatal screening, while the fetus is in the uterus. This type of screening is usually done by amniocentesis. Some sixty genetic defects can be detected this way. As mentioned above, recently the chorionic villi sampling method has begun to be tested as a preferred procedure of screening fetuses for genetic defects.

Screening of the newly born for some forms of inherited disorders is mandatory in most states in the United States. Early diagnosis of certain disorders, for instance, phenylketonuria (PKU), can lead to the initiation of treatment that can save lives and cure the disorders. Some hospitals screen the newly born for some thirty genetic defects on a voluntary basis.

Carrier Screening

Adults who are clinically well can be screened to determine whether they are carriers of recessive defective genes of certain genetic diseases. If both parents are carriers of a specific defective gene, there is a one-in-four chance that their children will have the disease. It is estimated that each of us carries from four to eight defective genes of some kind. Since individuals usually have different kinds of bad genes, the chance of procreating children with a genetic disease is quite small. Nevertheless, it happens sometimes and it is a worthy human goal to prevent any disease from occurring. The advocates of mass genetic screening are trying to achieve such a goal.

Their proposal is that every newborn child and every adult should be screened for major genetic disorders and should have a kind of genetic I.D. card or genetic passport.

According to recent statistics, physical and mental disabilities in newborns doubled in 25 years in the United States. Researchers at the University of California have said that in absolute numbers, this means that 140,000 babies born in 1983 will suffer from physical abnormalities, mental retardation or learning problems. The number of children affected by these infirmities was about 70,000 in the late 1950's. Some researchers speculate that the reasons for this growth are increased cigarette smoking by women, more frequent exposure to toxins, and improved medical care techniques that enable the weak to survive and pass on their defective genes. Others, however, argue that the increase is more apparent than real. In the past 25 years the diagnosis of congenital problems has improved, and this fact shows up in the statistics as an increase of the disabled.[5] Reports like this, even if the statistics can be questioned, are an impetus for proposing the introduction of mass genetic screening.

Mass Genetic Screening

The first major attempt at mass genetic screening in the United States was connected with sickle-cell anemia. This is a disease affecting black persons almost exclusively. It is a crippling and painful disease that leads to early death. Twenty-nine states and the District of Columbia had enacted mass genetic-screening laws for sickle-cell anemia, most of them compulsory. Most black legislators strongly supported them. Despite its praiseworthy intent, the mass screening produced a hostile response in the black population and created great confusion. Most states have already repealed the laws mandating the screening and replaced them with voluntary programs.

The unanticipated adverse reaction to the sickle-cell anemia screening brought to the surface several problems that had not been considered before. The public is not ready yet for compulsory mass genetic screening; the average person does not understand the difference between being a carrier of defective genes and having the disease. More education is needed before mass screening either of the whole population or of certain select groups can be undertaken without producing unnecessary anxiety and feelings of stigmatization.

Screening of Industrial Workers

In 1982, fifty-nine large American companies informed the Congressional Office of Technology Assessment that they planned to begin genetic screening of their workers in the next five years. E.T. du Pont de Nemours & Co., the Dow Chemical Company and fifteen other major companies had already used some form of genetic screening of their workers. Screening, the companies argue, can determine genetic predisposition to certain illnesses that might be caused by materials used at the places of work.[6] This kind of genetic screening, however, has aroused concern because "it could lead to discrimination against certain racial and ethnic groups, and because in most cases it is impossible to predict when a person with a given trait will suffer from exposure to a given substance."[7]

In addition to the socio-political problems, there are a number of ethical questions involved in screening. Many screening procedures are still in the experimental stage. It would be unethical to expose persons to these experiments without their informed consent and adequate protection. Confidentiality and privacy, too, are of special ethical importance. How will the data be handled? Who will have access to them? May insurance companies demand amniocentesis to find out whether a fetus has genetic defects, and, if it does, drop the health insurance of the family concerned unless they are willing to abort the child? A very disquieting question arises about what policy governments would follow once universal genetic screening has been accepted. Would "incompatible" men and women be forbidden to get married? Would they be allowed to get married but be "persuaded" not to have children? All kinds of economic pressures could be put on them to limit their freedom of choice in childbearing.[8]

As mentioned above, some of the screening tests are still in the experimental stage. It is a very complex task to "map" the genes and test them for their normalcy. Recently, however, the technique of gene splicing has been applied to the detection of disorders in the genes. Scientists are confident that this technique will substantially shorten the time for the detection of genetic disorders.[9]

Morality of Genetic Screening

Evaluating the morality of genetic screening, it can be stated that in itself it is a neutral means: it can be used for good or for bad purposes. It can be used to obtain information for the treatment of genetic disorders and to help prospective parents to make responsible decisions concerning childbearing. These applications of genetic screening are commendable and ethical. But the use of genetic screening for the purpose of abortion of "defective" fetuses or for limiting freedom of choice in marriage and childbearing would be a violation of basic human rights and unethical.

The introduction of mass genetic screening should be gradual, and at least at the beginning it should be voluntary. It should be limited to genetic defects that can be diagnosed with certitude and are greatly debilitating. The public should be adequately informed and educated about the essentials of genetic screening in order to avoid misunderstandings and stigmatization. As long as it is voluntary, it should be easily accessible for everybody from the financial organizational point of view.

Responsible Parenthood and Genetic Screening

What does responsible parenthood mean in the case of couples who carry defective genes and have a certain degree of probability of giving birth to children with congenital defects? As we have seen, the only justifying purpose of mass genetic screening of adults is the obtaining of information that can lead to the prevention of the birth of abnormal children. One has a duty not to cause suffering or injury to others by his actions even if the bad effects of his action will follow only at a later date. One may not plant a time bomb to cause injury. Procreation in this case is said to be an act that causes injury with some degree of probability. In order to assess the moral responsibility of assuming risk in this case, the question of possible or probable "injury" has to be clarified. Who is injured—the child, the parents or society? What is the severity of the injury? The question here is primarily about the quality or normalcy of the child's life. Should society set standards for normalcy? It would seem not. Genetic defects in themselves do not make a person abnormal. If we consider the child's suffering or difficulties caused by genetic defects, we also have to think about the many values and joys of his life. Nobody can objectively evaluate the two sets of values and disvalues to conclude categorically that such a life is not worth living.

Taking Risks

One should not draw the conclusion from this that prospective parents need not take into consideration the risk they are assuming. As we have seen in Chapter 2, the right of parenthood is not absolute and unlimited. The limitation of this right, however, must be justified. If the probability of greatly defective offspring is very high and the parents are not capable morally or physically of taking care of such children, it would not be ethically responsible on their part to take a chance. They should rather abstain from having children. It would not be right for them to take the high risk in this case and turn their children over to society to care for them. Nurture and education of children are primarily the duty of parents and not of society. According to the principle of subsidiarity, society must help individuals when they cannot cope with their duties alone, but individuals should not shift their personal duties to society when with careful planning they are capable of fulfilling them.

Genetic Counseling

Genetic counseling has the task of interpreting the data of genetic testing and evaluating the ethical responsibilities resulting from them. In the United States the number of genetic-screening laboratories and the various counseling services they offer is steadily growing.[10] Today there are more than 500 genetic counseling centers and satellite facilities in the United States.[11]

Most persons who undergo genetic screening want both an interpretation of the data of the testing and moral guidance in their decision. The ethical part of genetic counseling is not an easy task and, unfortunately, it surpasses the training and educational background of most genetic counselors. One would like to hope that more counselors will be educated who can understand the concrete ethical problems of the counselees. Counselors should be morally sensitive and intellectually capable of giving prudent advice so that the counselees can make their own ethically responsible decisions.

Positive Eugenics

The contemporary eugenic movement deals mostly with the elimination of genetic defects, that is, with negative eugenics. Nevertheless, some scientists as, for instance, the Nobel Prize winner, Herman J. Muller, also advocate the goals of *positive eugenics*, suggesting to breed human beings of "better quality" by bringing together the best of both sexes for reproduction.[12] In this they follow Plato, who supported the idea of positive eugenics in *The Republic*. The modern followers of Plato, however, would use *artificial insemination* as the principal means to achieve the goal of eugenics. According to some far-fetched proposals, legislation should regulate procreation and allow only fertilization of "superior women" by the semen of "superior men." This would allegedly assure the improvement of the human race and guide mankind's evolution to a brighter future.

Artificial Insemination

As it is today, artificial insemination is not used for the futuristic goals of positive eugenics, but recent improvements of the technique make certain limited objectives of positive eugenics possible. In modern times artificial insemination has been used with considerable success in animal husbandry. Through this technique, it is possible to produce superior cows for milk or meat, as well as other kinds of animals with specific characteristics. The theory of artificial insemination has been known for centuries, but its large-scale commercial application became possible only when the technique of freezing and storing sperm for future use became possible in the 1950's.

Artificial human insemination was successfully performed in several cases during the last quarter of the nineteenth century in England, France and the United States. The number of artificial inseminations by the semen of donors (AID) has been steadily growing since the end of World War II in America and other countries. The estimates of children born each year by AID range from ten thousand to twenty-five thousand in the United States alone.

Artificial insemination by donor is the combination of a remedy for sterility and a modern method of positive eugenics. There is an attempt, at least in theory, to select donors with excellent intellectual and physical qualities. Advocates of positive eugenics see the spreading of artificial insemination as a hopeful sign that the goals of breeding a better human race can be achieved. The time has arrived, they say, to concentrate our efforts on enlightened education and legislation regarding positive eugenics.

Sperm Banks

When the technique of freezing sperm had been developed, it became possible to establish sperm banks. There are nine non-commercial frozen sperm banks in the United States connected with university hospitals and clinics.[13] At the same time the number of commercial semen banks is growing steadily. Women requesting artificial insemination can choose from the semen of a great variety of donors, whose physical and intellectual qualities are listed by the bank. The identity of the donor, however, is kept strictly confidential and is not revealed either to the woman, to public authorities or to anybody else.

Sperm Bank for Super-Intelligence

In 1980, Robert K. Graham, a wealthy California business man, began to collect sperm from Nobel Prize winning scientists and offered it to young women with high I.Q.'s. William Shockley, who won the Nobel Prize for physics in 1956, openly admitted that he had contributed to this sperm bank.[14] Some two dozen women applied for the sperm of the anonymous Nobel donors and several had been artificially inseminated. The first baby in this eugenic experiment was born to a Chicago woman in April 1982. It later turned out that the mother and her husband had served time in prison for fraud and the husband had been charged with neglecting his wife's children from a previous marriage.

Many Nobel Prize winners took a dim view of Graham's project. There is no guarantee, they argue, that the children born will be super-intelligent and that high I.Q. persons produce better people and a better society.

Another unusual sperm bank opened in Oakland, California in 1983. It is run entirely by women and is dedicated to the ideals of feminism. Its purpose is to serve all women regardless of their race, genetic status or sexual orientation. Lesbians and single women are encouraged to participate.[15]

Artificial Insemination and the Single Woman

It is a serious ethical question whether single women should deliberately conceive and bear children and try to raise their offspring without the benefit of a normal family environment. It would be irresponsible for women to bear children without the resources to care for them.

It has been estimated that one out of ten AID recipients is unmarried or lesbian.[16] There have also been reports that a single woman on welfare had been artificially inseminated. As she became pregnant, she received pregnancy welfare assistance, and later she also received aid for child rearing when her child was born. One of the principles of responsible parenthood is that parents have the duty to take care of their children. They should not have more children than they can provide for. In addition to this question of financial responsibility, it is unethical deliberately to bring children into a home with only one parent. It is known that children whose parents die or are divorced suffer from the lack of normal family life. One has the duty not to expose children to an abnormal family life if one can avoid it.

Artificial Insemination by Husband

Artificial insemination is occasionally done with the husband's semen (AIH) because some physical or psychological problem hinders normal intercourse. Some husbands who undergo vasectomy for contraceptive purposes have their semen stored for eventual use in the future if, for some unforeseen reason, they will want to have a child later. Many moralists do not think it unethical to have artificial insemination by one's husband if, for medical reasons, it becomes necessary to help the couple to have their own genetic child. They argue that the unity and the purpose of marriage is preserved and science in this way only helps the couple to reach the natural goal of marriage. Some moralists, however, object to AIH because the unitive and procreative aspects of the natural generative act are separated.

Artificial Insemination by Donor

AID, on the other hand, presents greater ethical problems. Marriage is monogamous by its very nature, but AID brings a third party into this exclusive union in a very realistic way. One should not get involved here in the controversy about whether or not AID constitutes adultery. The answer to this question will depend on how one defines adultery. If it is carnal union with a partner outside of marriage, then AID is not adultery. But if it means conceiving a child by the semen of a man other than one's husband, AID should be judged adultery. This is, however, a controversy only about terminology. The unethical fact is that a third person is brought into the marriage, which is an exclusive union of one man and one woman for their mutual love and for the purpose of procreation.

The above reasoning can be criticized, however, by pointing out that AID helps to achieve one of the main purposes of marriage, namely the procreation of children. The question nevertheless remains as to whether parenthood is such an absolute right that a woman whose husband is infertile may have a child by any means, even going outside the marriage. One has to consider that fertility or infertility is not an individual question but a collective and mutual problem of a man and woman joined in marriage for better or worse. Nobody is fertile or infertile alone but only in regard to his or her marriage partner. If a marriage happens to be infertile, the partners should not alter the essential nature of marriage in order to bring a child into their conjugal society. This could be done without breaking the unity of their marriage by adopting a child. The basic equality of the spouses and the unity of the marriage is safeguarded in adoption and it can be seen as, in a way, remedying infertility.

AID might produce psychological problems for the husband, who would be reminded every day of his inadequacy as he sees the child who is not really his. The wife may have certain psychological problems, too, as she fantasizes about the real father of her child. As for the child, will he be told later of his origin, or will he be kept uninformed? In either case, a certain amount of tension may be caused between the child and the parents. All these factors tend to weaken the harmony of the marriage and counteract the fact that infertility was remedied in some way by artificial insemination.

Motherhood by Proxy

Recently, the media reported news about a new application of artificial insemination for bringing children into an infertile marriage. This is a modern version of the biblical case of Abraham's infertile wife, Sarah, asking her husband to have relations with her Egyptian slave girl, Hagar, to bear a child for her: "Perhaps she can bear a child for me" (Genesis 16:2). Hagar conceived and bore Ishmael.

Today some infertile wives enter into a contract with fertile women to bear children for them by proxy. The sperm of their husbands is used artificially to inseminate the hired women, who agree to bear a child for them and surrender the baby at birth. The fee for this "service," according to reports, is between $10,000 and $15,000.

Dr. Richard Levin of Louisville, Kentucky was the first to organize this surrogate motherhood arrangement when he opened Surrogate Parenting Associates in 1980. Dr. Levin claimed that thousands of childless couples sought his services and several thousand women were interested in becoming surrogate mothers.[17]

Dr. Levin accepts as surrogates only married women who already have their own children. The candidates must undergo extensive physical and psychiatric examination. They sign a contract that they will surrender the child at birth and that they will abstain from smoking, drinking alcohol and taking drugs during their pregnancy. The couple and the surrogate never meet face to face and never learn each other's names.

Noel Keane, an attorney in Dearborn, Michigan, believes that the surrogate mother and the couple should know each other. Mr. Keane has appeared on television several times and has stated that for a fee of $5,000 he will put surrogate mothers in touch with childless couples.[18]

From the ethical point of view, motherhood by proxy must be judged as an act of causing extramarital pregnancy. Although there is no carnal union between the infertile wife's husband and the surrogate mother, procreation is achieved outside a marriage which is an exclusive union between husband and wife.

In addition to the ethical problems, motherhood by proxy seems also to be illegal in most states. In essence, it includes a contract to sell a baby for money. For instance, Steven L. Beshear, the attorney general of Kentucky, maintains that paid surrogate motherhood contracts violate the state law that forbids payment for "the procurement of any child for adoption purposes."[19]

It seems that the whole idea of surrogate motherhood has not been well received by the general public either, as the common use of the derisive phrase "wombs for rent" also indicates.

A.I.D. and Eugenics

The practice of using the same donor for multiple insemination and the lack of records on true paternity may result in inadvertent marriages between half-sisters and half-brothers. Since the legality of artificial insemination and the legitimacy of children born by it are not clear, physicians are not very anxious to keep adequate records. (Only fourteen states in America have laws concerning the legal status of artificial insemination.) A survey conducted by geneticists and obstetricians at the University of Wisconsin in 1979 found that genetic screening of donors is inadequate and the same donor is frequently used for multiple insemination. Since one ejaculate can fertilize several women, a man donating semen only three or four times can have a large number of natural children. Most doctors recruit their donors from among medical students and young hospital physicians, but genetic screening in these instances mostly consists of asking questions about whether the donor or his family had any genetic disease. The survey found that very few doctors conduct tests to discover any inherited disease of the donor. In any case, since a donor is paid between $140 and $150 for one specimen, the monetary remuneration may induce him to be less honest in his answers.

The President's Ethics Commission has found that "little if any information is obtained about the genetic history or genetic risk of the donor . . . .This casual approach to obtaining donor samples poses several potentially serious problems."[20] Since there is only minimal record keeping, "when AID results in genetic disease, the source of the sample cannot be determined; semen from the donor may be used again and may result in another child with the disease. Indeed, the Commission heard testimony about just such a case."[21]

Responsibility of the Donor

Finally, the donor's act is hardly praiseworthy from the ethical point of view. He may be the father of a large number of children, but he shirks the duties and responsibilities of fatherhood. He just sells his semen and hides his fatherhood from the mother of the children. This flies in the face of the most intimate and deeply human and humanizing relationship of parenthood. His act is dehumanizing.

If artificial insemination for the purpose of positive eugenics became widespread, it would affect not only the humanity of the persons involved in it but also the whole society, as a special race could develop that would claim superiority for its members, having been specially chosen to be superior to the rest of humanity. Mankind has been struggling throughout history to eliminate or lessen discrimination and racism. New divisive elements must not be introduced into our society. Positive eugenics, the deliberate attempt artificially to breed a superior race, is unethical.

QUESTIONS FOR REVIEW AND DISCUSSION

1. What is the main argument of the eugenic movement presented by Francis Galton? How do you evaluate his argument?

2. What is meant by negative and by positive eugenics?

3. How did the development of molecular biology affect the eugenic movement?

4. How do you evaluate the compulsory sterilization of "genetically inferior" persons?

5. What is your ethical evaluation of sterilization of retarded young women to prevent their sexual abuse?

6. What is the morality of genetic screening to learn whether a person is a carrier of defective genes?

7. Should everybody be screened (a) soon after birth? (b) before marriage?

8. Should genetic screening be voluntary or compulsory?

9. What is the task of genetic counseling: scientific information or ethical guidance?

10. How do you evaluate the morality of AID?

11. How do you evaluate the morality of AIH?

12. Is it ethically or scientifically justifiable to produce "super-intelligent" children by using sperm of Nobel Prize winners as Robert K. Graham proposed? Does "the good of society" justify such a project?

Notes

1. Charles R. Kindregan, *The Quality of Life*. Milwaukee: The Bruce Publishing Co., 1969, p. 5.

2. George J. Annas, "Sterilization of the Mentally Retarded." *The Hastings Center Report*, August 1981, p. 18.

3. *The New York Times*. February 19, 1981, p. B 2.

4. Annas, *op. cit.*, p. 79.

5. *The New York Times*. July 18, 1983, p. A 1.

6. "Top 59 U.S. Companies Plan Genetic Screening." *The New York Times*. June 23, 1982, p. A 12.

7. Constance Holden, "Looking at Genes at the Workplace." *Science*. July 23, 1982, p. 336.

8. Cf. Marc Lappe *et al.*, "Ethical and Social Issues in Screening for Genetic Disease." *New England Journal of Medicine*, May 25, 1972.

9. Harold M. Schmeck, Jr., "Genetic Scientists Hail Gains in Field." *The New York Times*. August 14, 1983, p. A 28.

10. For information about the location of screening laboratories and counseling services one can turn to the National Genetics Foundation, 250 West 57th St., New York, New York 10019.

11. President's Commission for the Study of Ethical Problems in Medicine and Biomedical and Behavioral Research, *Screening and Counseling for Genetic Conditions*. Washington, D.C., U.S. Government Printing Office, 1983, p. 11.

12. Cf. Ted Howard and Jeremy Rifkin, *Who Should Play God?* New York: Dell Publishing Co., 1977, pp. 167–170. Joseph Fletcher, *The Ethics of Genetic Control: Ending Reproductive Roulette*. Garden City: Doubleday, 1974.

13. Richard M. Restak, *Premeditated Man*. New York: The Viking Press, 1973, p. 69.

14. "Superkids." *Time*, March 10, 1980, p. 49.

15. *The Hastings Center Report*, February 1983, p. 3.

16. *Ibid.*

17. Cf. "Pregnancy by Proxy." *Newsweek*, July 7, 1980, p. 72.

18. *Ibid.*

19. *The New York Times*. January 28, 1981, p. C 9.

20. President's Commission, *op cit.*, p. 68.

21. *Op cit.*, p. 69.

5 In Vitro Fertilization and Embryo Transfer

Experimentation with Animals

Fertilization of animal ova *in vitro*, that is, in a petri dish or test tube, is a good way to observe the fertilization process and gain scientific knowledge of the growth of an embryo. The ova of the animal can be obtained by surgical process or can be flushed out from the uterus. Laboratory animals are usually given hormones to produce superovulation so that several ova can be gained for the experiment at the same time. The ova then are placed in a petri dish containing nutrients and the semen is added to start the process of fertilization. The growth of the fertilized ova can be studied at various stages, as the embryo is easily observable in a petri dish and accessible to scientific instruments. If a functioning artificial womb could be developed, an animal could be produced in a laboratory. An incubator is basically an artificial womb that helps premature babies complete the time of gestation. Liquid incubators were used in experiments with lamb fetuses that were removed by a Cesarean, and an attempt was made to bring them to term in an artificial womb, but all such experiments have failed so far.

Artificial Womb

Experiments have been performed to make fertilized ova develop in modified test tubes or artificial wombs, but the embryos died long before they could reach the stage of premature fetuses, when they could have been transferred to an incubator to complete the process of gestation. It is not likely that the gap between the initial and concluding stages of gestation in artificial wombs can be bridged in the near future. Thus the time of hatching babies in laboratories had not yet arrived. Nevertheless, work continues in this field and one breakthrough may speed up the development of a working artificial womb.

Experimentation with Humans

There is no reliable record of how much experimentation has been done with human ova fertilized *in vitro*. One can only surmise that some scientists working with animal embryos have tried to experiment with human genetic material. Also Dr. Daniele Petrucci, an Italian geneticist and biologist, announced in 1959 that, after a number of failures, he successfully fertilized a human ovum *in vitro* and kept the developing embryo alive for twenty-nine days, after which he destroyed it because it had become deformed. Scientific and religious communities expressed their strong disapproval of such experiments with human embryos, but Dr. Petrucci continued his research and claimed later that he kept another embryo alive for fifty-nine days. Russian biologists claimed even better results, but scientific documentation is not available.

Test Tube Babies

Recent experiments with test tube fertilization of human ova have not been performed just out of scientific curiosity, but for the sake of helping sterile women bear their own genetic children. Female sterility is frequently caused by a blockage in the fallopian tubes, which prevents the ovum from passing through the tube where it could be fertilized and then descend to the uterus. Surgical removal of the blockage is very difficult or in most cases, impossible. Surgical removal of ova from the ovaries, however, is possible and this fact makes fertilization *in vitro* feasible. This minor, but very delicate, operation is done with the help of an instrument called a laparoscope. This device is guided through a small incision in the abdomen down to the ovary, where the surgeon can see the maturing ova and remove one with the help of the apparatus. The ovum then

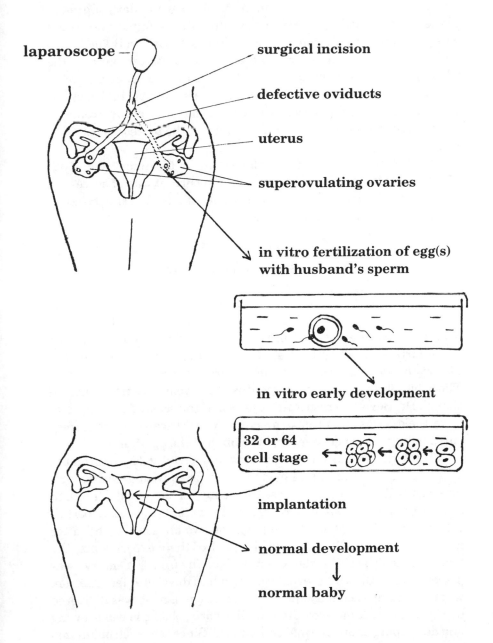

laparoscope

surgical incision

defective oviducts

uterus

superovulating ovaries

in vitro fertilization of egg(s) with husband's sperm

in vitro early development

32 or 64 cell stage

implantation

normal development
↓
normal baby

is placed in a petri dish, where it can be fertilized by the husband's semen. The fertilized ovum or embryo, after several days of growth in the test tube, is implanted in the wife's uterus, and if everything goes well, the embryo implants itself in the uterine wall and a normal pregnancy and childbirth can be expected. As can be seen, the whole process has been designed to help childless couples to have their own genetic children. The procedure seems simple in theory but a great number of practical difficulties have to be overcome to achieve a normal pregnancy and childbirth. The process is very delicate and costly.

In 1983 it cost about $7,500 for an initial treatment and about $5,000 for each additional attempt. At the current rate of success, it would require about $38,000 to ensure about a 50 percent chance of a live birth for a particular woman.[1]

The First Test Tube Baby

Dr. Douglas Bevis, of Leeds University in England, a gynecologist, announced in 1974 that he had successfully implanted human ova, fertilized in test tubes, in the wombs of three women who had given birth to healthy babies. He refused to reveal, however, the identity of the women or the babies in order to protect their privacy. The babies were already eight months to one year old at the time. Although Dr. Bevis is a respected researcher, the scientific community nevertheless was unwilling to accept his claim because of the secrecy surrounding his experiment and the birth of the children.[2]

The birth of Louise Brown in England, on July 26, 1978, on the other hand, was announced by the world press with great fanfare. She was hailed as "the first test tube baby" of the world. Her birth had been eagerly awaited by reporters, the parents and Dr. Robert G. Edwards and Dr. Patrick C. Steptoe, the two physicians who, after many failures, finally achieved the goal of their experiments, the birth of a healthy child who was conceived *in vitro*. The embryo was placed in Mrs. Brown's uterus two and a half days after fertilization, when it had reached only the eight-cell stage. Louise was delivered by Cesarean section. According to all reports, she has been growing and developing as any normal child would. Since the much publicized birth of Louise, at the time of this writing, the births of over 180 test tube babies have taken place. The United States, Australia, West Germany, France, Austria, India and Sweden have joined England in being successfully involved in human *in vitro* fertilization (IVF). At present, there are some 40 clinics in the United States alone that do IVF. It is expected that this number will grow to 200 within a year because of the great demand for this kind of medical service.

"Surrogate Mothers"

So far, *in vitro* fertilization and embryo transfer have been performed to help childless couples to have their own genetic children. No person outside the marriage was involved in the process of procreation. Embryo transfer, however, opens the way to a number of possibilities and combinations in which persons outside the marriage could somehow participate in the procreation of a child. Some of these possibilities are: donations or selling of ova to infertile women, carrying the fertilized ova of other women to viability, carrying embryos to which the ovum and semen were donated by anonymous strangers.)

Artificial Inovulation

Recent research in animal breeding has resulted in a technique slightly different from fertilization *in vitro*. Pure-bred cows, for instance, are given hormones to superovulate and then are fertilized by artificial insemination with the semen of pure-bred bulls. The fertilized eggs or embryos are flushed out and the best specimens arc transferred to the wombs of common cross-breed cows, which carry them to term and give birth to pure-bred calves. A cow normally can produce only about six calves in her reproductive life. By this method, however, she can produce thirty or more offspring in a year. Embryo transfer in cattle breeding is obviously quite rewarding financially.

This type of embryo transfer has been suggested as a possibility to remedy infertility for human beings as well.

Donating Ova

It was reported in October 1978[3] that Drs. Randolph W. Seed and his brother Richard, physicians in Chicago, had developed a technique to transplant an embryo from the womb of one woman to the womb of another by a non-surgical method. The transplant procedure is said to be quite simple so that it can be done in the physician's office. In this procedure, the sperm of the husband of an infertile woman is used to inseminate an anonymous donor. If the donor woman conceives, five days later, the fertilized ovum is flushed from the donor's uterus and is implanted in the uterus of the infertile woman who carries it to term. The flushing out and the implantation of the embryo is said to be so simple that it can be done in two thirty-minute sessions. The technique avoids the difficult and costly procedure of fertilization *in vitro*, but the baby's genes are made up of those of the husband's and of the donor's. The wife only carries the child to term. The child is genetically not hers. This is a counterpart of artificial insemination by donor and could be called artificial inovulation. It is not a satisfactory remedy for infertility from the ethical standpoint because the child genetically belongs to only one of the spouses, and a third person, the donor, is brought into the exclusive union of two persons in marriage.

A medical team headed by Dr. John E. Buster, professor of obstetrics and gynecology at the U.C.L.A. Medical Center in Torrance, used this system to achieve two pregnancies. They reported the event in the July 22, 1983 *Lancet*. They made 14 attempts to fertilize the fertile donors' eggs by the sperm of the husbands of infertile women who wanted to receive the embryos. Five embryos resulted from the artificial insemination and two of the embryos "took" in the wombs of the infertile women. The two pregnancies were progressing normally at the time of their report.[4]

Possible Applications
of Embryo Transfer

For the ethical evaluation of embryo transfer it will be useful to classify its possible applications in the following way:

1. The method by which Louise Brown was born.

2. Donation of ovum to an infertile woman, the donated ovum fertilized by her husband's semen. Dr. Alan Trounson, who works at Monash University's fertilization program in Melbourne, Australia, told delegates of an international symposium on IVF that some 15 eggs had been donated at his center to infertile women who could not produce healthy ova. The ova were obtained from women undergoing IVF for themselves and who could anonymously donate an extra egg to infertile women to be fertilized with their husbands' semen.[5]

3. The case of a woman who can produce normal ova, but whose health would be endangered by pregnancy. Her ovum could be fertilized by her husband's semen either *in vitro* or *in vivo*, and after three to five days of growth, the embryo could be transferred to the uterus of a healthy woman who, either out of friendship or for payment, would carry it to term. After delivery, she would give the baby to the couple who are the genetic parents of the child.

4. The same kind of embryo transfer as in the preceding instance, only done in the case of a career woman who wants to have her own genetic child but does not want to be tied down by pregnancy. These last two possible combinations are mentioned in recent literature by the catchy phrases "surrogate mothers" and "wombs for hire."

5. A more far-fetched variation, namely, the establishment of commercial ova banks, which would be the counterpart of the already existing sperm banks. Some even speak of the possibility of frozen embryo banks, where infertile or eugenically motivated women could shop for embryos whose characteristics would be listed for the shopper's convenience.

Embryo Banks

In order to decide whether embryo banks are feasible or are in the realm of science fiction, it is useful to mention that the freezing, thawing and implanting of animal embryos have already been done successfully.[6]

Experiments with animal embryos led to the discovery that fertilized ova can be frozen and thawed with less damage than unfertilized eggs. Animal embryos are now frozen commercially, but the success rate of embryo transfer is still greater with unfrozen embryos than with frozen ones.

Healthy lambs have developed from embryos that were frozen for two and a half years. Frozen and thawed cattle embryos were implanted in cows that then produced healthy calves. Researchers believe that frozen embryos will survive indefinitely.

Freezing livestock embryos is done mostly to facilitate the shipment of pure-bred animals, or animals with new strains that have some highly profitable quality. Before the technique of embryo freezing was developed, rabbits were used to transport cattle embryos which had been implanted in their wombs. The embryos survived a few days, long enough to have the rabbits flown overseas. Arriving at their destination, the embryos were surgically removed from the rabbits and transplanted to the wombs of cows.

In addition to facilitating commercial cattle breeding, the establishment of frozen embryo banks can also serve the purpose of various research projects concerned with transmitting desirable traits and producing new varieties of animals. Freezing livestock embryos is a costly procedure, but it is very profitable.

Human Embryos Frozen

At Monash University Center in Melbourne, Australia, a limited number of human embryos have been frozen, thawed and transferred into receptive wombs. A successful pregnancy was reported in early May 1983. The ova were obtained from women taking part in IVF. Since hormonal stimulation before laparoscopy produces several mature eggs, some of the fertilized eggs can be frozen and stored for later use if the first attempt at embryo transfer does not succeed. In such a case the woman does not have to undergo another operation for extracting a ripe ovum from her ovaries.[7]

Dr. Robert Edwards and Dr. Patrick Steptoe, the British pioneers in fertilization research, announced in early 1982 that they planned to freeze "spare" embryos for use later by the natural mother or for donation to infertile women. If a fair number of embryos were frozen and stored for a longer period of time, we would have embryo banks. Dr. Michael Thomas, the chairman of the British Medical Association's Ethics Committee, assailed this plan. "Modern technology is running ahead of morality," he said.[8]

Frozen embryos could also be used for research to improve the techniques of IVF and embryo transfer. There are no data available about the number of frozen embryos and about the purpose of their storage. The British Medical Research Council does not forbid the freezing of embryos but states that "tests of animal embryos in appropriate animal models are necessary before it can be assumed that freezing and storage of the embryo does not cause harm to the conceptus."[9] The guidelines of the Australian National Health and Medical Research Council simply point out that there may be some biological and social risks in freezing embryos, "restricts storage for transfer to early undifferentiated embryos," and sets a time limit of ten years for storage.[10]

Interspecies Fertilization

Another combination has to be mentioned that has been spoken of in some publications. In 1979, a hybrid ape was born in the Grant Park Zoo in Atlanta.[11] The hybrid ape is the offspring of two species of apes. Some scientists believe that this fact indicates the possibility of hybridization between other distantly related primates, including man and a great ape. *In vitro* fertilization and implantation could facilitate these experiments, as some scientists have remarked. So far, however, no one has seriously suggested that the hybridization of man and a great ape should be attempted or that a human embryo be implanted in the uterus of an ape.

It seems that some scientists do research trying to fertilize animal ova with human sperm, e.g., hamster eggs. Such experiments are not necessarily done for producing a new species between man and animal. They can be done for diagnostic purposes also. The British Medical Research Council states that animal ova fertilized with human sperm should not be allowed to grow beyond the early cleavage stages.[12]

The Ethics of IVF

It seems that the first method, the one by which Louise Brown was born, did not cause much moral concern in England. In the United States on the contrary, research involving human fertilization *in vitro* and embryo transfer came to an almost complete halt in 1975 when the federal government banned new grants for this form of experiment. The National Commission for the Protection of Human Subjects in Biomedical and Behavioral Research, established by Congress in 1974, was given the specific task, among others, to examine the morality of *in vitro* fertilization and advise the government as to the acceptability of this kind of research. When the mandate of the National Commission expired, the Ethics Advisory Board of the Department of Health, Education and Welfare (H.E.W.) took up the task, and after several months of hearings and deliberations, on March 16, 1979 it reached the decision that human *in vitro* fertilization under certain conditions is ethically acceptable.[13]

In the opinion of the Ethics Advisory Board, research involving human *in vitro* fertilization is "ethically acceptable." This term, the Board explained, simply means that "it is ethically defensible but still legitimately controverted." The Ethics Board is of the opinion that research should be done on non-human primates as much as possible to "obtain a better understanding of the process" and eliminate risks for humans. "If the research involved human *in vitro* fertilization without embryo transfer," the persons whose genetic material is used must be informed of the nature and purpose of the experiment; it is necessary to obtain their informed consent to their role in the research. In addition, the embryos must not be sustained in the test tube beyond fourteen days after fertilization. The fourteen days were agreed upon because it is believed that the embryo implants itself in the uterine wall around that time, and it is then that it is considered to be firmly established on its way toward full human development. If the research also involves embryo transfer, the ovum and the sperm must be obtained from lawfully married couples. This condition is intended to exclude any role for "surrogate mothers" and is aimed at helping married but childless couples to have their own genetic child.

To facilitate our ethical analysis concerning the previously mentioned procedure of *in vitro* fertilization and embryo transfer, we must distinguish the ethical problems of fertilization without implantation from the problems of fertilization in connection with implantation.

IVF without Embryo Transfer

In vitro fertilization without implantation necessarily involves the destruction of a number of incipient human lives. As we have seen in Chapter 2, certain arguments may be proffered for the theory that human life is not present before implantation, but good reasons can be offered for the contrary position as well. When we have a doubt about the presence of human life, the safer course has to be followed and human life must be given the benefit of the doubt. Consequently, a fertilized ovum has to be treated with the respect that is due to human life. One has to conclude that the bringing into existence and destruction of human embryos for the sake of experimentation is unethical. It is equally unethical to try to grow a human embryo *in vitro* because it cannot be brought to viability. Even if it could be at some future date, the fetus still would be exposed to risks and would be used as an experimental object rather than a human subject.

IVF with Embryo Transfer

As for *in vitro* fertilization with embryo transfer, one could argue that it respects human life and that it is only good medicine to help childless couples to have their own genetic children. If the natural law is not simply the functioning of biological laws, but the rational action of man in pursuance of his existential goals, intervention in biological processes can be justified to achieve one of the natural goals of marriage, that is, the procreation of children. One could even argue that the procreative part of the conjugal act is not permanently separated here from the unitive aspect; it is only delayed, which is likewise the case in the process of normal conception.

One might be willing to accept the previous reasoning if the procedure were safe for both the developing fetus and the mother. It seems, however, that the technique is still in the experimental stage.

Dr. Steptoe admitted that the birth of Louise Brown came only after "roughly a hundred unsuccessful efforts."[14] Could the procedure be improved by animal experimentation to make it safe for humans, so that no more human embryos have to be wasted before a successful implantation than as occurs in natural procreation?

The rate of successful pregnancies by IVF is approaching 17 percent. This fact, however, does not mean that 83 percent of fertilized ova are deliberately destroyed. Many of these fertilized ova are transferred into recipient wombs but fail to implant themselves in the uterine wall and thus are naturally aborted. In the natural process of fertilization about 45 percent of fertilized ova achieve implantation. An argument, therefore, can be offered in defense of IVF as a moral means of good medicine helping to achieve one of the important goals of marriage.

Another concern is the confusion of values that would prevail if the country spent large sums of money for research on new procreative methods and at the same time continued the destruction of over a million babies by abortion every year.[15] *In vitro* fertilization and embryo transfer are expensive procedures, and the limited resources of a country would be better spent on more important and more urgent health care programs that would benefit a wider range of the population. Distributive justice demands spending of public funds for projects that benefit everybody in some way. Problems that are not vital and are isolated should be attended to after the vital and more universal needs of the population have been met.

The Ethics of Surrogate Motherhood

As for the situations listed under items 2 to 5, the ethical dilemmas they pose seem less complex. Giving an ovum to a sterile woman to be fertilized by her husband's sperm is the same, from the moral point of view, as AID. Whether the donor remains anonymous or not, a third person is introduced into the marriage, which by its nature is the exclusive union of one man and one woman. "Renting a womb" to carry one's genetic child to viability is even more objectionable. Even certain advocates of AID turn against this idea, and rightly so. If a woman, for whatever reason, is not willing to put up with the inconvenience of pregnancy, she should not have children and should not be a parent. Many of the cares and problems of parenthood come only after the birth of children. The woman who is not willing to make the sacrifice of bearing her children probably will not make the sacrifice of educating and caring for them either. In addition, the woman who carries somebody else's child to viability probably will become attached to that child, and this may complicate the life of the child if the identity of the "hired mother" becomes known. It seems that the child is here being used as a means for satisfaction of some desire to the genetic mother and is not being brought into existence primarily as a person for his or her own sake.

Adopting Embryos

The fact that successful pregnancies have been achieved with frozen and defrosted embryos poses another ethical dilemma. Would it be ethically acceptable to adopt a baby while it is still in the embryo stage instead of adopting it when it is fully developed and born? It has been argued that the adopting parents would be more naturally connected with the adopted child because the wife, although it is not her genetic child, would carry him or her in her womb to viability.

This proposal, however, is laden with great difficulties. Such a baby would be bought from embryo banks, and hence treated as a commerical object and not as a human being. Even if embryos were offered free for adoption, somebody would have to provide a large sum of money to "produce" and maintain these embryos. In addition to the financial consideration, the danger of malformation of frozen and defrosted embryos should not be overlooked. This would be an unjustified experimentation with human subjects for the sake of adoptive parents. The idea of embryo banks, looked at from a moral point of view, should be abandoned.

The hybridization of man and ape, or any other animal, which is a far-fetched possibility, would be entirely dehumanizing. It should not be attempted for whatever reason. Similarly, the transfer of a human embryo to the uterus of animals for the sake of experimentation or the attempt to bring it to viability should not be done at all. There is no need to amplify the idea of how dehumanizing, and consequently unethical, such a manipulation of human life would be.

QUESTIONS FOR REVIEW AND DISCUSSION

1. Describe the technique of IVF.

2. What is the success rate of IVF? Is it approaching the rate of natural fertilization?

3. What are the ethical arguments for and against IVF or "test tube babies"?

4. What is the morality of donating ova to infertile women or of buying ova from ova banks?

5. How do you evaluate "surrogate motherhood," i.e., transferring an embryo into a "rented womb"?

6. What is the morality of buying an embryo from an embryo bank and adopting it? Would it be ethically different if the embryo were donated without any remuneration to a childless couple?

7. What is your ethical evaluation of freezing and storing ova and embryos?

Notes

1. Clifford Grobstein, Michael Flower, John Mendeloff, "External Human Fertilization: An Evaluation of Policy." *Science*, October 14, 1983, p. 130.

2. David Rorvik, "The Embryo Sweepstakes." *The New York Times Magazine*, September 15, 1974, p. 17.

3. *United Press International*, October 13, 1978.

4. *Science News*, July 30, 1983, p. 69.

5. *The New York Times*, October 28, 1983.

6. *Ibid.*, September 15, 1974; *The Wall Street Journal*, May 9, 1979; *The New York Times*, July 26, 1978.

7. Clifford Grobstein, *et al.*, *op. cit.*, p. 129.

8. *Associated Press*, January 28, 1982.

9. "In Britain and Australia, New In Vitro Guidelines," *The Hastings Center Report*, February 1983, p. 2.

10. *Ibid.*

11. *Science*, July 20, 1979.

12. *Ibid.*

13. Margaret O'Brien Steinfels, "In Vitro Fertilization: 'Ethically Acceptable' Research." *The Hastings Center Report*, June 1979; "Ethics Advisory Board: In Vitro Fertilization Is 'Ethically Acceptable.'" IRB, *A Review of Human Subjects Research*, April 1979. See also *BioScience*, May 1979, p. 321.

14. *The New York Times*, December 1, 1978.

15. Andre E. Hellegers and Richard A. McCormick, "Unanswered Questions on Test Tube Life." *America*, August 19, 1978.

6 Anomalous Forms of Procreation

The ethical questions of multiple parenthood, parthenogenesis and cloning will be examined in this chapter. None of these techniques have been used for human procreation as yet. The possibility of using them, however, is not entirely in the realm of science fiction. Animal experimentations in these fields have been successful, and some scientists believe that the techniques can be applied to human beings as well.

Cell Fusion

Fusion of mature germ cells (gametes) of the same species occurs in nature during fertilization. Somatic cells (body cells that are incapable of reproduction) fuse spontaneously only in exceptional cases. Cell fusion, as a controlled laboratory manipulation of cells, was achieved only in the 1960's. The technique enables scientists to produce hybrid cells. In 1972, biologists at Brookhaven National Laboratory succeeded in growing hybrid plants from artificially fused cells. The plants have grown to full maturity and remained fertile. At the same laboratory in 1975, human and tobacco plant cells were fused and grown in combination.[1] A Hungarian group reported about the same time that they had successfully fused and grown HeLa (tumor cells derived from a cancer patient many years ago) human cells with those of carrots.

Recently, a new technique of cell fusion has been developed to produce uniform antibodies in large quantities. The antibodies can be used to diagnose a variety of medical conditions and to attack foreign substances that penetrate the human body and cause illness.

The technique was developed by Cesar Milstein and his colleagues at the Medical Research Council in Cambridge, England. They fused some mouse cancer cells with other mouse cells that produce antibodies. "The result was a malignant cell that can proliferate indefinitely under laboratory conditions but that also makes antibody. Each cell and all its descendants (clones) make identical antibody that binds to the same target . . . . The cells are called hybridomas and their product is called a monoclonal antibody."[2]

"Mosaic" Mice

Cell-fusion technique can be applied to young embryos *in vitro*. In 1965, Dr. Beatrice Mintz experimented with embryos of mice and succeeded in fusing them. She then placed the fused embryos in the wombs of mice that carried them to viability. The result was individuals with four, rather than two, natural parents. The experiments worked with rabbits, rats and sheep as well. The biological structure of the offspring in these cases, however, looks like a mosaic. Sometimes the internal organs have two different kinds of cells, with two different genetic types; sometimes a whole organ comes from only one set of parents and another organ from the other set. Also, the external appearance of the offspring shows heredity traits from the multiple parents; some mice, for instance, have black and white striping.

It is believed that multiple parenthood would be possible for human beings also. It is not known, however, whether any experimentation is going on that attempts to fuse human embryos. The cost and technical difficulties of this kind of experiment have most likely prevented any attempt to produce "mosaic" human beings.

Parthenogenesis

Parthenogenesis (Greek word for virgin birth) is the opposite of multiple parenthood. It is reproduction without fertilization by a male germ cell; that is, the offspring has only one parent. It spontaneously occurs in certain lower plants and certain animals.

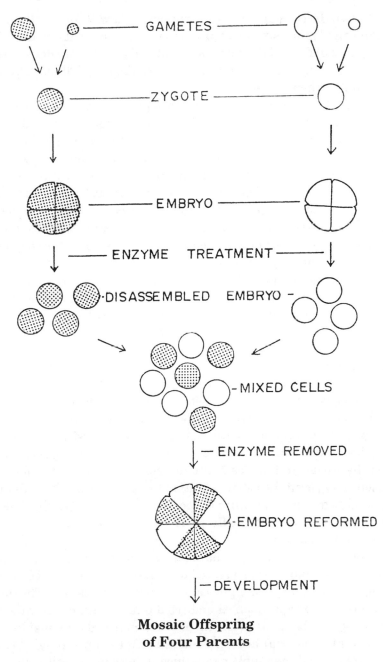

PARENTS A   PARENTS B

——— GAMETES ———

—————ZYGOTE—————

——— EMBRYO ———

—— ENZYME TREATMENT———

·DISASSEMBLED EMBRYO ·

-MIXED CELLS

— ENZYME REMOVED

·EMBRYO REFORMED

—DEVELOPMENT

**Mosaic Offspring
of Four Parents**

Cell fusion technique applied to embryos.

117

Oskar Hertwig and his wife experimented with sea-urchin eggs in 1896 and found that strychnine added to the sea water containing the eggs would set off their development and growth into normal sea-urchins. No sperm fertilized these eggs, so the couple have achieved artificial parthenogenesis.

Since then, a great variety of techniques has been worked out to produce sea-urchins without fertilization. Experiments with frog, turkey and chicken eggs also have resulted in parthenogenesis.

The first mammalian experiments in virgin birth took place with rabbit eggs. Gregory Pincus and his team, in the United States, produced the first parthenogenetic rabbit in 1939. This experiment, however, has never been successfully repeated. Dr. Pincus was primarily interested in contraceptives, and the parthenogenetic rabbit was only a by-product of his research in contraception, the control of fertilization and implantation.

Dr. Pincus performed certain experiments with human ova in connection with his contraceptive research, but artificially produced parthenogenesis of human beings has not yet occurred.

Dr. Stanley Rienan also did some experiments with human ova in the late 1930's. He succeeded in mechanically activating a human ovum, but it soon died without developing into an embryo.[3]

It is generally held that spontaneous parthenogenesis does not occur in human beings. Some scientists, however, do not exclude this possibility. Dr. Landrum Shettles, who in 1978 was involved in a dispute over an uncompleted attempt to produce a "test tube baby" in America,[4] found that three out of four hundred human eggs removed from their ovarian follicles had undergone cleavage in the follicles without any possibility of fertilization by spermatozoa. This finding would indicate the possibility of spontaneous human parthenogenesis. But there is no scientific proof of an actual parthenogenesis among human beings.

The British science journal *Nature* reported on May 26, 1983 that scientists have experimented with human ova and succeeded in producing an embryo of eight cells without fertilization. The chromosomes of the experimental embryo did not spontaneously double (as sometimes happens in parthenogenetic animals) to enable it to develop into a normal human being. The embryo had only 23 chromosomes, half of the number contained in human somatic cells. The fact that only one in four embryos they experimented with was free of chromosomal abnormalities indicated that the experiment to produce a normal parthenogenetic baby is far from succeeding.[5]

The idea of artificially induced human parthenogenesis does not generate as much interest among scientists or the general public as does artificial insemination or *in vitro* fertilization. The reason is that, aside from scientific curiosity, it would not have much practical value and the procedure would be very involved and costly. One benefit perhaps would be the control of sex-linked genetic disease because all children by parthenogenesis would be female. It would be possible, therefore, to avoid hemophilia, for instance, a disease that affects only male offspring.

Cloning

Cloning has become known in recent years through sensational, informative articles in the daily press and weekly magazines. The Greek word *clone* means twig. In many cases the cutting of a plant stuck in the soil is able to grow into a new plant of the same genetic composition. Grafting, too, produces the exact genetic copy of the plant from which the scion was taken. This form of asexual plant propagation has been known from ancient times. It also has been observed that certain simple multicellular animals, e.g., jellyfish, reproduce asexually by releasing a group of cells that can regenerate the organism. The offspring is a *clone*. Individuals reproduced this way are generically identical.

Higher plants and animals have two kinds of cells, genetic cells and somatic cells. The union of the germ cells, i.e., sperm and egg, is sexual reproduction. The offspring is genetically different from both parents, the union of the two germ cells producing a mixture of characteristic traits. The idea of the possibility of asexual reproduction of plants from an isolated cell, of animals, or even of man, emerged in the 1930's. It was suggested that every somatic cell of a living organism contains in its nucleus the genetic code of the entire organism. In 1938, Hans Spemann, a German biologist and Nobel Prize winner, proposed the experiment of removing the nucleus from an egg and replacing it with the nucleus of a somatic cell to see whether the egg would develop into a normal offspring that would be the exact copy or clone of the individual from which the nucleus was taken.

Carbon Copies of Frogs

In 1952, Drs. Robert Briggs and Thomas J. King, at the Carnegie Institute in Washington, experimented with frog eggs. They removed the nuclei of freshly fertilized eggs and replaced them with nuclei from the embryonic tissue of one individual of the same species. The eggs began to develop and the result was a group of genetically identical tadpoles, "carbon copies" of the donor of the cell nuclei. This procedure is called cloning or nucleus transplantation. Dr. F.C. Steward had similar success with root cells of carrot. He stimulated single differentiated root cells to reconstitute the whole carrot plant. The technique opened the way to commercial application of cloning. Identical flowers and other plants can be produced this way from an outstanding specimen of the species.

Dr. John B. Gurdon, of the University of Oxford, went further with the experiments of Dr. Briggs, transplanting an intestinal cell nucleus of an adult toad into a toad egg, from which he had removed the nucleus. Some of his transplants produced normal toads. It has been proved, therefore, that cloning somatic cells of adult vertebrate animals is possible.

Cloning of Fish and Mammals

Biologists at the University of Oregon achieved the first mass cloning of fish. Their technique was to inactivate the chromosomes in the sperm from fish by using ultraviolet radiation. The sperm then were used to fertilize the eggs. Each fertilized egg had only half the number of chromosomes of a normal fish, that is, the chromosomes of the mother's germ cells. The doubling of the chromosomes was achieved by pulses of pressure or heat. The number of cloned fish in one of the experiments was as high as 874.[6]

Karl Illmensee of the University of Geneva, Switzerland, and Peter Hoppe of the Jacksons Laboratory in Bar Harbor, Maine, reported in January 1981 that they had cloned mammals for the first time. After 316 tries, they succeeded in cloning three mice. They transplanted mouse embryo cells into enucleated eggs, from which normal mice developed.[7]

Two American scientists, Dr. James McGrath and Dr. Davor

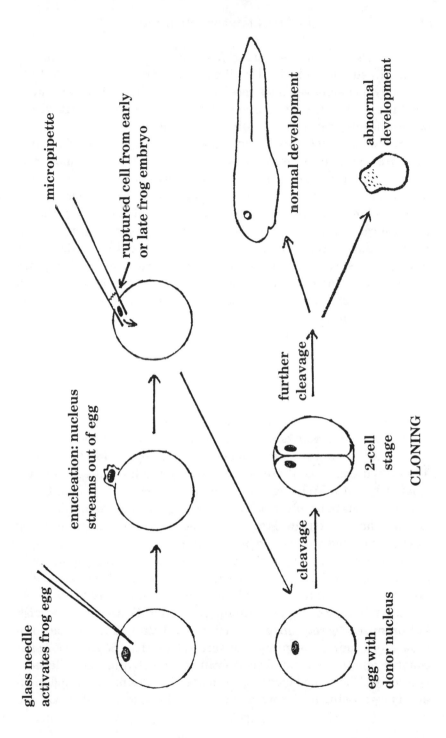

glass needle activates frog egg

enucleation: nucleus streams out of egg

micropipette

ruptured cell from early or late frog embryo

normal development

abnormal development

further cleavage

2-cell stage

cleavage

egg with donor nucleus

CLONING

Solter, of the Wistar Institute of Anatomy and Biology in Philadel-phia, refined the method of Dr. Illmensee and reported in June 1983 that they had achieved a success rate of more than 90 percent in re-moving the pronuclei from a mouse embryo and replacing it with a donor nucleus from a genetically different mouse.[8]

Soviet scientists have been engaged in another type of cloning. They are trying to defrost and isolate living cells from mammoth car-casses found in Siberia. The goal is to remove the nucleus of a living mammoth cell and transplant it into an enucleated elephant egg which would be placed in the womb of an elephant hoping that it would normally develop there to viability. As is known, the mam-moth became extinct about 10,000 years ago and some 36 frozen mammoth bodies have been found in Siberia. Some are 40,000 years old and have been fairly well preserved by a natural process of deep freezing in the icy Siberian climate. If the Russian scientists succeed in cloning a mammoth, they would bring back into existence an ex-tinct species.[9]

The Cloning of Man

These results in cloning gave rise to speculation about whether cloning of human beings would be possible. In general, biologists be-lieve that the cloning of human beings is possible, at least in theory. The difficulties are only technical because the human egg is much smaller than the frog egg and, in addition, nuclear transplantation of humans has to be followed by implanting the embryo in the uterus of a woman at the right stage of the menstrual cycle, whereas frog eggs are hatched outside the body of frogs.

David Rorvik, author of several books on new developments in the sciences, claimed in his book, *In His Image: The Cloning of Man*,[10] that he had been asked by a bachelor millionaire to assemble a group of scientists to produce his clone. Rorvik accepted the task but promised secrecy about personal identities and the actual pro-cedure of cloning. Laboratories were set up in a Southeast Asian country and, after a number of failures, the cloning has allegedly succeeded. The cloned embryo is reported to have been carried to vi-ability by a young native woman who gave birth to a healthy boy, the

"carbon copy" of the millionaire. The boy is allegedly well and growing normally.

The scientific world received the news with great skepticism.[11]
Some even went so far as to call it a hoax. Since Rorvik is not willing
to break his pledge of secrecy about the persons involved in the alleged cloning, there is no reliable proof of whether the first human
cloning has occurred or not.

Cell Fusion and Cloning

Cell fusion could be combined with clonal reproduction. The
fused nuclei of two different species could be implanted into an enucleated egg that, at least in theory, could develop into some new species. As some writers speculate, this procedure also could be
attempted with the fused nuclei of human and animal cells implanted into an enucleated human or animal ovum.

Ethical Evaluation

What is the morality of these anomalous forms of reproduction?

Cell fusion to create new species of plants or animals can be very
useful in horticulture, agriculture or animal husbandry. One has to
be careful, however, to avoid creating new kinds of organisms whose
spread or propagation could not be controlled and would become
harmful.

The fusion of human cells with plant cells may also prove to be
a useful scientific experiment. Human-type enzymes, for instance,
could possibly be produced by plants and used in medicine.

The attempt to fuse human and animal cell nuclei, however, and
transplant them into either a human or animal enucleated ovum to
produce a new half-human, half-animal species cannot be judged fa-
vorably from the ethical point of view. This is a kind of experimentation that should not take place.

Some argue, however, that if such an experiment ever succeeded, it would be beneficial both to the animals involved and to
mankind. The evolution of these animals would be artificially

speeded up. The animals would become more "intelligent" and this would be to their advantage. Mankind, too, would gain because we could use these "intelligent" animals for all kinds of monotonous and "dirty" work. Thus man would be freed for higher types of activities. The crux of the question is whether these intelligent animals would be human rather than merely animal. Would mankind be introducing a new kind of slavery and a new form of discrimination? If these new kinds of beings had some form of human intelligence, they should be treated as human beings and their human rights should be protected. In reality, human beings would be degraded and dehumanized, not animals elevated. For similar reasons, the hybridization of man and a great ape should not be attempted. As far as is known, no experiments of this nature are being performed. Had it not been cited as a possibility, the question would be entirely academic.

The fusion of two human embryos promises a greater probability of success than hybridization of man with other organisms. Nevertheless, there would seem to be no valid reason to justify such an experimentation from the ethical point of view. Scientific curiosity is not a valid reason to experiment with human beings, using them as guinea pigs. Some argue that it would be a new way to blend more genes within one individual and that it could introduce a new means of bringing about greater variety in the human species. These arguments are not really convincing even from the scientific point of view. Instead of improvement in the genetic make-up of man, weaker individuals and even monsters could be the result. The risks for harming the offspring are quite real and, according to a solid ethical principle, one has to take the safer course when there is doubt about causing harm to human life. The safer course in this case is to refrain from these experiments.

As for the morality of *parthenogenesis*, some argue that it could be justified in human beings for bypassing sex-linked genetic defects and for the advancement of our knowledge of the process of procreation. Some even say that women could assert their independence by thus freeing themselves from male participation in the process of procreation. These reasons are not convincing. Again, one would be experimenting with human life, risking the well-being of the possible offspring; human beings would be treated as experimental objects and not as human subjects. No one can foretell whether children born through parthenogenesis would be biologically normal. Further, women during the last months of pregnancy, and while their children are small, need the financial and loving support of a husband. Otherwise, they would be forced to take a job to support themselves and their children, with the result that their children would not have adequate care. Parthenogenesis could advance only a spurious independence for women, something not even worth considering seriously. Scarce financial and medical resources are better spent on delivering better health care with proven means than on questionable and risky experimentations.

Clonal reproduction has many advantages in horticulture, agriculture and animal husbandry. Advocates of human clonism argue that it would bring great benefits to human beings as well. The genotype of talented persons, great artists, musicians, superior and successful individuals could be copied and immortalized. Their exact genotype could be transmitted from generation to generation and the human race would be that much richer. Beautiful persons, actors and actresses, great sportsmen, physically strong individuals could be duplicated or produced in an indefinite number of copies. Parents who may have lost their child in an accident would be able to have a duplicate of the beloved child. Similarly, a person successful in business or some other human enterprise could "carbon copy" his own person and transmit his business possessions to his own duplicate.

Another suggestion is that a number of identical humans could be produced for a certain type of work where mutual understanding and cooperation are essential.

Further, by cloning, one could control the selection of the sex of the offspring. Another advantage would be risk-free transplantation of organs among clones, as there would not be any danger of rejection. One could continue these fantasies and other scenarios at length.

Some of these speculations are clearly far-fetched. Nevertheless, the morality of cloning has to be considered seriously since experiments to clone human beings will probably be attempted in the not too distant future.

All the reasons favoring cloning imply in some way that man is just a means for certain societal goals or for the satisfaction of individual or parental wishes. The clones would be mere products of the laboratory, in the hands of selfish men. The clones would become a new kind of slave, produced for the performance of certain express tasks. Even if these tasks were highly intellectual or artistic, they still would have the characteristic of being forced labor. Aside from the fact that it has not been proved that talents and skills are inherited, the clones would be expected to perform as the nucleus donor did. Their freedom of choice concerning their careers would be curtailed, for they would be expected to imitate the scientific genius or the great musician from whom they were cloned. Whether the clones are regarded as geniuses or as slaves, a new class of human beings would be created that would introduce novel forms of division and discrimination into our society, a society that has been trying for the past centuries to eliminate social differences.

Cloning experiments would involve the destruction of a number of embryos and would also run the risk of producing malformed or monstrous children. Experimentation of this kind with human life is degrading and dehumanizing. Again, man would be treated as an object and not as a person.

Further, clonal reproduction would threaten the values of human parenthood, conjugal love and family. Cloning would not eliminate the sexes, and mankind would still remain divided into male and female. Marriage, an exclusive union in love between a man and a woman, would still be the "natural" cell and component of a larger society. The removal of procreation from marriage, and from a loving union of husband and wife, would weaken the bond of love between married people. It would impair parenthood as the basic organization of humanity. It would be *dehumanizing* and, consequently, unethical.

QUESTIONS FOR REVIEW AND DISCUSSION

1. Describe the techniques of cell fusion, parthenogenesis and cloning.

2. What are the applications of these techniques in agriculture and animal husbandry?

3. What is the ethics of creating new species of plants and animals? Is it wrong to "play God" in this sense?

4. What is the morality of fusing human cells with plant or animal cells?

5. How do you evaluate the morality of experimenting to produce a half human—half animal by cell fusion?

6. What is the morality of experimentation with human ova to produce a parthenogenetic baby?

7. What are the reasons for and against cloning man?

Notes

1. C. Weldon Jones, *et al.*, "Interkingdom Fusion Between Human (HeLa) Cells and Tobacco Hybrid (GGLL) Protoplasts." *Science*, Vol. 193, July 30, 1976, pp. 401–403.

2. Julie Ann Miller, "Antibodies for Sale." *Science News*, May 7, 1983, p. 123.

3. Robert T. Francoeur, *Utopian Motherhood*. Garden City: Doubleday and Co., 1970, p. 140.

4. *The New York Times*, July 18, 1978.

5. *Ibid.*, May 28, 1983, p. A 14.

6. Edward Edelson, "Large Scale Cloning of Fish in Oregon." *The Daily News*, June 3, 1981.

7. *Science*, 23 January 1981, p. 375.

8. James McGrath, Davor Solter, "Nuclear Transplantation in the Mouse Embryo by Microsurgery and Cell Fusion." *Science*, June 17, 1983, p. 1300.

9. Craig R. Whitney, "Russians Aim to Create Live Specimen of a Mammoth." *The New York Times*, March 4, 1980.

10. David M. Rorvik, *In His Image: The Cloning of Man*. Philadelphia and New York: J.B. Lippincott Co., 1978.

11. "Scientists Dispute Book's Claim That Human Clone Has Been Born." *Science*, Vol. 199, March 24, 1978, p. 1314.

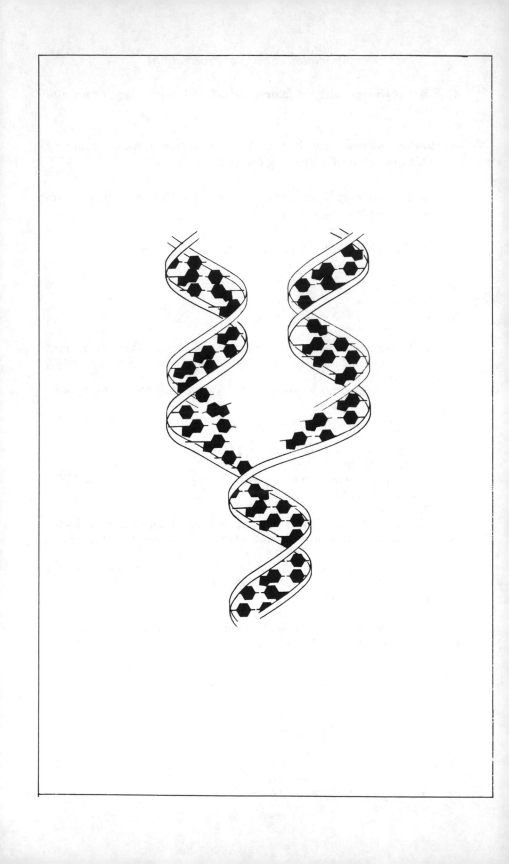

7   Gene-Splicing, Genetic Engineering

The term genetic engineering can be understood either in a broad or in a strict sense. The media usually use it in its broad meaning, calling genetic engineering any manipulation of life or intervention in human nature such as *in vitro* fertilization, artificial insemination, eugenic methods or cloning. Strictly understood, genetic engineering means direct intervention in the genetic make-up of a living being, the replacement of genes or the addition of new genes to the genetic "code" or "blueprint" of an organism. In this chapter the term will be used in its strict meaning.

Chromosomes, DNA, and Genes

It has been known for some three centuries that living beings are composed of cells. In 1882, Walther Flemming, a German biologist, studying the process of cell division, observed that the nuclei of cells contained certain structures that could pick up a certain red dye. He named those structures *chromosomes*, which is Greek for "colored bodies."

Before a cell divides in the process of *mitosis* (from the Greek word for "thread"), pairs of the threadlike chromosomes duplicate, then separate and occupy the opposite sides of the dividing cell. When the process of cell division is completed, each new cell has an equal number of chromosomes of the same genetic structure. As cell division continues, each new cell of a growing multicellular organism acquires the same chromosomal structure.

Most original cells that start a new living being are the result of a combination of two germ cells, male and female. Germ cells, how-

129

ever, only have half of the chromosomes that are characteristic of the species. Thus when two germ cells are joined, the new being has the full number of chromosomes that are a distinctive mark of that kind of being. For example, human germ cells, that is, sperm and ovum, have twenty-three chromosomes each. The fusion of these two cells in fertilization results in a *zygote* with forty-six chromosomes. Through countless subsequent mitoses, these same forty-six chromosomes will be replicated into all body cells of the developing human being. The fusion of sperm and egg, however, produces a new combination of chromosomes and a new unique combination of characteristics of a new human being. The traits of this person will be a mixture of the traits contained somehow in the chromosomes of the germ cells. But because a human being has more than forty-six different characteristics, biologists have abandoned the early assumption that each chromosome is responsible for only one trait. Instead, they assume that each chromosome contains a great number of genes, which are considered responsible for the great variety of specific traits. Recent estimates put the number of genes at one hundred thousand.

Modern biologists began some exciting scientific detective work to find the chemical substance and structure of the genes whose existence had been assumed. In 1944, Oswald T. Avery, Colin McLoud and Maclyn McCarthy, at the Rockefeller Institute (now Rockefeller University) in New York, demonstrated for the first time that *deoxyribonucleic-acid* (DNA) is the hereditary substance of living cells. It was proved later that the long DNA molecule is composed of sections, which are the long-sought-after genes responsible for the different characteristics found in all organisms.

The Double Helix

In 1953, an Englishman, Francis H.C. Crick, and an American, J.D. Watson, working at Cambridge University and using the technique of X-ray diffraction, were able to construct the model of the DNA molecule. It is shaped like a double helix or a pair of corkscrews nested one within another. There are only four types of nitrogenous bases in the DNA, adenine (A), cytosine (C), guanine (G) and thymine (T). Each of these is composed of carbon, nitrogen, oxygen and hydrogen, and each is attached to a chain of alternating sugar and phosphate molecules. A genetic code or a genetic language means the sequence of the four kinds of nitrogenous bases along the sugar-phosphate chains. Thus, one sequence could read like this: ATTTGTCCA-CAGATACGG.[1]

DNA Database

In 1982, the National Institutes of Health (NIH) awarded a $3 million contract to Bolt, Beranek and Newman, a company specializing in computer communications, to set up a national database of DNA sequences.[2] The database has been set up at the Los Alamos National Laboratory in New Mexico. It is called the Genetic Sequence Data Bank, simply named GenBank.

The locations of about 800 of the estimated 100,000 genes have already been mapped. It is hoped that by the end of this century a list of all human genes and their structures will be compiled and recorded on the DNA database and will be available to scientists. A European facility, the Nucleotide Sequence Data Library at the European Molecular Biology Laboratory in Heidelberg, Germany, became functional in April 1982. Japan, too, began compiling a DNA database several years ago.

Gene-Splicing, Recombinant DNA

A further development in the knowledge of genes was the discovery that bacterial cells, in addition to the main circular DNA molecule, i.e., chromosome, also have small circular DNA molecules called plasmids, which likewise contain genes. It was further found, in 1962, that substances called restriction enzymes can cut DNA molecules into fragments. A restriction enzyme, contained in bacterial cells, was purified by Dr. Herbert Boyer and his team at the University of California Medical Center in San Francisco, and it was used in 1972 by Janet Mertz and Ronald Davis to cut DNA molecules and splice the fragments together with another chopped DNA. The fragments joined readily because they have "sticky ends."[3] The process, known now as *gene-splicing*, opens new paths for genetic engineering.

Gene-splicing makes it possible to produce hybrid plasmids, that is, to introduce a new chain of genes *in vitro* that can command the production of new traits when taken into an organism. A hybrid plasmid can be reintroduced into a bacterium where the recombined DNA will replicate as part of the bacterium. The bacteria, dividing as often as four times an hour, will continue to manufacture the introduced gene and its product in great quantity. *Recombinant* DNA technology uses bacteria as factories because bacterial cells are easier to manipulate than cells of higher organisms.

Gene Transplants

How is the hybrid plasmid reintroduced in a bacterium? The technique is called *transformation*. The bacterium is heated in the presence of calcium chloride that, apparently, makes holes in the cell wall so that the hybrid plasmid can penetrate the cell through these holes. Also, pure DNA can be given to the cells and the cells integrate the new genes into their gene pool. This technique was tried with mammalian cells and it was found that some specially treated cells absorbed the purified DNA and replicated. The success rate, however, was not very high. The technique of *cell fusion*, mentioned in Chapter 6, can also be used to introduce genes into cells.

Another method of inserting genes into a host organism is the technique of *transduction*. This method uses viruses as carriers. The desired gene is attached to the DNA of a non-pathogenic virus, which easily penetrates the host cell that then integrates the new gene into its gene pool. The fact of viral infection shows, at least in theory, that this method could be used in *gene therapy*. A virus can infect an entire organism, and if it carries the correct gene, a genetically diseased organism can be restored to its normal genetic health. This kind of genetic therapy has been successfully tried with bacteria. Bacterial genetic defects are routinely corrected by laboratories by altering the defective DNA of the bacterial cell by transduction.

In 1982, Gerald Rubin and Allan Spradling, of the Carnegie Institution in Baltimore, devised a new technique of transplanting

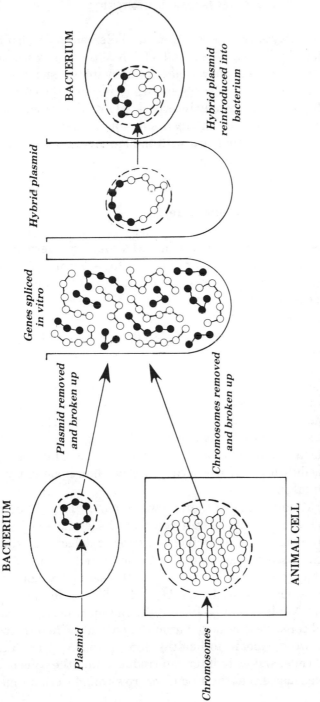

BACTERIUM

Plasmid

ANIMAL CELL

Chromosomes

Plasmid removed and broken up

Chromosomes removed and broken up

Genes spliced in vitro

Hybrid plasmid

BACTERIUM

Hybrid plasmid reintroduced into bacterium

GENE-SPLICING. Bacterial plasmid (containing genes) and chromosomes of animal cell (containing genes) are removed and cut into fragments by restriction enzyme. Genes are spliced *in vitro* to form a hybrid plasmid. The new chain of genes is reintroduced into the bacterium where the recombined DNA will replicate as part of the bacterium.

genes. They employed transposon, a natural element of the fruit fly genetic material. This is a segment of DNA that moves around within the chromosomes. They isolated a movable segment, called the P element, and used it to carry specific genes into the embryo of a fruit fly. The genes were stably incorporated into the chromosomes, correctly expressed and inherited in subsequent generations. Researchers are experimenting now with the P element to carry genes into species other than fruit flies.[4]

Gene Therapy

In 1975, an international attempt was made by German and American scientists and physicians to cure three German sisters by the method of transduction. The bodies of the three German children failed to produce the enzyme arginase, which resulted in the debilitating genetic disease, arginanemia. The three sisters are the only known victims of this genetic disease. American scientists at Oak Ridge National Laboratory, hearing of the case, supplied Dr. H.G. Terheggen, the physician of the children, with the virus called the Shope papilloma virus, that is known to produce arginase. The virus was injected in the sisters in the hope that the genetic information of the virus would become integrated into the cells of the children and order the cells to produce the enzyme. Dr. Terheggen, however, told an international conference of the Association for Children with Learning Disabilities that the virus injection had apparently not helped the children.[5]

Another attempt at gene therapy was made in 1980. Martin J. Cline and Winston Salser, heading a team of scientists at UCLA, conducted an experiment to correct the genetic defect that causes thalassemia, a disease that is similar to sickle cell anemia and is common in Mediterranean countries. A 21 year old woman was treated in Jerusalem on July 10 and 11, and a 15 year old Italian girl was treated in Naples on July 15, 1980. Bone marrow cells, which produce blood cells, were removed from the patients. Then the bone marrow cells were exposed to healthy genes capable of producing normal blood cells, and were later reintroduced into the bone of the patients. It was hoped that their bone marrow would work normally and would produce healthy blood cells. Unfortunately, the experiment did not succeed and the researchers were rebuked for having violated the federal guidelines of Recombinant DNA Research.[6]

Dr. Timothy J. Ley, Dr. Arthur W. Nieuhuis and their seven colleagues reported in *The New England Journal of Medicine* on December 8, 1982 that they had successfully altered the activity of genes in the human body to correct the hereditary blood disorder, thalassemia. This seems to be the first successful gene therapy.

Scientists are making promising progress in locating the defective genes of several diseases. For instance, the November 19, 1983 issue of *Nature* reported that a multi-disciplinary team had located the gene that causes Huntington's disease. This opens the way to isolating the defective gene or genes. It should then be possible to learn more about them and prevent them from being expressed or from causing the terribly debilitating effects of the disease.[7]

Medical Products

As it stands now, the technique of recombinant DNA applied to *bacteria* has produced good results and created a fast-growing industry. Pharmaceutical companies see the possibility of making bacteria manufacture insulin, enzymes and other drugs that are very costly to synthesize chemically or can be obtained only from slaughtered animals. It was announced on September 7, 1978 that a joint effort of two five-man research teams, using the recombinant DNA technique, succeeded in making the intestinal bacteria Escherichia coli produce human-type insulin.[8] One of the teams worked at the City of Hope National Medical Center in Duarte, California, under Dr. Keiichi Itakura, and the other was led by biologist, David Goeddel, of the biochemical firm, Genentech, Inc., in San Francisco. There are some 60 million diabetics in the world and a great percentage of them require insulin injection to survive. Insulin has been extracted until now from cattle and swine. The steadily growing number of diabetics, however, has caused some concern about sufficient supplies of insulin. In addition to the problem of supply, there is the problem that animal insulin causes an allergic reaction in about 5 percent of diabetics.

The Eli Lilly Company marketed the human-type insulin in 1982.

Further progress was made by researchers at the University of California at San Francisco when, using bacteria as factories, they succeeded in producing the human *hormone required for normal growth*. The scientists used pituitary-gland tumors, removed from patients, to make a hybrid plasmid that was transferred into bacteria E. coli, which then began to produce the human growth hormone. This hormone is the only known treatment for pituitary dwarfism, which affects about twenty thousand Americans. The only source of the hormone until then was pituitary glands removed from cadavers. It took about fifty cadavers to obtain enough hormone for one child for a year.[9]

The production of *interferon* is another achievement of recombinant DNA research. Interferon, which was discovered in 1957, is a natural protein that helps cells defend themselves against virus infection. Researchers until recently had not succeeded in producing it in purified form in large enough quantities to experiment with it.

Large and well-known American corporations are heavily investing in research on *gene transplants*. Some objectives of their research are "a number of hormones, simple proteins, vaccines, antiviral compounds, antibodies and industrial enzymes that could be used either to produce chemicals or to break down industrial waste."[10] In its 1982 report to Congress, the Office of Technology Assessment listed among other achievements the following pharmaceutical products of the application of genetic engineering: human insulin, interferon, growth hormone, urokinase (for the treatment of blood clots), thymosin-d1 (for controlling immune response) and a vaccine for foot-and-mouth disease.[11]

Agricultural Research

Agricultural research aims at developing crops that produce their own fertilizer. As is known, legumes such as clover, alfalfa, peas and beans produce their own fertilizer. Nodules grow on their roots in which bacteria abound that can "fix" nitrogen and thus produce fertilizer. It has been known for a long time that by rotating wheat and other crops with legumes, the need for artificial fertilizers can be reduced. If bacteria could be manipulated into a symbiosis with wheat to fix nitrogen, it would greatly benefit food production all over the world.[12]

Another application of the gene-splicing technique is to prevent the formation of ice on crops. Frost damage in the United States runs about one billion dollars a year; it is about five billion dollars worldwide. Frost damage only occurs if ice crystals are formed when the temperature is below 0°C. It has been found that crystallization of the supercooled water takes place only when "a special material, called nuclei, cell or seed," is present to trigger the formation of ice. "Two types of bacteria have been found that can serve as seeds for ice crystals." When these bacteria lacked the gene that is the key to ice formation, they did not produce frost damage even at temperatures below 29° Fahrenheit and as low as 21°. The ice seeding genes of the bacteria can be eliminated by bacteria-infecting viruses, called bacteriophage. Viruses that infect only the two types of bacteria that act as seeds for ice formation have been developed and their effectiveness proved in laboratory tests.

It is estimated that it would cost about $100 to spray one acre of crops with these viruses to achieve frost protection. Scientists were ready to have a field test in California in the fall of 1983 but a law suit delayed the experiment until the spring of 1984.[13]

Recombinant DNA Research

New developments in the technique of manipulating genes indicate that researchers in genetic engineering are making steady progress in the practical application of recombinant DNA. Dr. Har Gobind Khorana, a Nobel Prize winning organic chemist, and his team at the Massachusetts Institute of Technology, constructed a gene and implanted it in a living bacterial cell where it functioned as if it had been the natural part of the cell's DNA. He had previously constructed a yeast-cell gene, but it did not function in a living cell. This time the team duplicated a gene of the common intestinal bacterium Escherichia coli and succeeded in synthesizing also the regulatory portions of the gene that make it function as a living gene. It took them six years to make this gene, but as a result of their experiments they have developed a more efficient method of synthesis that enables them to produce the same gene in half the time.[14]

Computerization and automation of the gene-splicing technique was developed in 1981. Vega Biotechnologies, a division of Vega Laboratories, Inc., of Tucson, Arizona, and BioLogicals, Inc., of Toronto, Canada, in competition with each other, marketed a "gene machine" that can link nucleotides to the DNA string in just 45 minutes. This used to take weeks and months for scientists to do manually.[15] Unfortunately, the first gene machines developed technical problems. BioLogical got out of the business, and Vega Biotechnologies had to retool its first machines at a considerable cost. In spite of the initial setbacks, four more American companies entered this limited market of an estimated 7,000 potential users. In addition to the American companies, a British, a West German and a Swedish company are also producing gene machines. The new improved models seem to work satisfactorily.[16] Automation will obviously greatly facilitate and speed up the pace of biological revolution.

Harvard Medical School researchers reported in the September 15, 1983 issue of *Nature* that they had made artificial chromosomes.[17] European and American scientists have learned also to construct artificial genes that can be turned on and off.[18]

Significant progress was also made by Dr. Paul Berg and his colleagues, Richard Mulligan and Bruce Howard, at Stanford University, when they successfully transplanted a rabbit gene into monkey cells. This was the first transplant of a functioning mammalian gene. The transfer was achieved by inserting the rabbit gene into the DNA of the virus SV–40, that formed a recombinant molecule. The altered virus then was used to infect cultured monkey cells, that is, the virus carried the rabbit gene into the monkey cells.[19]

Scientists have developed a reliable method of micro-injecting genes into the germ cells of experimental animals and making those genes work there. Richard Palmiter and his team at the Howard Hughes Medical Institute of the University of Washington transferred a rat growth-hormone gene into a mouse embryo. The gene from the rat growth-hormone was incorporated into the mouse embryo and caused the mouse to grow twice its normal size.[20] Experimentation with fruit flies has proved that micro-injected genes are transmitted to successive generations of fruit flies.[21]

There is no reason to doubt that the technique of gene transplant, further refined, could be applied also to human beings.

Brave New World?

Although molecular biology has made remarkable and exciting progress during the past decades, some publicists have been carried away by their imagination describing the scientifically engineered future man and the "Brave New World" that is supposedly just around the corner. As we have seen, the technique of recombinant DNA has not reached the sophistication (if it ever will) that would enable us to custom-make human beings according to our whims, or, worse, according to a masterplan of a dictator. Nevertheless, the recombinant DNA technique has already made significant contributions in the area of applied science that can greatly benefit mankind. As we have seen, some important hormones and antibodies can be produced by this method. In addition, the production of medically and industrially useful chemicals can be revolutionized. We can foresee the manufacture of vaccines by constructing specific bacterial strains that can produce the desired antigenic material. In the fields of agriculture and energy production the projections are very realistic.[22]

In regard to the practical application of the recombinant DNA technique, it is important to note that there is a great difference between transplanting a gene into a single-celled bacterium and altering the genetic code of human beings who consist of many billions of cells. The latter possibility exists, but it will take a great deal of work and experimentation before significant results can be expected.

The next development will likely take place in what is called "genetic surgery." About 5 percent of the population is born with genetic defects. Some of these are slight while others are seriously debilitating. Some of the defects are monogenic, that is, caused by one gene; others are polygenic, the result of several defective genes. If the one defective gene can be mapped and replaced by a normal gene, a diseased person can be cured. For this surgery the defective gene must be located in every organ or cell group where it is active. Then the healthy gene must be introduced in all of those millions of cells where they have to be taken up into the DNA of the malfunctioning cells and suppress the defective gene. Genetic surgery in the case of polygenic defects is obviously much more complicated. Presently no one considers it seriously as a possibility.

Other forms of speculation concerning the transformation of man are even more far-fetched. The altering of healthy characteristics as, for instance, the color of eyes and hair, is an interesting topic for science fiction but is not on the list of priorities of serious science.

Hazards of Gene-Splicing

Gene-splicing has many practical applications, but at the same time experimentation with recombinant DNA may cause much harm. Scientists themselves have become keenly aware of biohazards and of the ethical problems connected with gene-splicing experiments. In the early 1970's, Dr. Paul Berg proposed an experiment that involved splicing SV–40, a tumor-causing virus, into the DNA molecule of a laboratory specimen of Escherichia coli, the ordinary bacterium found in the human intestine.[23] Some researchers became concerned at the possibility of SV–40 virus accidentally escaping from the laboratory and infecting E. coli in the human intestine, where it could propagate itself in limitless numbers. Because of this possible danger the experiment was postponed.

In June 1973, the Gordon Conference on Nucleic Acids further discussed the ethical implications of gene-splicing experiments. The Conference sent a letter to the National Academy of Sciences expressing its concern about the possible hazards of the experiments. The National Academy then asked Dr. Berg to convene a meeting to consider the problem. Ten distinguished scientists met in April 1974. As a result, Dr. Berg wrote an open letter to scientists that was simultaneously published in *Science, Nature* and the *Proceedings of the National Academy*. Dr. Berg made several recommendations: an international conference should be convened on the problem; in the meantime there should be a voluntary moratorium on recombinant DNA experiments; and the National Institutes of Health should devise safety guidelines for experiments with recombinant DNA. According to all reports, the moratorium was observed by all scientists during the seven months before the international meeting convened in Asilomar, California, in February 1975.

The Conference lifted the moratorium but voted for restrictions on certain experiments with recombinant DNA. The NIH were asked to publish guidelines on containment procedures and to rank the experiments according to probable danger. With these resolutions scientists, in fact, agreed to the regulation and policing of their activities in the field of DNA research.[24]

The "N.I.H. Guidelines for Research on Recombinant DNA Molecules" was issued in June 1976. Controversy, however, continued, as some cities and states in America passed even stricter laws than the N.I.H. Guidelines for the building and operating of gene-splicing laboratories. The N.I.H. safety regulations deal in detail with laboratory conditions that make the escape of viruses or new organisms impossible. In addition to strict laboratory construction rules, scientists must use weakened bacteria that cannot survive outside the laboratory. Certain types of experiments are forbidden altogether, for instance, the transfer of genes for drug resistance into microorganisms which do not acquire them naturally. It has to be noted, incidentally, that the N.I.H. guidelines apply only to federally funded research, but private companies pledged themselves to follow the same rules.

The press reported widely on the possible dangers of recombinant DNA research. Hazards both laymen and scientists are mostly concerned about are: (1) the creation and escape of new life forms that could endanger man and the environment; (2) the creation of virulent microorganisms that would be resistant to antibiotics. These organisms could destroy other forms of life, producing an "Andromeda Strain" scenario.

One concrete example of possible dangers was the production of cellulase-containing Escherichia coli by Dr. A.M. Chakrabarty, of the General Electric Research and Development Center at Schenectady, New York. Dr. Chakrabarty planned also to introduce a methane-forming gene into a bacterium "so that it would be able to turn wastes, such as sewage sludge, directly into usable methane gas."[25] After having produced these "bugs," it has occurred to Dr. Chakrabarty that the bacterium could easily get into human intestines and "every time you ate a lettuce you might have a lot of gas in the stomach and that is not a very bright prospect." Because of these and other possible dangers the transformed bacteria were destroyed before they could have gotten out of the laboratory.

Social Control of Gene-Splicing

Genetic researchers have observed the safety rules for recombinant DNA technology that were made mandatory in 1976. Nevertheless, as the technique of genetic engineering was developing, most scientists became convinced that the rules were too stringent and the hazards were not as grave as initially thought. At their insistence, the original guidelines have been relaxed repeatedly, but the National Institutes of Health have kept the rules mandatory in its latest revision of the rules in 1982.[26]

It can be concluded from our previous consideration of genetic surgery that the immediate ethical problems concern the safety of the techniques employed. When the possibility of danger to the human race or the environment arose, scientists acted responsibly and cooperated in designing safety regulations. It is obvious that there is a moral duty not to cause harm to anybody and to prevent possible dangers. Even if a certain experiment promises great benefits, but involves a risk to human beings, one has the duty not to perform the experiment or to change the procedure in such a way that hazards are eliminated. One is obliged to take the safer course when the safety of human life is involved.

Freedom and Restraint of Scientific Research

No responsible scientist would disagree with the moral duty to avoid danger. Controversy continues, however, about another aspect of the activity of scientists, namely judicial control and public regulation of research. Modern science, whose origin goes back only about three hundred years, enjoyed almost unlimited freedom of research in most countries. Some scientists argue that there is no need for legal control of DNA research because scientists are responsible persons and peer supervision is sufficient to regulate their activities. One can admit that most scientists are responsible persons, but this does not make social control unnecessary. Modern scientific research deals with much more dangerous and possibly devastating matters than the science of the past. Any mistake or negligence in the field of nuclear power or genetic engineering can have far-reaching consequences and can cause incalculable harm. On the occasion of the controversy following the Asilomar Conference, a number of scientists mentioned the occurrence of negligence and carelessness in laboratories. When the experts are divided concerning the possibility of danger, we are faced with a serious doubt as to the admissibility or supervision of an experiment. In cases of serious doubt of this type, according to basic ethical principles, one is obliged to take the safer course with respect to both the performance and the supervision of the experiments. Erwin Chargaff, professor emeritus of biochemistry at Columbia University, stated succinctly: "Anyone affirming immediate disaster is a charlatan. But anyone denying the possibility of its occurring is an even greater one."[27]

It is a sound ethical principle that rights are not unlimited but are restricted by the rights of others and by duties that come into conflict with the exercise of those rights. The right to freedom of research is limited by the rights of human beings to safety and undisturbed living. Since the primary purpose of civil society is to protect the rights of individuals and promote the temporal welfare, society has the moral power and duty to protect the safety of its citizens by legislation when it becomes necessary. It seems to me that public interest in the case of genetic research must be protected by society and must not be left in the hands of individual researchers. Well-designed laws can reconcile the safety of the public and the benefits of scientific progress more efficiently than individuals could. Scientists immersed in their own research and motivated by the fame derived from important discoveries can easily overlook the interest of their fellow citizens.

Risk-Benefit Ratio

Researchers like to speak about risk-benefit ratio in connection with dangerous experimentation, claiming that dangerous research should be allowed when the possible benefits for mankind outweigh the risks. One of the problems with the application of this principle is that the terms of risk and benefit are not clearly defined and can be subjectively interpreted by the researcher. I think that the question of risk has to be considered first. If it is likely that human subjects could be seriously harmed by an experiment, no possible benefit would justify the research. The good end does not justify the bad means.

The *conclusion* is, then, that freedom of research, like every right or freedom, is a limited right. Society and prudent legislation will have to see to it that a balance between the right of freedom of research and the right of the public to safety is maintained and that basic human rights are not sacrificed for the less important rights to "progress" and free research. This means that regulation and proper control should be extended to all research involving possible danger, publicly or privately funded.

Domestic control of hazardous research obviously will not prevent dangers to the whole human race if other countries do not regulate research. Western Europe has established several supranational scientific groups to oversee European research in recombinant DNA, but these groups have no authority to enforce guidelines. What is needed is an international agreement, possibly through the United Nations, that would oblige all countries to regulate all hazardous research effectively. The difficulties of obtaining such an agreement must not be underestimated. Biological research can and does turn out biological weapons. Thus international control of biological research becomes part of international armament control. Unfortunately, attempts at international armament agreement have had very limited success so far.

The Ethics of Gene-Splicing

The President's Commission for the Study of Ethical Problems in Medicine and Biomedical and Behavioral Research stated in its report of November 1982 that gene-splicing technology is not "intrinsically wrong or contrary to important values" but certain of its applications or consequences may be undesirable. The enterprise should continue for its great potential benefits for mankind but efficient regulation and oversight should be established to prevent any harm. "The continued development of gene splicing approved in this Report will require periodic reassessment as greater knowledge is gained about the ethical and social, as well as the technical, aspects of the subject."[28]

The cure of genetic defects through genetic surgery, if it can be done safely, causes no ethical problems. It would be good medicine and obviously a great benefit to mankind. On the other hand, other applications of gene-splicing that appear futuristic now create serious moral concern. Producing superman by inserting genes for greater mental or physical abilities could create a special elite class unless the whole population is changed. Either case would mean an unethical manipulation of man. The manipulators would be trying to use an elite or a specially designed group of human beings as a means for their own goals. This would be a violation of the inherent right of persons for self-determination. If the "upgrading" of man were to affect everybody, it is obvious that the whole population could not be changed without a massive totalitarian manipulation of every individual. This would involve the total suppression of freedom. In addition, who would decide what kind of characteristics should be injected into the whole population? And who knows whether those traits would improve the quality of human life or rather destroy it? We need not speculate about the ethics of this scenario because no scientist seriously anticipates the possibility of this happening in the foreseeable future.

Most inventions of human ingenuity can be used for good or evil. Recombinant DNA technology is no exception. The technology in itself is not in conflict with any ethical value. Its potential benefits for humankind are exceptionally great and the common good would suffer if the technology were stifled. On the other hand, social oversight of the technology is not only ethically justified but seems to be advisable in order to prevent any possible harm.

QUESTIONS FOR REVIEW AND DISCUSSION

1. What are chromosomes, DNA and genes?

2. Describe the technique of gene-splicing.

3. Is the use of recombinant DNA technology ethically right or wrong?

THE MAIN ISSUES IN BIOETHICS

4. What is gene therapy? Is it possible to eliminate and replace defective genes by gene therapy? What are the possibilities at present?

5. Is it right or wrong to change the genetic code of man? Is "playing God" wrong?

6. What are the hazards of genetic engineering? Is social control of genetic engineering ethically justifiable?

Notes

1. Cf. Isaac Asimov, *The Genetic Code*. New York: Clarkson N. Potter, 1962, Chapter 9.

2. Roger Lewin, "Long-Awaited Decision on DNA Database." *Science*, Aug. 27, 1982, p. 817.

3. Richard Hutton, *Bio-Revolution: DNA and the Ethics of Man-Made Life*. New York: New American Library, 1978, p. 36.

4. "New Vehicle for Reliable Gene Transplant." *Science News*, Oct. 23, 1982, p. 260.

5. *The New York Times*, March 1, 1979.

6. See "UCLA Gene Therapy Racked by Friendly Fire." *Science*, Oct. 31, 1980, p. 509; and "Gene Therapy Caught in More Entanglements." *Science*, April 3, 1981, p. 24.

7. "Huntington's Disease Gene Located." *Science*, Nov. 25, 1983, p. 913.

8. *United Press International*, September 6, 1978.

9. *The New York Times*, July 17, 1979.

10. *The Wall Street Journal*, May 10, 1979.

11. Cf. "On the New Frontier of Biotechnology." *The Hastings Center Report*, October 1982, p. 7.

12. P.R. Day, "Plant Genetics: Increasing Crop Yield." *Science*, Vol. 197, September 30, 1977, pp. 1334–1336.

13. Cf. J. Miller, "Microbial Antifreeze: Gene Splicing Takes to the Field." *Science News*, Aug. 27, 1983, p. 124; and Colin Norman, "Legal Threat, Cold Delay U.C. Experiment." *Science*, Oct. 21, 1983, p. 309.

14. *The New York Times*, August 28, 1976.

15. Cf. Barnaby Feder, "Automating Gene Splicing." *The New York Times*, January 15, 1981, p. D2.

16. Cf. Marilyn Chase, "After Slow Start, Gene Machines Approach a Period of Fast Growth and Steady Profit." *The Wall Street Journal*, December 13, 1983, p. 33.

17. Cf. *Science*, Oct. 7, 1983, p. 41.

18. Harold M. Schmeck, Jr., "Artificial Gene Can Be Turned On and Off." *The New York Times*, Oct. 4, 1983, p. C3.

19. *Science*, Vol. 202, 1978, p. 610.

20. Jean L. Marx, "Building Bigger Mice through Gene Transfer." *Science*, December 24, 1982, p. 1298.

21. "New Vehicle for Reliable Gene Transplant." *Science News*, October 23, 1982, p. 260.

22. Stanley Cohen, "Recombinant DNA: Fact and Fiction." *Science*, Vol. 195, February 18, 1977, pp. 654–657.

23. Daniel J. Sullivan, "Gene-Splicing: The Eighth Day of Creation." *America*, December 17, 1977, pp. 440–443.

24. Cf. Richard Hutton, *op. cit.*, Chapter 2.

25. Nicholas Wade, "Dicing with Nature: Three Narrow Escapes." *Science*, Vol. 193, January 28, 1977, p. 378.

26. J.F. Miller, "DNA Rules Eased but Kept Mandatory." *Science News*, February 13, 1982, p. 104.

27. Tabitha M. Powledge, "Recombinant DNA: The Arguments Shift." *The Hastings Center Report*, April 1977, pp. 18–19.

28. President's Commission for the Study of Ethical Problems in Medicine and Biomedical and Behavioral Research, *Splicing Life*. Washington: Government Printing Office, 1982, pp. 77–79.

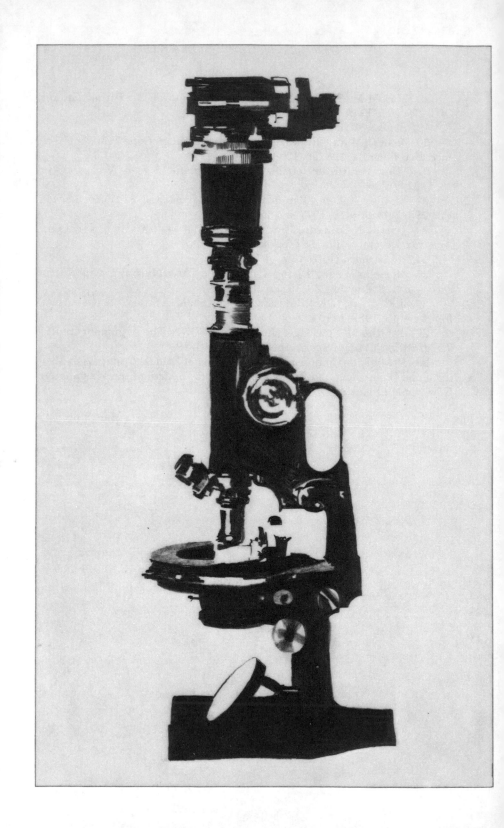

8 Human Experimentation

Medicine is an experimental science by its nature. Primitive men and ancient healers, trying to treat diseases, must have acted on a trial-and-error basis until an accepted medical practice had developed with respect to the cure of certain illnesses. The history of human experimentation is as old as the history of medicine. Even in our own times, the diagnosis of an illness and its recommended treatment contain a certain element of experimentation in them since individuals may react differently to the same medicine. The physician has to evaluate the patient's reactions to a medication, increase or lessen the dosage, or prescribe another medicine as the case may be. It is true that the physician will move only within certain limits which have been established by the previous experience of other physicians or researchers. Nevertheless, medicine always retains a certain component of experimentation.

The occurrence of contagious diseases, pestilence, plague, famine and other natural calamities were always occasions for experimentation. Various treatments were tested in the attempt to stop the spread of contagion and cure the already afflicted. Human experimentation today, however, means more than simply the attempt to cure a patient by various treatments. It involves deliberate research in which human beings are used to gain medical knowledge. The human subject may be harmed or at least inconvenienced in such deliberate experiments in order to help others later. Ancient physicians believed that the dissection of the dead in order to learn human anatomy was not sufficient to gain knowledge about the malfunctions of the body. Aristotle was of the opinion that one had to study the living body in order to understand biological functions and malfunctions. Hence the Alexandrian physicians experimented with

149

vivisection to advance the science of medicine. The subjects of vivisection were always condemned criminals. It seems that this Egyptian practice set a precedent because we also find instances in later centuries in Europe, where princes and kings gave permission to use condemned criminals as experimental subjects.

Scientific Experimentation

Modern medicine could not have developed without experimentation. The development of smallpox vaccination, the conquest of yellow fever, the defeat of typhus, polio vaccination and many other advances in the treatment of diseases and in the care of public health are due to experimentation with human beings.

The story of the first smallpox inoculation is especially interesting for Americans since it took place in the Boston area in 1721. The Rev. Cotton Mather learned that African natives believed that any person who had the scars of smallpox would never have the disease again. For this reason they occasionally and purposely gave each other the disease. He further learned that the Turks also did this. Since the Boston area was affected several times by lethal smallpox epidemics, Mather thought that inoculation with smallpox could prevent the spread of the disease. He convinced Dr. Zabdiel Boylston to experiment with the inoculation. Boylston did not inoculate himself because he had already had smallpox, but first inoculated his own child who developed a mild case of smallpox and got well. He then inoculated 286 people, only 6 of whom died. Boylston, however, thought some of these may have been infected before inoculation. Toward the end of 1721 and in the early months of 1722 there was another smallpox epidemic in the Boston area. According to the notes of Dr. Boylston, 5,759 persons who were not inoculated had the disease, and out of these 844 died. Thus the mortality rate of the inoculated persons was only 2 percent while the other group had a 15 percent mortality rate. This was clearly an experiment with human subjects based only on primitive knowledge. Nevertheless, the procedure gave some protection to a large number of people inoculated in the revolutionary army of General Washington, until the cowpox vaccination of the English physician Edward Jenner in the 1790's provided better protection against smallpox.[1]

The Use of Statistics

Boylston used statistics to evaluate the result of his smallpox inoculation. Statistics, however, as a tool of scientific research, did not fully develop until the late eighteenth century. Pierre Simon LaPlace, a French mathematician, was the first to suggest, in 1814, the application of systematic statistics to experimentation. He proposed using two groups of subjects, one receiving treatment and the other not, the second group serving as a control. Statistical evaluation of the incidence of illness or healing occurring in the two groups was expected to be of help in determining the efficacy of medication used in the experiment. A few controlled studies were conducted in the eighteenth and nineteenth centuries, but such studies have become widely used only in the twentieth century. In 1908, President Theodore Roosevelt established a board to study the effect of boric acid and saccharine on human beings. This was one of the first controlled biomedical studies organized by the American government. Studies organized along these lines have become the customary procedure in America and in other countries in testing drugs and nutriments.[2]

In the late nineteenth and early twentieth centuries, a revolutionary change in the practice of medicine took place as experimental application of technology, biology and chemistry to medicine grew to vast dimensions. Experiments sponsored by governments and private organizations multiplied in the industrialized world. Biomedical research could be conducted on laboratory animals only to a certain degree because drugs and treatments ultimately must be tested on human beings whose reactions to certain drugs differ from the reactions of animals. The realization of this fact then led to a widespread use of human subjects in experiments.

Reports of Abuses

The media published reports on human experimentation only occasionally before World War II. The prosecution of Karl Brandt and of other German physicians by the Nuremberg Military Tribunal for experiments on prisoners, however, was widely publicized. The reports of alleged abuses called world attention to the fact that human experimentation had been going on for many years, not only in German concentration camps but also in other parts of the world. The German physicians at the trial quoted, as part of their defense, cases of experiments on prison inmates that took place in the United States and in other parts of the world.[3]

As the number of biomedical studies has enormously increased and their scope has expanded during the last few decades, reports on successes and on alleged abuses have multiplied, too. There is hardly a week one does not find an account of some biomedical research in the daily press or in popular magazines. The media undoubtedly have played a prominent role in increasing the ethical sensitivity of the public to the use of human subjects in experiments.

Robert M. Veatch and Sharmon Sollito list eleven cases of experiments, some involving large numbers of people, which took place since 1966 and which raise disturbing ethical questions.[4] In one case, for example, twenty-four persons were given LSD to study the long-range changes in their personality, performance, value judgments and attitudes. All twenty-four had answered an advertisement and were paid at the rate of $2 per hour. They were not informed as to the possibility of personality changes and other dangers connected with the experiment. Some of them had never heard of LSD and others had only a slight knowledge of it.

The case of the Tuskegee Syphilis Study has been widely publicized. It first came to public attention in 1972, forty years after its inception, exposed to public view by the media. In 1932, the U.S. Public Health Service began an experiment in Alabama to study the natural course of untreated syphilis. Two groups of black males took part in these experiments, which came to be known as the Tuskegee Study. One group consisted of 399 syphilitic men who remained untreated and were not informed of the nature of their illness. The other group, consisting of 201 men, did not have syphilis but participated in the experiment as a control group. All 600 men received periodic placebo injections. They were also treated for occasional diseases other than syphilis. By the late 1940's penicillin, an effective remedy for syphilis, became available, but none of the participants was treated with penicillin or any other medicine for syphilis. When Associated Press reporter Jean Heller broke the story in 1972, the Health, Education and Welfare Department ordered an investigation of the study. The ad hoc advisory panel to the Assistant Secretary for Health concluded in 1973 that the experiment was ethically unjustified. By that time there were only seventy-four known survivors of the experiment. As a result of subsequent litigation on behalf of the survivors and the heirs of the deceased, an out-of-court settlement was reached according to which syphilitic survivors received $37,500 each and living non-syphilitic survivors of the experiment received $15,000 from the federal government.[5]

Quite different is the story of polio vaccine. Experimentations with the vaccine and its successful development in 1954 have been open to review and have been well reported in the scientific literature. The National Foundation for Infantile Paralysis supported the cooperative research program that was open to scientific scrutiny. In addition, the public was informed about the procedure involved in developing the vaccine and about the safety aspect of the vaccination before it came to the point of the inoculation of about 440,000 children in the United States in the spring of 1954.

As experiments on human beings greatly increased and investigative reports concerning their ethical aspects began to appear in the press, the moral sensitivity of the public was awakened and sharpened. As a result, pressure has been building up to bring human experimentation under social control in order to protect the dignity and rights of human subjects.

The Nuremberg Code

It was at the Nuremberg trials by the International Military Tribunal after World War II that a comprehensive statement on the ethical aspects of human experimentation was formulated for the first time. As is well known, twenty-three German physicians were accused of "war crimes and crimes against humanity" for having performed experiments on inmates of concentration camps. The Nuremberg court, trying war criminals, accepted a natural-law mode of reasoning as a basis for judging the guilt of the defenders.[6] A special court opinion was prepared concerning the conditions under which experimentation on human subjects may be approved and ethically carried out. This court opinion, prepared to help the judges in the formulation of their judgment, has become known as the *Nuremberg Code*.[7] The Code, as did the Nuremberg court in general, follows a natural-law mode of reasoning in justifying the prosecution of the doctors. Special emphasis is placed by the Code on *informed voluntary consent* as the primary condition for any ethically acceptable experiment on human subjects.

The Nuremberg Code formed the basis of the so-called Declaration of Helsinki of the World Medical Association in 1964. It was adopted by the eighteenth World Medical Assembly held in Helsinki, Finland, and is entitled "Recommendations Guiding Doctors in Clinical Research."[8] The American Medical Association (A.M.A.), on November 30, 1966, adopted a similar directive entitled "A.M.A. Ethical Guidelines for Clinical Investigation."[9]

What are the *general ethical principles concerning experimentations* on human subjects which are valid for any person involved in experimentation?

Voluntary Consent

First we have to ask the question whether there is a duty to experiment on human subjects. The question may seem unusual but it has to be asked because some scientists may feel obliged to carry out human experimentation.[10] Experimentation on human subjects is necessary in many cases *if* we want to develop new drugs, new therapies or new preventives for serious diseases that beset the human race. Looking back into history, we can say that, in a certain way, it was necessary for the sake of the common good of mankind to develop certain vaccines and drugs that stop the spread of contagious diseases. If human experimentation was a necessary prerequisite for development of these vaccines, then the conclusion must be that, in a certain way, there was a duty to experiment on humans.

This conclusion, however, appears quite strict and rigid, and it seems to impose a duty on all of us to submit to experiments since, as members of the human community, we all are obliged to work for the common good. In practice, however, the duty to experiment loses its theoretical rigidity. It cannot be proved that a certain drug or a concrete therapy is absolutely necessary for the common good. We may accept the existence of a general duty imposed upon the members of society to cooperate in the promotion of the common good, and this may include the obligation to promote the state of public health, for example, by assuming the responsibility of being immunized. The "social imperative," however, to participate in the development of therapies can be, and usually is, fulfilled by volunteers who are either scientists working on a project or are subjects of experiments. It is necessary to have a police force in civil society, but the duty to join the police force can be fulfilled by volunteers. There is no need to enlist everybody as long as there are enough volunteers.

It follows from this that voluntary consent is the basic ethical condition for human experimentation.

Therapeutic and Non-Therapeutic Experiments

Classification and clarification of the different kinds of experiments that are performed on human beings will greatly help us in the matter of their ethical evaluation. One of the most frequently mentioned classifications in bioethical literature is the distinction between *therapeutic* and *non-therapeutic* experiments. Therapeutic experiments are designed and conducted for the benefit of the subject, either to diagnose or to treat his illness. Non-therapeutic research refers to an experiment designed not to benefit the research subject directly but only to gain knowledge that can be used in the treatment of other persons.

The National Commission for the Protection of Human Subjects of Biomedical and Behavioral Research has recently abandoned the distinction between therapeutic and non-therapeutic research. One of the reasons for dropping this distinction is the fact that some types of research cannot be clearly defined as either therapeutic or non-therapeutic. For example, research designed to explore the cause of a disease can be put on the borderline between therapeutic and non-therapeutic experiment. The patient may or may not benefit by the research depending on the circumstances.[11]

Accepted and Non-Validated Practice

The Commission replaced the therapeutic and non-therapeutic distinction with the terms accepted, routine practice and non-validated practice of medicine. The introduction of this distinction was prompted by the fact that it is difficult to distinguish between clinical research and the practice of good medicine. Every diagnosis and treatment of a patient is a small research project carried out by the physician. Individual persons are different and react differently to drugs and thus adminstering a certain drug to a patient amounts to an experiment. The conclusion of the Commission is that it is preferable to use the terms standard or accepted and non-validated medical practices.

The Commission's reasoning is well founded, and it is important to keep in mind the meaning of its terminology when one reads its reports and documents. Nevertheless, there are also strong arguments for retaining the distinction between therapeutic and non-therapeutic research. It is important for the ethical evaluation of an experiment to know whether the project has been designed to benefit the subject or whether it is not meant to help the participant here and now. This can be ascertained easily. Unusual and non-validated medical practices, for example, to save a patient in a desperate situation, can be called therapeutic. The physician's sincere intention and effort to help the patient is an important aspect in the ethical evaluation of the procedure. It seems that it is not too difficult, in most cases, to determine whether an experiment is therapeutic or not because the design and the purpose of the experiment imply its therapeutic or non-therapeutic character.

Informed Voluntary Consent

Consent cannot be a human and intelligent act without proper knowledge of the purpose, the procedure, possible inconvenience, pain and risk of the experiment. Information about an experiment and free consent to it may be problematic, however, in many cases. Even educated persons may lack the scientific background to understand the purpose and procedure of an experiment. Uneducated persons or children may have even greater difficulty in grasping fully what is involved in a certain research project. It is obvious that the experimenter has a grave obligation to inform prospective subjects in non-technical language of all aspects of the experiment. He must adjust the information to the educational level of the subjects involved in the research. It is especially important to be candid about inconveniences and the likelihood of risk. With good will and honesty, this kind of information can be prepared and imparted to the subjects. Deliberate deception is morally wrong. To give false or less than full information in the recruitment of volunteers for experimentation is ethically unjustifiable. The good end of the experiment does not justify the evil means of lying and deception.

Experimentation with Incompetents

If a person cannot understand the information given in nontechnical language at his educational level, he is unable to give consent, because he does not know the object of his consent. This is the situation in experiments on infants, on children and on the mentally defective.

Does it follow then that no experiments may be ethically permitted on children and the mentally defective? According to most ethicians, therapeutic experiments that by their very nature intend to benefit the incompetent person may be ethically justified. Nevertheless, it is generally held that in order to avoid abuses it is necessary to get the "proxy consent" of the parents or of the guardians of these persons. The National Commission for the Protection of Human Subjects in Biomedical and Behavioral Research prefers the term "permission" of the parents or guardians to the term "proxy consent." Therapeutic experiments in the case of those incapable of giving informed consent may be performed only if there is no proven alternative for the treatment of their illnesses.

As for the permissibility of non-therapeutic experiments on incompetents, opinions are divided. For example, Richard A. McCormick, S.J., of the Kennedy Center for Bioethics, Georgetown University, Washington, D.C.,[12] states that it may be ethical for parents and guardians to give proxy consent to experimentation if the experiment is well designed, has no discernible risk, causes no discomfort and the subjects are minors. He justifies his opinion by a natural law argument that children are members of the human community and it is reasonable to presume that they would want to consent to such experiments for the benefit of others if they could express their wishes.

Paul Ramsey, of Princeton University, rejects McCormick's position "which is bound to weaken the protection of children in this age of research medicine."[13] Ramsey defends the principle "that protects the individual human person from being used for research purposes without either his expressed or correctly construed consent."[14] He holds that it is immoral to use children in research unrelated to their treatment to which they cannot themselves consent. There is no valid reason to presume that they would consent to the research.

The arguments on both sides have a certain validity. The weight of arguments, however, could be shifted in favor of the parental *permission* for experiments in certain cases if we consider that certain experiments may later benefit the subjects themselves. In addition, it is a normal exercise of parental authority to induce children to do what is objectively good even before they can understand what good is. It is obviously assumed that parents will not give permission for useless and risky experiments and will keep the good of their children and the genuine interest of the human community before their eyes.

The Department of Health and Human Services addressed the question of participation of children in research and published its regulations in the *Federal Register* on March 8, 1983. It stated that researchers must obtain both the permission of the parents or guardians and the "assent" of the children. The regulation, however, does not specify the age of assent but instructs the Institutional Review Boards to determine whether the children involved are capable of assenting.

Could the same reasoning be applied to experiments with comatose and dying persons? It seems that in their case the weight of the arguments is shifted to the position which opposes experiments on these persons. The dying individual needs all our compassionate help in the last hours of his life. It would be unethical and inhuman to disturb him with experiments unrelated to his treatment even if the experiments might benefit others. The experiment would distract and inconvenience the dying person and, therefore, it would be an ethically impermissible means for an otherwise good end.

The *need and competent design* of experiments has obvious ethical connotations. Useless and badly designed experiments only waste scarce scientific and economic resources. In addition, they are an abuse of the good will of the experimental subjects, who are being deceived as to the value of their cooperation in the research.

The *integrity and competence of the researcher* is also an evident condition for the ethical permissibility of an experiment. Although this condition appears obvious, it has to be mentioned explicitly because the pressure for promotion in the academic and scientific world, the availability of public and private funds for research, great economic rewards for inventions, and the allurement of national and international fame may influence some scientists to be less scrupulous in their experiments.

Experimentations Involving Prisoners

On January 9, 1976, Joseph Stetler, president of the Pharmaceutical Manufacturers Association, at a hearing of the National Commission for the Protection of Human Subjects of Research, stated that about 85 percent of all "phase-one" testing of new drugs is done on prisoners.[15] Phase-one testing is the initial study to find out what effects a drug will have on the normal human body. Researchers like to use prisoners for experiments because their controlled diet, uniform activities and daily regimen make the evaluation of such testing more reliable and easier to perform than the evaluation of tests with non-institutionalized persons.

Prisoners have been used for various sorts of biomedical research in the United States since before World War I. Recently, however, concern was expressed by various groups and individuals about the morality of such experiments. The Nuremberg Code has clearly stated the ethical principle that no human beings, not even prisoners, may be forced to be subjects of experimentation. The widespread use of prisoners, especially for testing new drugs, brings up the question of whether or not large numbers of prisoners are being forced into experimentation, which is a violation of their basic human rights, rights which they have not been deprived of even in jail.

Is it possible in the controlled prison environment to safeguard the genuine freedom of inmates to volunteer or not for experiments? In medium and maximum security institutions where most of the experiments are conducted, there are many ways to exercise pressure on inmates to volunteer. Just a break in the monotony of prison routine or the hope of some reward constitutes a great inner pressure, the opponents of prison experiments state, to induce somebody to "volunteer." Pressures have undoubtedly been exerted on prisoners, and the possibility of forcing them to submit to experiments is very real in the prison atmosphere. On the other hand, we must admit that procedures and conditions can be worked out that assure a genuine freedom for volunteering and giving informed consent to experiments. A number of prisoners themselves have argued that it is possible to set up conditions that guarantee their freedom of choice to participate in experiments.

From the ethical point of view, non-therapeutic experiments on prisoners may be permitted if their informed and truly free consent can be obtained. The conditions of prison experimentation recommended by the National Commission for the Protection of Human Subjects in Research are aimed at assuring such a free consent. These recommendations were made in October 1976 and contain the following essential points: non-therapeutic experiments should not be conducted on prisoners unless "(a) the type of research fulfills an important social and scientific need and the reasons for involving prisoners . . . are compelling; (b) the involvement of the prisoners . . . satisfies conditions of equity; and (c) a high degree of voluntariness on the part of prospective participants and of openness on the part of the institutions . . . would characterize the conduct of the research . . . ."[16]

It has been estimated that it costs about $70 million to bring a new drug to the market. It is obvious that using prisoners for testing is less costly than the use of non-prisoner volunteers. Nevertheless, many pharmaceutical companies, in order to avoid the problems of voluntary consent of prisoners, turn now to non-prison volunteers who are cloistered for periods of up to eight weeks. Some monetary inducement is necessary, however, to recruit a sufficient number of volunteers. It can be questioned, in turn, whether monetary inducement restricts the freedom of consent. In order to obviate this difficulty, monetary rewards are usually kept to such a degree that no "excessive" inducement occurs.

Fetal Research

Public concern has also been expressed about the morality of fetal research when certain cases of this type of human experimentation have become widely publicized. As the number of abortions has been growing, it has become easy to obtain fetuses for experimentation prior to abortion. The National Commission for the Protection of Human Subjects was charged in 1974 to study the question of fetal research and make recommendations to the Department of Health, Education and Welfare for the ethical conduct of fetal research. It has been found that most fetal experiments have been performed for therapeutic purposes, i.e., for the benefit of the fetuses involved in the experiments. But also some minimal-risk non-therapeutic experiments have occurred prior to normal birth or prior to abortion. In addition, a number of risky non-therapeutic studies have also been performed on fetuses before abortion. There have been a few even more questionable experiments performed on living fetuses following abortion. Researchers in all cases justified the experiments on fetuses by the goal of advancing fetal medicine, that is, ultimately by the goal of saving lives.

What is the morality of fetal research as a means to attain the praiseworthy goal of advancing fetal medicine? As we have seen in Chapter 3, the fetus is a human being. From the ethical point of view, then, experiments done on fetuses must be judged as if they were small children who cannot give their consent to the experiments.

As we have seen before, therapeutic and non-therapeutic but minimal-risk experiments may be performed on children with parental permission if the experiments are necessary for the advancement of pediatric medicine. Similar conditions are required for the permissibility of experiments on fetuses. The reason is that children, even fetuses as human beings, are members of the human community and they have the general duty to promote the common good as much as they can. What their cooperation with the common good may or should be at the beginning of their life is up to their parents to decide. In natural law reasoning, it is the parents' duty to guide the actions of their children before they reach the age of reason. Fetuses who will be aborted may not be treated differently from those who complete their term. There are no ethically extenuating conditions to treat them differently. Abortion is a grave injustice done to the fetus. This wrong should not be aggravated by the injury of using the fetus for risky, non-therapeutic research.[17]

Recommendations of the National Commission recognize the

human dignity of the fetus and provide protection to the fetus which is similar to that given to infants and children. H.E.W. has accepted the Commission's recommendations with one exception. Agreeing with the Commission, H.E.W. judged it unethical to keep a fetus *ex utero* artificially alive for research purposes if there is every reason to assume that the fetus is about to die. But it judged permissible to maintain the vital functions of a fetus *ex utero* for research purposes when the goal of the experiment is "to develop new methods for enabling fetuses to survive to the point of viability."[18] It seems that except on this one point the H.E.W. regulations are ethically well founded.

The Use of Placebos

The use of *placebos* in experiments produces special ethical problems from the point of view of informed voluntary consent. Placebo, a Latin word meaning "I shall please," is a medically ineffective substance that is customarily used in testing new drugs when it is given to a control group. The problem arises from the fact that the control group is not informed of the worthless nature of the medicine being administered. For example, a group of American soldiers crossing the Atlantic during World War II was given a new motion-sickness medicine; the other group, however, received only placebos. By using placebos, the medical and military authorities tried to find out whether the new medicine was pharmacologically effective or had only psychological effects. It has been an age-old custom to give "sugar pills" also in cases when no effective medicine is available but a patient expects some medication from a physician.

Is the use of placebos unethical? It seems that experimental volunteers who are given placebos are clearly misled and deceived. Deception, no matter what its purpose, cannot be approved morally. Researchers, however, object that the use of placebos is necessary and experimental subjects cannot be told whether they receive placebos or medically effective medicine because the knowledge of receiving placebos would invalidate the experiment. The great benefits, the researchers argue, justify the harmless deception. It can be pointed out, however, that some experiments involving placebos are not entirely harmless (for example, in the case of sick persons as research subjects, one group of whom does not get a drug to alleviate or prevent the worsening of an illness) and that the good end does not justify the evil means.

What would happen if all members of a test group were honestly told that some of them will receive the new drug and others only placebos? Would it invalidate the result of testing? Some argue that it would not. It is a fact that pharmacologically ineffective placebos frequently produce the alleviation of pain or cure an illness. Recent studies indicate that placebos frequently work because they trigger specific biochemical changes in the body. This fact is a proof that there is an interaction between mind and body, that there is no real separation between them. The placebo is only an occasion for the human mind effectively to order the body to produce certain biochemical changes. If this is true in the case of illnesses, the use of placebos in experiments on healthy persons can be misleading too, because it is possible that the placebos cause biochemical changes that are similar to those caused by drugs. If these facts are true, the argument for blind or double-blind experiments involving placebos loses its scientific weight. Apart from this, however, the ethical argument should always prevail that we are not allowed to use deliberate deception even for a good purpose.[19]

The ethical problem of placebo use in research could perhaps be solved if the volunteers were told that some members of the group may receive placebos and the administration of placebos would follow the double-blind method.

It has been proved that placebos frequently lessen pain or even heal a patient. Is it ethically wrong to use a lie that cures? One investigation revealed that in a hospital 41 of 47 physicians, that is, 87 percent, had used placebos on patients who requested more pain killers than the doctors thought necessary.[20] It seems that the use of placebos by doctors is quite widespread. Some argue that their use is unethical because it involves deception. Other doctors, however, defend the ethical use of placebos because they maintain that they can be administered without deception. The patient can be given the placebo with these or similar words: I will give you a medicine which, although without known chemical activity, frequently has very positive healing effect.[21]

As we have seen in the previous chapter, peer review is not always sufficient to assure the ethical conduct of research. Public policy and carefully designed regulations are needed. In the United States the National Research Act (P.L. 93–348, 88 Stat. 342, 1974) mandated the establishment of *Institutional Review Boards* (I.R.B.) at every institution conducting research on human subjects that is federally funded. The purpose of the I.R.B.'s is to assure that the experiments meet federal standards based on ethical and legal principles.[22] Most institutions have voluntarily established Institutional Review Boards even if they do not receive federal funds.

Well-designed positive laws and regulations are important for the protection of citizens and for public order. One must not make the error, however, of assuming that well-intentioned positive regulations are always the correct expression of sound ethical principles. One needs to continue with the ethical analysis of regulations, procedures and all aspects of experimentation with human beings so that the rights of human subjects, as the first condition for any morally justifiable research, are safeguarded.

Some researchers have complained that the necessity of getting I.R.B. approval for a project makes experiments cumbersome and slows down useful research. It is a fact, however, that since the establishment of the Institutional Review Boards, abuses of human subjects have completely stopped. Supervision by I.R.B.'s is a small price to pay for the effective protection of human rights.

Privacy and Confidentiality

Man needs to communicate with his fellow human beings in order to get help or just to share his joys and worries. Most of this communication deals with private matters that are not meant for public airing. It follows from the individual nature of man that we have a right to privacy. We turn to our friends or professionals to get assistance, and we rightly assume that discussion of our private affairs will not be divulged.

It would be a violation of our rights if social or scientific researchers pried into our private life without our knowledge or permission.

Privacy means the right to control access to information concerning our private life. *Confidentiality*, on the other hand, means that information gained from an individual will not be revealed to others without his permission, but will be "kept in confidence."

It is assumed that professional persons, physicians, lawyers, priests, will keep confidential what has been entrusted to them even if there is no explicit written agreement to that effect. In experimentations with human beings, however, it is customary that written guarantees are given concerning the revelation and use of data gained from individuals in the course of the experiment.

QUESTIONS FOR REVIEW AND DISCUSSION

1. What is the role of human experimentation in medicine? Would it be sufficient to perform only animal experiments?

2. If human experimentation is necessary for the public welfare, is there a duty to submit to experimentation?

3. Why is voluntary consent the first condition of an ethically correct experiment?

4. Does voluntary consent presuppose full information about the details of an experiment?

5. If informed voluntary consent is necessary for the ethical conduct of experiments, is it ever permissible to experiment with children and incompetents?

6. Can prisoners ever freely consent to experiments?

7. Is it ethical to experiment with fetuses?

8. Is the use of placebos ethically justifiable (a) in experiments, (b) in therapeutic treatments?

9. Is government regulation of human experiments ethically justifiable, or is it an unjustified governmental intrusion into the field of science?

Notes

1. Cf. Francis D. Moore, "A Cultural and Historical View," in *Experiments and Research with Humans: Values in Conflict.* Washington, D.C.: National Academy of Sciences, 1975, pp. 15–20.

2. Cf. Nathan Hershey and Robert D. Miller, *Human Experimentation and the Law.* Germantown: Aspen Systems Corporation, 1976, p. 4.

3. Cf. M.H. Pappworth, M.D., *Human Guinea Pigs.* Boston: Beacon Press, 1968, p. 61.

4. Robert M. Veatch and Sharmon Sollito, "Human Experimentations—The Ethical Questions Persist." *Hastings Center Report,* June 1973.

5. Cf. Charlotte L. Levy, *The Human Body and the Law.* Dobbs Ferry: Oceana Publications, 1975, p. 1.

6. Cf. Andrew C. Varga, *On Being Human,* New York: Paulist Press, 1978, p. 104.

7. See the full text in Appendix I.

8. See the full text in Appendix II.

9. See the full text in Appendix III.

10. Cf. Leon Eisenberg, "The Social Imperatives of Medical Research." *Science,* Vol. 198, December 16, 1977, pp. 1105–1110.

11. Robert J. Levine, "Clarifying the Concepts of Research Ethics." *The Hastings Center Report,* June 1979, pp. 21–26.

12. Richard A. McCormick, "Proxy Consent in the Experimentation Situation." *Perspectives in Biology and Medicine,* Autumn 1974, pp. 2–20.

13. Paul Ramsey, "The Enforcement of Morals: Non-Therapeutic Research on Children." *Hastings Center Report,* August 1976, p. 21.

14. *Ibid.*

15. *The New York Times,* January 10, 1976.

16. Roy Branson, "Prison Research: National Commission Says 'No, Unless . . . .' " *Hastings Center Report,* February 1977, pp. 15–21.

17. Cf. Richard A. McCormick and Leroy Walters, "Fetal Research and Public Policy." *America,* June 21, 1976, pp. 473–476.

18. Barbara J. Culliton, "Fetal Research: HEW Rules Depart from Commission's Recommendations." *Science,* Vol. 190, October 17, 1976, pp. 251–253. HEW regulations were published in *Federal Register* 40, no. 154, August 8, 1975, pp. 33526–33552.

19. Cf. Sissela Bok, "The Ethics of Giving Placebos." *Scientific American,* Volume 231, November 1974; Norman Cousins, "The Mysterious Placebo." *Saturday Review,* October 1, 1977, pp. 9–16.

20. Cf. Lindsey Gruson, "Value of Placebo Being Argued on Ethical Grounds." *The New York Times*, February 13, 1983, p. 21.

21. Cf. Reginal W. Rhein, Jr., "Placebo: Deception or Potent Therapy?" *Medical World News*, February 4, 1980, pp. 39–47.

22. Robert M. Veatch, "The National Commission on IRB's: An Evolutionary Approach." *Hastings Center Report*, February 1979, pp. 22–28.

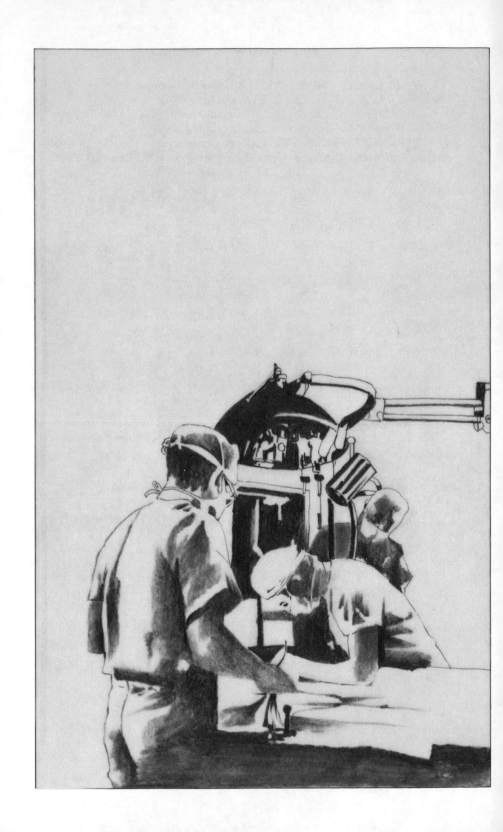

9 Psychosurgery and Behavior Control

Psychosurgery can be described as brain surgery to correct mental and behavioral disorders. *Normal behavior* has never been satisfactorily defined. Nevertheless, persons in authority as well as the common man have been passing judgment on certain forms of conduct as being deviations from the normal, i.e., as being *abnormal behavior*. It seems there is a vague common understanding of what normal and abnormal behavior is. The application of the ambiguous rules of normalcy to particular cases, however, may result in contradictory appraisals of a person's behavior. Is a man with new and strange ideas a prophet or a mentally deranged person? Totalitarian regimes judge dissidents to be mentally disturbed and lock them in lunatic asylums. It happens in open societies, too, that the political and social gadfly is regarded as eccentric and abnormal.

Psychiatry

In ancient times mental illness was thought to be caused by the malign influence of evil spirits. Various forms of exorcism were applied to expel demons in order to restore the normal self-control of the patient. Modern man and modern medicine do not believe in demons and their harmful influence on human beings. Nevertheless, psychiatry, the new science of the late nineteenth century, taught that the cause of abnormal behavior was to be found in mental or psychological factors hidden in the subconscious stratum of man's psyche. Psychoanalysis and other techniques were supposed to be able to bring these evil things to the surface of consciousness and "exorcise" them. Expelling the cause of an obsession or deviant behavior in this way is believed to cure the patient. There is no intention here of agreeing with the unflattering comparison of a psychiatrist with a witch doctor, or of calling him a "head shrinker" as popular language does. Psychiatry has made many contributions to the understanding of mental illness and has developed certain effective methods of alleviating mental disorders. Nevertheless, psychiatrists themselves admit that their art is still greatly experimental. Their techniques are uncertain and very slow to produce results.

Brain Surgery

While psychiatry has been looking for the causes of mental illness in the subconscious, certain scientists and physicians have turned to the exploration of another possible cause of abnormal behavior, namely, an illness of the brain. The brain is assumed to be the means by which human beings control all their activities, thoughts and ideas—in other words, their whole personality. If the brain is sick, the human mind is sick as well. The brain is the center of the human person. A comparison is often made between organs of the body, for example, the kidneys and the liver, and the organ of the mind, i.e., the brain. If the liver malfunctions, the body becomes sick; if the brain malfunctions, it is the mind that becomes sick. It is difficult, however, to prove the theory that mental illness is the result of a malfunctioning brain. Biology does not know enough about the functioning or malfunctioning of the brain to draw well-founded conclusions. Nevertheless, constant progress is being made in "mapping" the brain, that is, identifying certain parts that seem to be the *loci* of specific vital functions, for example, of seeing and of hearing. The *loci* of emotions and mental disorders, however, have not been clearly identified. Yet operations performed on the brains of animals, and the subsequent modifications of their behavior, have encouraged a few surgeons to operate on the human brain, too, in order to modify the abnormal behavior of the patients. These operations have given rise to the emergence of psychosurgery that, at the beginning of the twentieth century, was called by the emotionally less charged term brain surgery. Such an operation consists of the destruction of the diseased part of the brain that is assumed to cause abnormal behavior.

The first known instance of brain surgery took place in Switzerland in 1891. It was performed by Gottlieb Burckhardt, the superintendent of a mental institute.[1] He operated on six patients to reduce their impulsive behavior, which he thought was the result of excess neural activity in the cerebral cortex. He removed certain parts of the cortex to lessen this neural activity. One patient died but the survivors became more peaceful in their conduct and easier to manage. Nevertheless, they remained psychotic and had to be kept in the mental institute.

Lobotomy

Brain operations did not become an accepted method of treating mental disorders until 1935. In that year, at the Second International Congress of Neurology, held in London, two American brain researchers, Carlyle F. Jacobsen and John F. Fulton, reported on the results of their experiments with brain operations on monkeys and chimpanzees. Destruction of the prefrontal regions of the brain produced marked behavioral changes in these animals. Their reactions to certain stimuli became subdued in contrast to the previous explosive agitation caused by the same stimuli. There were other changes as well that resulted in an overall calm and subdued behavior in the animals.

Antonio Egas Moniz, a Portuguese participant at the Congress, asked the question about whether similar operations might not be performed on mental patients to relieve their anxiety and agitation. Despite the negative reaction of the neurologists present, Moniz decided to experiment with the operation. Returning to Portugal, he developed a method of brain operation that later became known as a *lobotomy*. Moniz and his colleague, Almeida Lima, claimed a high rate of success achieved by the operations they performed. Several agitated and violent patients who underwent the surgery became calm and easier to manage. The operation slowly gained favor with neurosurgeons, so much so that, according to some estimates, as many as 70,000 lobotomies were performed in the United States and

Britain alone from 1935 to 1955. This happened despite the many undesirable side effects of the operations and outright failures to cure
the patients. Many of the persons who were operated on became ap-
athetic, asocial and irresponsible in their conduct.

Electrical Stimulation of the Brain (ESB)

Around the mid-1950's, the technique of lobotomy became almost completely abandoned as a tool for helping the mentally disturbed. New techniques emerged, however, attempting to improve
the art of brain surgery for the modification of behavior.

The history of the new technique began in 1908 when the British
neurosurgeon, Dr. Victor Horsley and his associate, R.H. Clarke, developed the so-called Horsley-Clarke stereotaxic device. Basically,
this instrument consists of a very thin needle or wire which, except
for the tip, is insulated. Through tiny holes drilled in the skull of animals or human beings electrodes can be inserted into almost any
part of the brain. The placing of the electrodes is done with the aid of
three-dimensional anatomical maps, so-called stereotaxic atlases.[2]
The wires can be used to measure electrical signals coming from different parts of the brain. In addition, they can be used to pass weak
electric currents through them and electrically stimulate specific
parts of the brain. Dr. Walter Rudolph Hess, of Switzerland, and Dr.
Stephen W. Ransom, of the United States, did a great deal of research
and recorded the responses elicited by *electrical stimulation of the
brain (ESB)*. In 1949, Dr. Hess was awarded the Nobel Prize for this
work of mapping of the responses elicited by electrical stimulation of
about 4,500 neural sites in 480 cats.[3]

Wiring Up the Brain

A great many experiments with various animals have demonstrated that changes in the behavior and the mood of animals can be
produced by electrical stimulation of various parts of the brain. With
the development of radio technology and miniaturization, it has become possible to attach a small radio receiver to the ends of wires inserted into various regions of the brain. Through the radio receiver

these regions can be stimulated in sequence from a distance. José M.R. Delgado and his team at Yale University have improved the devices of electrical stimulation and have expanded the range of research in this field. Delgado described a number of typical reactions to electrical stimulation of the brain of both animals and human beings.[4] One of the devices he used in his research is called "*stimoceiver*." This is an instrument for radio transmission and reception of electrical messages to and from the brain of animals or human beings. The stimoceiver is plugged to the head sockets of the patient who has been fitted with electrodes. He remains unrestrained and can continue his activities while under constant medical observation through radio messages emanating from his brain. At the same time the patient's brain can be manipulated at a distance through radio messages from the doctor or therapeutic stimulation can be administered by computerized automatic programming.[5]

Effects of ESB

The following are some of the reactions observed. Electrical stimulation of the right side motor cortex of a cat produced bending of one hind leg. The performance was repeated as many times as the electrical stimulation was applied. A monkey sitting in its cage picking at some food received a radio stimulus to its thalamus, got up and began to walk. When the stimulation ceased, he sat down, but repeated the performance as many times as the stimulation was applied. A complex motor response was induced by ESB in another monkey. The response consisted of a series of different actions that were repeated in the same order as many times as ESB was applied. Sleep was induced in a monkey. After thirty seconds of stimulation of the septal area, the animal fell asleep.

ESB can immobilize an animal in the middle of ongoing activities. A cat lapping milk was immobilized with its tongue out. A great variety of inhibitory effects were produced on experimental animals by stimulation of certain parts of their brains. One of the most spectacular experiments performed by Dr. Delgado was the stopping of a bull in full charge. By radio stimulation of the bull's brain, its aggressive behavior was inhibited and the bull stopped abruptly. It seems that the sudden halt of the bull was the result of a combination of "motor effect, forcing the bull to stop and to turn aside, plus behavioral inhibition of the aggressive drive." Repeated stimulation of the bull's brain rendered him less aggressive. In another experiment, electrical stimulation of certain parts of a monkey's brain inhibited maternal affection.

It seems that stimulation of a specific area of the brain can produce pleasant feelings. Experimental rats, cats and monkeys voluntarily chose to press a lever repeatedly which caused electrical stimulation. The animals obviously enjoyed the stimulation because, although they were hungry, they preferred electrical self-stimulation to food within their reach.

The reactions of human beings to electrical stimulation of the brain are similar to those of animals. Delgado described experiments in which, for example, "electrical stimulation of the depth of the brain" induced pleasurable feelings.

Patients suffering from schizophrenia or Parkinson's disease became "relaxed and at ease" after stimulation of the septal region. The narcolepsia of one man was greatly relieved by pressing his "septal button." An important part of research is aimed at the inhibitory effects induced by electrical stimulation of the brain. The symptoms of epilepsy, Parkinson's disease and chorea are involuntary movements that are caused by neural discharges originating in specific parts of the brain.[6] If these discharges could be prevented or counteracted by electrical stimulation of those parts of the brain, suitable therapies could be developed. Constant and intractable pain as well might be alleviated by ESB.

Brain "Pacemaker"

In 1973, Dr. Irving S. Cooper, a world-renowned neurosurgeon, at that time working in St. Barnabas Hospital in the Bronx, New York, developed a brain "pacemaker" to help patients suffering from epilepsy, Parkinson's disease and other severe neurological disorders.[7] The pacemaker consists of two sets of electrodes that are placed over the front and the rear of the cerebellum, with wires running under the skin to the chest, where two miniature radio receivers are implanted. A circular antenna is taped to the skin of the patient above the receivers. The antenna is connected with a battery-powered transmitter that fits in a breast pocket or shoulder harness. When activated, the transmitter sends a small electric current to the cerebellum, which produces an inhibitory effect, neutralizing the neural discharges that seem to cause epileptic seizures. "Wayne A.," the first epileptic Dr. Cooper fitted with the pacemaker, improved considerably and was able to resume working. After the surgery, he had several seizures, but it seems that all of them took place because a wire leading to the battery was broken. When the wire was repaired, the seizures stopped.

Delgado speculates[8] that a stimoceiver implanted in a patient could be linked to a computer. Localized abnormal electrical activity of the brain which precedes an epileptic seizure could be picked up and transmitted by the stimoceiver to a distant computer, programmed to recognize abnormal electrical patterns preceding a seizure. The computer could automatically send signals to the stimoceiver to stimulate a specific part of the brain, preventing the epileptic attack. Delgado reported that his speculation was supported by his experiments on chimpanzees. A more advanced instrument developed by Delgado and his team at Yale University is "the multichannel transdermal stimulator." A miniature radio receiver and transmitter are implanted under the skin. The instrument does not need batteries. It does not have terminals protruding through the skin. "Energy and signals are transferred through the intact skin by radio induction."[9]

Electrical stimulation of the brain does not destroy any part of the brain. It is also painless. The electrodes can remain implanted or they can be removed at any time. This is a great advantage over brain surgery, which is irreversible, frequently unpredictable, and may have undesired side-effects. The relatively easy maneuverability of ESB instruments renders them suitable tools for diagnosing the malfunctioning of certain parts of the brain that seem to cause abnormal behavior, such as compulsive moments, uncontrollable rage or aggressive fits. For example, if the stimulation of a specific part of the brain always causes a patient to fly into a rage, it is concluded that that particular part of the brain is the cause of the spontaneous outbreaks of rage. It is thought that the removal of that "diseased" part of the brain can cure the patient and permit him to return to his normal social environment. The surgery in this case may be simply the application of a stronger electric current, which would burn and destroy a small part of the brain tissue previously diagnosed as diseased.

Dr. Vernon H. Mark and Dr. Frank R. Ervin used Delgado's stimoceiver to determine what part of the brain of a young woman, Julia S., caused her frequent and uncontrollable fits of rage.[10] The rage was precipitated when a particular area in the amygdala was stimulated. Having performed several experiments, the two doctors drew the conclusion that there was a definite connection between this part of the brain and her fits of violent rage. They made a destructive lesion in Julia's right amygdala, the assumed source of her disorders. According to the two surgeons, Julia had only two mild cases of rage in the first year after the operation and none in the second year. Her epileptic seizures, however, had not been eliminated.[11]

Violence and Psychosurgery

Can psychosurgery control violent behavior? When ESB and the new methods of psychosurgery gained publicity, the idea emerged that it would be better to perform operations on the brains of violent criminals than send them to prison. A simple surgery would rehabilitate them and turn them into useful members of society. Drs. Mark and Ervin argued that some violent behavior can be caused by brain dysfunction and could be controlled by psychosurgery. Their book, *Violence and the Brain*, raised a storm of criticism from those who believe that human behavior is modified much more by individual self-determination and social influence than by biological processes. Clarifying his ideas in an article,[12] Dr. Mark stated that the domain of psychosurgery is very narrow, but that it is legitimate in certain cases when psychotherapy and drug therapy are ineffective or have serious side-effects. Dr. Mark defends himself and other neurosurgeons against accusations implying they were involved in many thousands of cases of brain surgery in an attempt to control the behavior of persons who betray some traits of abnormal behavior. According to a survey conducted by the American Psychiatric Association, only about five hundred psychosurgery procedures are performed annually in the United States.[13]

Brain surgery as a panacea for controlling or eliminating violence is regarded with disdain by scientists and medical communities. Nevertheless, certain law enforcement agencies thought it worthwhile to try it in penitentiaries. In 1972, the Law Enforcement Assistance Administration of the U.S. Department of Justice gave a grant of $109,000 to aid the work of the Neuro-Research Foundation in identifying prison inmates with habitual violent behavior coupled with evidence of brain damage.[14] One project for psychosurgical treatment of violent inmates was stopped in 1973 because of public protest prompted by publicity in the media. This project has become known as the Vacaville project. According to the plan, violent inmates were to be taken to medical facilities at Vacaville and then to the University of California at San Francisco Medical Center to be diagnosed as to whether the source of their aggressive behavior was located in the central parts of their brain. Inmates diagnosed as being aggressive because of brain damage were then supposed to undergo psychosurgery. On November 30, 1974 the U.S. Senate Subcommittee on Constitutional Rights issued a 651-page report on federal funds used in behavior-control tests. The Subcommittee, headed by Senator Sam J. Ervin, Jr., found that "the federal government, through a number of departments and agencies, is going ahead with behavior modification projects, including psychosurgery, without a review structure fully adequate to protect the constitutional rights of the subjects." The Subcommittee expressed doubt that "the government should be involved at all in programs that potentially pose substantial threats to our basic freedoms."[15]

Psychosurgery and Prisoners

In 1974, the case of Louis Smith, the first instance of psychosurgery to be adjudicated by a U.S. court, attained national publicity. These are the facts of the case. In 1955, while a mental patient at Kalamazoo State Hospital, Smith was accused of raping and murdering Marilyn Kraai, a student nurse. Instead of being brought to trial, he was committed to Ionia State Hospital as a criminally insane sexual psychopath. In 1972, he was transferred to the Lafayette Clinic in Detroit and was asked by the Director of the Department of Health to participate in a state-funded experiment. Smith was thirty-six years old at that time and had already spent eighteen years in mental institutions. The experiment was to test two methods of eliminating aggressive behavior in violent mental patients. One method was designed to use drugs, the other involved psychosurgery, the destruction of certain areas of the brain. Louis Smith and his parents gave written consent to his involvement in the experiment. Gabe Kaimowitz, a Michigan Legal Services attorney, however, brought suit to enjoin the state from performing psychosurgery on Louis Smith or any other person in a similar situation. Louis Smith, however, was freed before the hearing of the case and withdrew his consent to the experiment. The court, nevertheless, continued to hear arguments about brain surgery of mental patients detained in state institutions.[16] The court ruled that "patients involuntarily committed in state institutions are incapable of giving legally competent, voluntary, and knowledgeable consent to experimental psychosurgical operations."[17]

The "Detroit Case," as it became known, received wide publicity and called public attention to the ethical problem of controlling human behavior. As a result, correctional institutions have become more careful about the use of radical methods of behavior control. In 1974, the Behavior Control Research Group of The Institute of Society, Ethics and the Life Sciences sent a questionnaire to the Commissioners of Correction in all fifty states. Regarding psychosurgery, "all states reported that psychosurgery was not being used as a treatment procedure, although one qualified with 'not at this time.' "[18]

Controversy about the ethical use of psychosurgery is not limited to its application in correctional institutions. Opponents of psychosurgery point out that basically it is nothing else than experimentation with the human brain, and that the results so far are of very dubious value. In 1973, Dr. Peter Breggin, Director for the Center for the Study of Psychiatry, an opponent of psychosurgery, argued at hearings before the Subcommittee on Health of the Senate that psychosurgery has not achieved any real cure of mentally disturbed persons. Psychosurgery blunts the individual's emotions, makes him more docile and subject to the control of others. It destroys the highest capacity of man, which amounts to the destruction of the "self."[19]

The National Commission for the Protection of Human Subjects of Behavioral and Biomedical Research agreed with the opinion of those who hold that psychosurgery is an experimental procedure. Nevertheless, the Commission stated in its report, issued on March

14, 1977, that in certain cases psychosurgery could have therapeutic effects. For this reason, it maintained that subjects should not be prohibited from undergoing psychosurgery. The operation may be permitted, however, only when it is safe and effective according to competent medical assessment, and when the subject has given informed consent.[20] According to the recommendation of the Commission, psychosurgery should be performed only at an institution where there is an Institutional Review Board (I.R.B.) approved specifically for reviewing proposed psychosurgery cases, and where there are competent surgeons and staff to perform the operation and to care for the patient after the operation.

Electroconvulsive Therapy (ECT)

Electroshock therapy is another form of psychosurgery. It was first used in 1938 by two Italian psychiatrists, Dr. Ugo Cerletti and Dr. Lucio Bini. Searching for a treatment for schizophrenia, they induced a convulsion in a patient by an electrical apparatus. The condition of their patient improved after the therapy. The original apparatus has been refined, but the method has basically remained the same. Electrodes are fastened to one side of the head or to both temples of the patient. He receives a muscle relaxant and is anesthetized with a short-acting barbiturate. Then electric current is applied for 0.1 to 0.5 of a second, which produces a convulsion. Dr. Stuart Yudofsky, of the New York State Psychiatric Institute, has estimated that about "80 percent of the depressions that do not respond to drugs do respond to convulsive therapy."[21]

The 1975 film, "One Flew Over the Cuckoo's Nest," strengthened the popular opinion that electroconvulsive therapy is cruel and inhuman. Its safety and efficacy, however, have been reasonably well established. About 100,000 Americans each year undergo ECT to alleviate depression and schizophrenia. According to Dr. Richard Abrams, vice chairman of the Chicago Medical School's Department of Psychiatry and Behavioral Science, a number of controlled studies have proved that the treatment is safe and that its side-effects are few and less severe than those of drug treatments.[22]

Nevertheless, there are dissenting opinions on the part of some physicians. For instance, Dr. John Friedberg, author of the book,

Shock Treatment Is Not Good for Your Brain, questions the safety of ECT.

A referendum in the city of Berkeley, California, proposed to ban the use of electroshock therapy by psychotherapists within the city limits. It won a 61% majority in the November 1982 elections, so that the administration of ECT became a misdemeanor. That law, however, was voided when the Alameda County Superior Court issued an injunction restraining the city of Berkeley from enforcing the prohibition. The State of California already has a law requiring a patient to give two consecutive consents before ECT can be administered to him.

It is not known how ECT affects the brain and how it works. Some researchers think that it increases the patient's levels of beta endorphin, one of the "natural opiates" produced in the brain that combats pain and stress.[23]

The ethical problem with ECT is that it is still an experimental therapy. Thus all the conditions for licit human experimentation must be fulfilled before it can be administered. In addition, the patients in many cases are not entirely competent to give informed consent to the therapy and thus a proxy consent or the permission of a guardian must be obtained.

Ethical Evaluation

From the ethical point of view, the main problem with psychosurgery is its experimental nature. Can neurosurgeons judge in good conscience that a certain lesion of the brain is safe and effective? Data are inadequate in this regard; the few known facts are not reassuring. In addition, the question of informed consent causes considerable difficulty. The subject of the proposed psychosurgery is mentally disturbed or, at least, unbalanced. According to accepted conditions of a free and voluntary decision, he cannot make an informed consent. It follows from this that, in the present state of our knowledge of the human brain and its functions, psychosurgery can morally be justified as an experimental therapeutic intervention only when other forms of therapy have failed and one is dealing with a desperate situation. One may conclude that it is better for the patient to be calmed by a permanent lesion of his brain than to be in a straitjacket for the rest of his life. In addition, the patient's informed consent has to be replaced or completed by the permission of his parents or guardians because, in most cases, he is not capable of giving genuine consent to the operation.

The goal of psychosurgery is the improvement of the humanity of the patient. The main characteristics of humanity are rationality and sociability. The restoration of both of these distinctively human traits is the ideal end of psychosurgery. However, if improvement can be achieved only in one aspect of the patient's humanity, that progress is still a worthwhile result.

There may be cases when a habitually violent patient has the ability to think and reason more or less rationally. Would it be ethically permissible to calm him by a brain operation that, at the same time, would blunt his intellect? One could perhaps argue that his humanity might be improved by enabling him to live in peace with his fellow human beings. It seems, however, that the source of our humanity is rational thinking. If it has to come to choosing between the two characteristics of man, rationality should be preserved; it should not be destroyed in favor of sociability.

There is no need to argue here that psychosurgery may not be considered as a means to eliminate violence from society or to empty the prisons. Mentally or emotionally abnormal persons, in any case, should not be condemned to jail or detained there. If, nevertheless, they happen to be there because of judicial mistakes, with respect to psychosurgery, they should be treated in the same way as mental patients in general.

Psychosurgery should not be used in an attempt to improve man "beyond the normal." Such an experiment would seem to be unethical at least on two counts:

1. The operation would be too risky; instead of improving the abilities of a person, the intervention might reduce his normality.

2. Who is to determine what is normal and what would constitute improvement beyond the normal? One would rightly be hesitant to entrust this task to neurosurgeons or to any authority or individual.

The Ethics of ESB

Electric stimulation of the brain or the implantation of a stimoceiver does not seem to cause any permanent lesion or damage to the brain. The electrodes and the instrument can be removed at any time. Consequently, therapeutic application of ESB or of brain "pacemakers" to prevent epileptic seizure, to stop involuntary movements, or to reduce intolerable and intractable pain is within the realm of good medicine in the hands of competent neurosurgeons. It is true that this type of medical treatment is still experimental, but it is less risky than a permanent lesion of the brain. In addition, in many cases the patient is capable of giving informed consent to the treatment. He can judge whether it is worthwhile to attempt such a procedure instead of using other kinds of therapy.

As we have seen, electric stimulation of the brain can change the mood of a person; it can produce pleasant feelings and force a person to perform certain movements. Theoretically, it would be possible to control another person's will to a certain degree. Science fiction books and movies, inspired by new biological developments in this field,[24] fantasize about the time when an entire population is wired up and a dictator, pressing buttons on a console, controls the whole nation. Unfortunately, dictators have easier methods than this to control a nation. They practice their trade very competently without resorting to the practically impossible procedure of sinking electrodes into the heads of every citizen. The possibility of abusing psychosurgery in individual cases, however, cannot simply be dismissed. Soviet Russia locks many of its dissidents in mental institutions and subjects them to treatments designed to return them to "normality" and to control their behavior. There is no need to dwell on the obvious immorality of any attempt to subjugate the wills of others, be it by electrodes, drugs or any other means.

We could speculate that someone might like to have electrodes in his brain so that he could control his own mood, get rid of anxiety or depression, by pressing the button of electrical stimulation himself. Could this be approved from the ethical point of view? It could be approved only in cases when a person cannot cope with his psychological problems and is incapable of regaining his psychic balance through his will power. Otherwise, one of the moral tasks of a person is to exercise self-control and to manage his own life, including his moods and anxieties, by self-determination. Reliance on electrodes or on drugs to do this for us in ordinary situations would be the surrendering of a part of our personhood as free and moral agents. The use of electrical stimulation and of drugs is morally justified only to regain our self-control, not to eliminate it.

QUESTIONS FOR REVIEW AND DISCUSSION

1. What are the causes of abnormal behavior?

2. Can brain surgery restore normalcy?

3. Describe the technique of ESB. Can ESB change or control the behavior of animals and human beings?

4. What are the therapeutic applications of ESB and stimoceivers?

5. Can psychosurgery cure violence?

6. Describe ECT. Is it an effective therapy to alleviate depression? Why is there a debate about the efficacy of ECT?

7. Is the application of the various forms of psychosurgery ethically justifiable?

8. Would it be ethically justifiable to use ESB to change or control one's mood?

Notes

1. Elliot S. Valenstein, *Brain Control*. New York: John Wiley and Sons, 1973, p. 266.

2. Valenstein, *op. cit.*, p. 25.

3. *Ibid.*, p. 28.

4. José M.R. Delgado, *Physical Control of the Mind: Toward a Psycho-civilized Society*. New York: Harper & Row, 1969, pp. 76–176.

5. *Ibid.*, pp. 86–91.
6. *Ibid.*, pp. 103, 106, 108, 157, 169, 141, 142, 143, 169.
7. David Hendin, "Pacemaker for the Brain." *Saturday Review*, January 26, 1974, pp. 66–69.
8. *Op. cit.*, p. 91.
9. José M.R. Delgado, "Brain Manipulation." *The Humanist*, March/April 1972, p. 11.
10. Vernon H. Mark, M.D. and Frank R. Ervin, M.D., *Violence and the Brain*. New York: Harper & Row, 1970, pp. 97–108.
11. *Ibid.*, p. 107.
12. Vernon H. Mark, "A Psychosurgeon's Case for Psychosurgery." *Psychology Today*, July 1974, p. 28.
13. *Hastings Center Report*, February 1979, p. 33.
14. Stephan L. Chorover, "Big Brother and Psychotechnology." *Psychology Today*, October 1973, pp. 43–52.
15. *The New York Times*, December 1, 1974.
16. *Kaimowitz v. Department of Mental Health*. Civil No. 73–19434–AW Circ. Ct. Wayne County, Mich., July 1, 1973.
17. Charlotte L. Levy, *The Human Body and the Law*. Dobbs Ferry: Oceana Publications, 1975, p. 76.
18. Helen Blatte, "State Prisons and the Use of Behavior Control." *Hastings Center Report*, September 1974, p. 11.
19. Peter Breggin, "The Return of Lobotomy and Psychosurgery." *Hearings before the Subcommittee on Health of the Committee on Labor and Public Welfare, United States Senate*, 93rd Congress, First Session, on S. 974, S. 878 and S. J. Res. 71, February 23, and March 6, 1973, Part 2, pp. 455–480.
20. George J. Annas, J.D., M.P.H.; Leonard H. Glantz, J.D.; Barbara F. Katz, J.D., *Informed Consent to Human Experimentation: The Subject's Dilemma*. Cambridge: Ballinger Publishing Co., 1977, pp. 240–241.
21. "Comeback for Shock Therapy?" *Time*, November 18, 1979, p. 76.
22. Richard Abrams, M.D., Letter to *The New York Times*, November 25, 1982, p. A 22.
23. Cf. J. Greenberg, "Findings Shed Light on How ETC Works." *Science News*, May 21, 1983, p. 325.
24. For example: In the movie made from Michael Crichton's *Terminal Man*, Harry Benson has forty electrodes implanted in his brain. He learns to live with it and even to love the electrical charges he gets from the terminals.

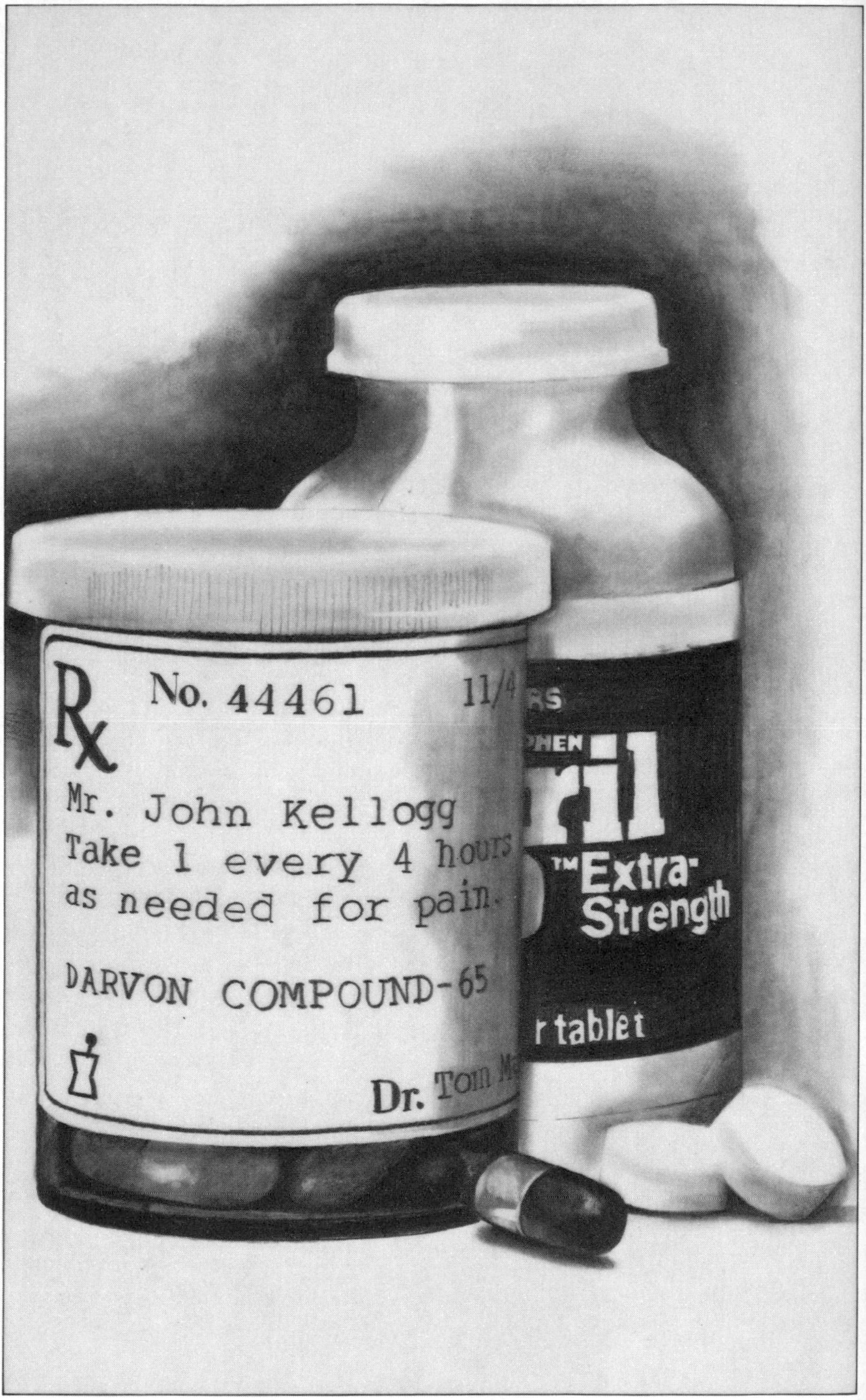
No. 44461 11/4
Mr. John Kellogg
Take 1 every 4 hours
as needed for pain.
DARVON COMPOUND-65
Dr. Tom M
™Extra-
Strength
r tablet

10 Drugs and Behavior Control

In the previous chapter we discussed the use of physical means to control behavior. In this chapter we will consider drugs, that is, chemical substances employed to manipulate behavior. The application of psychotropic drugs can be found in two main areas: (1) treatment of mental illness; (2) changing the mood of the user.

Psychotherapeutic Drugs

Drug treatment of mental illness is based on the assumption that mental illness may have biochemical causes. The development and the use of psychotherapeutic drugs in the mid-1950's had a dramatic effect on the treatment of mental patients. There were 559,000 mentally ill patients in public mental institutions in the United States in 1955. The introduction of psychotherapeutic drugs, however, reduced this number to less than 200,000 by 1979. This reduction took place despite the fact that both the rate of admission and the size of population had increased. Many patients respond quickly to drug treatment. They can then be discharged and continue therapy as outpatients.[1]

It is not the purpose of this book to describe the various drugs used in the treatment of different forms of mental illness. Our concern is with the ethical issues involved in drug treatment. One such issue emerges when we consider the fact that these drugs are not effective in every case, and that sometimes they produce irreversible side-effects. One of these side-effects is tardive dyskinesia. Prolonged use of certain psychotherapeutic drugs, especially neuroleptics, results in involuntary twitching of facial areas and other parts of the body.

Psychotherapeutic drugs still involve a certain element of experimentation. The ethical problem will have to be solved according to the principles of experimentation with human beings discussed in Chapter 8. Since these drugs are effective in the majority of cases and relieve a great deal of suffering, it can be assumed in individual cases that the specific drug will have a salutary effect. The medical staff must then carefully monitor the patient's reactions, however, and watch for possible side-effects.

Involuntary Treatment

The main ethical problem, however, in respect to psychotherapeutic drugs is not the one raised by their experimental character, but the question of involuntary treatment of mental patients.

Is it morally permissible to force mental patients to undergo treatment for the control of their behavior? Mentally disturbed persons who are a threat to themselves and to their community, or who seriously disturb the life of the community, must be protected from themselves and must be prevented from harming others. Society has a duty to defend individual rights and to promote the welfare of its citizens; consequently, it has the right to the means by which it can achieve these goals. If institutionalization of the disturbed person is the best way to achieve these goals, the state has the power to commit him to a mental institution.

The traditional theory that civil society has the *parens patriae* ("country's parent") power can be applied here. It is obvious that safeguards have to be taken so that citizens will not lose their freedom without justified reason. Most countries commit mentally disturbed persons to institutions only with the approval and at the recommendation of a committee of competent persons.

The U.S. Supreme Court ruled on June 26, 1975 that mental patients may not be confined in institutions against their will and without treatment if they are not dangerous to anyone and are capable of surviving on the outside. The ruling clearly intends to protect citizens from involuntary confinement and treatment when they are capable of fending for themselves and of making informed consent to their treatment.

Although it may be difficult to judge in individual cases whether a person can really survive on the outside as a rational human being, one can agree with the principle behind the Supreme Court's decision, namely, that it is the morally competent individual who is entitled to decide what treatment he is to receive. Some argue, however,[2] that individuals may not be involuntarily confined in institutions and treated against their will even if they are potentially dangerous to themselves or to society. Individuals should be free to determine their own conduct and the course their life should take. The problem with this defense of human freedom is that these persons are not really free to make a responsible decision. We do not hold the severely mentally disturbed person responsible for his actions and do not punish him. Confinement and treatment are intended to restore his freedom so that he can take over the control of his own life.

Civil society has the duty and, consequently, the right to look after the interests of its citizens who cannot do this on their own. It would follow from this that the duty and the right to commit mentally deranged and dangerous citizens to institutions implies the duty and the right of society to treat these patients. Confinement alone, keeping the patient in the "snake pit," falls short of the duty of society to help unfortunate citizens to regain the control of their own lives. It is understood that this duty and right of society is valid only in cases in which the patient does not have the ability to give or withhold informed consent to the treatment.

In June 1982, in *Youngberg v. Romeo*, the Supreme Court ruled that the Constitution guarantees certain rights to mentally retarded citizens who have been committed to institutions. "Habilitation" is one of the rights listed in the ruling. This means that society has the duty to help its unfortunate members to become as self-sufficient as possible.[3]

The goal of rehabilitation is to enable mental patients to live outside institutions. Authorities should be careful, however, not to discharge patients prematurely, forcing them to fend for themselves when they are not really ready for it. Between 1965 and 1981, the number of adult patients in mental institutions of the State of New

York declined from 85,000 to 23,000. "It is estimated that 47,000 were dumped in New York City, burdening local mental health services."⁴ It appears that many of these former inmates of mental institutions were not ready to live on their own. It is not fair to burden a community with their care when it is not equipped to do so.

The principles governing the confinement and treatment of mental patients seem to be clear and convincing in theory. Their practical application, however, may create considerable difficulty. There are no clear criteria by which to judge whether a patient in a certain case is competent or not to make a responsible decision.⁵ In addition, involuntary confinement and treatment can become instruments in the hands of the relatives of the patient or of state officials to control the behavior of a person with whom they disagree. Prudent legislation must see to it that this cannot occur.

Mood Drugs

It was discovered in prehistoric times that certain substances can change the mood of man. The Bible describes the effect wine had on Noah. References to the art of wine-making and the consumption of wine on various occasions can be found in all ancient literature. Beer was brewed by the Babylonians some four thousand years ago. Christopher Columbus found that the Indians smoked tobacco, and other explorers observed that the Incas chewed coca leaves and the Aztecs drank an intoxicating potion made from cactus. Tea had already been an ancient drink in China when returning travelers acquainted the Europeans with it. Coffee was brought to Europe from Arabia and Turkey. The kola nut, which contains caffeine, had been used in Africa for many centuries. Today it is the source of caffeine in cola drinks. Marijuana, also called cannabis or hemp, was known in ancient times as a very useful plant. It was cultivated for its fiber and used in making ropes and linen. References are made to it throughout recorded history. As early as the third millennium B.C., it was also known as a drug or intoxicant.

The use of opium goes back to prehistoric times. It is obtained by scraping the unripe capsule of a kind of poppy that will exude a milky juice. The dried juice can be taken orally or "smoked," that is, heated so that its vapor can be inhaled. It relieves pain and produces euphoria, a sense of well-being. It seems that it has been widely used in many parts of the world. The chief active ingredient of opium was isolated in 1808 by Friedrich Serturner in Paderborn, Germany. He named it "morphium" after Morpheus, the Greek god of sleep. Morphine, as it is called today, is an even more powerful pain reliever and narcotic than opium. It was soon learned, however, that morphine is addictive. Chemists, working to find potent non-addictive pain relievers, developed a number of drugs related to morphine. In 1898, a team of research chemists in Germany produced a synthetic derivative of morphine that proved to be four to ten times more potent a pain reliever than pure morphine. They also thought that the hero of their research, which they named heroin, was non-addictive and that it even could cure persons who had become addicted to morphine. Unfortunately, it soon turned out that heroin was just as addictive as the other narcotics. Morphine and heroin are either sniffed or injected under the skin into the muscle or directly into the vein.

The number of mind-affecting drugs has increased considerably in recent times. They can be classified according to the chemical reaction they produce in the body and according to the psychological effects the drug users experience.

The major groups are: narcotics, stimulants, sedatives, LSD and LSD-like drugs (also called hallucinogens by some), marijuana and hashish, tobacco.[6]

Narcotics

The most frequently used drugs of this group are: *opium, heroin, methadone, codeine.* They act on the central nervous system, relieve pain, produce sedation and euphoria. Used for a certain period of time, they *cause dependence.* The person addicted to narcotics becomes passive, withdrawn and lethargic. The "high," the euphoric effect that is initially produced, ceases when narcotics are taken regularly because the user develops tolerance to these drugs. Why, then, does the addict continue to take the drug? To escape the very painful and tormenting symptoms of withdrawal that are caused by lack of the drug in the user's system. The unfortunate addict is driven to support his addiction by any means in order to avoid suffering and to be able to blot out reality while the effect of the drug lasts. It costs over $200 a day to maintain a heroin addiction. Many of the addicts turn to crime and become drug pushers just to be able to get their daily dosage of the needed drug. It is estimated that 50 percent of the crimes committed in New York City are drug related.[7]

It is extremely difficult to overcome drug addiction. "Kicking the habit," going through the phase of "cold turkey," is a frightening experience for the addict. The will to endure it would need much greater psychological motivation than the addict, who is used to running away from reality, can build up.

Addiction and Withdrawal

One theory explains the sufferings of withdrawal the following way. The human brain produces its own opiates to relieve pain and build up the feeling of well-being. Narcotics, for instance morphine, flood the brain with artificial opiates and the brain stops producing natural ones. When the addict stops taking drugs, his neurons are deprived of both natural and artificial opiates. The result is pain and a miserable feeling until the brain can resume the production of natural opiates. This may take from several days to two weeks depending on the kind of drug the addict was using.

A person addicted to one kind of narcotic develops *cross-tolerance* to other kinds of narcotics, that is, he can substitute one narcotic for another to prevent the symptoms of withdrawal. The cross-tolerance phenomenon is the basis of the so-called methadone treatment for heroin addicts, the largest group of drug addicts. Instead of several daily injections of heroin, the addict can take a single daily oral dose of methadone to forestall withdrawal symptoms. This enables him to develop a more balanced life and to strengthen his motivation to overcome his dependence on methadone.

Stimulants

Cocaine, the amphetamines, caffeine and nicotine are the main representatives of the family of stimulants.

Cocaine is extracted from the leaves of the coca plant (Erythroxylum coca). The shrub grows on the eastern slopes of the Andes mountains and in the Amazon Basin. Indians of the Empire of the Incas and their descendants have chewed coca leaves for more than a thousand years. The Spanish conquistadores initially forbade the use of coca, but chewing coca soon became widespread, and coca was introduced also to Europe. Cocaine, the active ingredient of coca leaves, is a stimulant of the central nervous system. Dr. Sigmund Freud was enthusiastic about the effects of cocaine and prescribed it for the treatment of morphine addiction, stomach disorders and depression.

The use of cocaine produces a "high." The person feels that he is smarter, more competent, more energetic, better and more perfect all around. The illusion lasts some 30 minutes. Cocaine produces a false sense of superiority, which quickly disappears, and a "crash," a letdown, sets in when the drug wears off. The user naturally wants to get out of this state of depression by using more and more cocaine. One never has enough of it. Thus the user becomes dependent on cocaine not so much physically as psychologically. Although the physical symptoms of withdrawal from cocaine are not as severe as from heroin, "kicking cocaine" can be more difficult than withdrawing from heroin.

During the past five years or so, the use of cocaine has spread to all strata of the American population. Although it is readily available in low-income areas, it is considered the rich man's drug. It is used by executives, professionals, actors, students, athletes and the "common man." Sniffing cocaine is going on openly at the workplace, at parties, in parks, public lavatories, discos, clubs, bars, cocktail lounges and private homes. It is estimated that in 1982 the sales of cocaine exceeded $30 billion in the United States. Two decades ago only a small percentage of the population experimented with cocaine. By 1982 some 22 million Americans used it. According to government figures, during April 1983, 1.5 million adults, aged 26 or older, used cocaine.[8]

Amphetamines are a group of synthetic drugs. Their effects are similar to those of cocaine; they stimulate the central nervous system. An amphetamine was first marketed in 1932 under the name of Benzedrine. Amphetamines alleviate fatigue, produce a feeling of well-being and a cheerful mood, and heighten endurance. They can be taken orally in tablet form and absorbed in the gastrointestinal tract. "Pep pills" are used by students before examinations and by businessmen and executives to increase alertness. Athletes can increase their achievement by taking amphetamines. At international competitions, athletes are usually examined for the use of illicit "speed" drugs. Although cocaine is now the preferred drug, amphetamines are still widely used and are sold on the black market.

Caffeine, too, is a stimulant of the central nervous system. It is widely consumed in the form of coffee, tea, cocoa and "cola" drinks. Coffee was brought to Europe from Arabia and Turkey, tea from China, and cocoa from Mexico. Moderate use of these substances can increase alertness but heavy use may produce excessive tolerance, physical dependence and a craving for them.

Tobacco. It is well known that the first Europeans to become acquainted with smoking tobacco were Christopher Columbus and the early explorers of the New World. They were amazed to see the Indians inhale the smoke of lighted rolls of dried tobacco leaves and the smoke drawn from pipes. The early settlers tried it and many of them liked it. Sailors brought the seeds of tobacco to Europe, the Philippines, Asia and Africa, and smoking soon spread to many parts of the world. Despite many church and state laws against smoking, the custom became fairly well established in Europe by the beginning of the seventeenth century.

Since 1972 there has been a modest yearly decrease in the total use of tobacco in the United States. The Department of Health, Education and Welfare disclosed, however, that in 1979 the number of girls taking up smoking exceeded that of boys. In the twelve to eighteen year old category, for "the first time in the history of the nation, smoking among women in a major age group actually exceeds smoking among men." "Among the 17 and 18 year olds, only 19% of the boys smoke as against 26% of the girls, and girl smokers outnumber boy smokers in the 12 to 18 year old group by 1.7 million to 1.6 million."[9] According to the 1983 report of Surgeon General C. Everett Koop, daily smoking among high school seniors dropped from 29 percent in 1977 to 20 percent in 1981.

The psychoactive ingredient of tobacco is nicotine. It produces a strange combination of effects. When stimulation is needed, the smoker finds it stimulating; when a person is nervous, smoking may relax the user and act as a tranquilizer. Tobacco smoking is highly addictive, as all smokers who attempt to quit can testify. The person who tries to break the habit goes through very unpleasant withdrawal symptoms.

It has been well established that smoking is harmful to one's health. It may cause lung cancer, emphysema, aggravate heart disease and cause respiratory problems. It is evident that tobacco smoking harms non-smokers as well. Filters reduce the amount of poison inhaled by the smoker, but smoke coming from the lighted end of the cigarette contains at least twice as much poisonous material. All this and the smoke exhaled by the smoker must be inhaled by non-smokers in a smoke-filled room, car or train. The American Cancer Society noted: "A growing amount of evidence indicates that smoking constitutes a health hazard to non-smokers as well as smokers, particularly in a closed environment."[10] State Mutual Life Insurance Company of America studied the statistics of one hundred thousand insurance policy holders since 1964 and "found that death rates among smokers at all ages were more than twice as great as those of non-smokers and, for certain causes such as respiratory cancer, ran as much as 15 times higher."[11]

The first federal report on smoking was issued in 1964. It was a 1200-page documentation on the harmful effects of tobacco smoking. Eighteen years later, on February 22, 1982, the Surgeon General of the United States, Dr. C. Everett Koop, issued a new report. He declared smoking "the most important health issue of our time."[12] According to the report, smoking was the chief cause of lung cancer, which accounts for 25 percent of all cancer deaths. Smoking causes about 130,000 deaths from cancer each year. It is the major cause of cancer of the lung, larynx, oral cavity and esophagus. Smoking is a "contributing factor" to bladder, kidney and pancreatic cancers.[13] In addition to cancers, smoking causes heart disease. Smoking is the cause of about 30 percent of all heart disease deaths in the United States each year.[14]

Sedatives

Sedatives include tranquilizers (e.g., Miltown, Librium, Valium), barbiturates, methaqualone (Quaaludes), alcohol. Antineurotic or minor *tranquilizers* are used to lessen anxiety and tension.

Barbiturates relieve insomnia and have a sedative effect. When used to excess, barbiturates produce drunkenness very similar to alcohol intoxication. The habitual user becomes addicted, manifesting all the symptoms of alcoholism. Methaqualone, popularly called *Quaaludes*, is the fashionable new drug of the "disco set." It is a sedative and a hypnotic. Initally it produces euphoria, which later turns into severe confusion, apathy and withdrawal from reality. Its use has recently taken on epidemic proportions in the United States.[15]

The minor tranquilizers, on the other hand, when used moderately, do not create the danger of severe addiction. Their frequent use, however, may produce physical and psychological dependence and symptoms similar to that of alcohol drunkenness.

Alcohol, customarily classified as a depressant, has a variety of apparently contradictory effects. Observing a cocktail party, one can see that people at various levels of drinking begin to have different reactions. Alcohol may depress or stimulate, tranquilize or excite, release inhibitions or induce sleep.

Alcohol is part of modern life. Seven out of ten Americans drink regularly. The number of teenagers who drink is increasing steadily. Unfortunately, many of the drinkers become addicted to alcohol and develop the disease of alcoholism. The National Institute on Alcohol Abuse and Alcoholism estimates that there are over 12 million adult problem drinkers in America. In addition, there are 3.3 million youth aged fourteen to seventeen who have drinking problems. The abuse of alcohol is more widespread than that of any other mind-affecting drug.

Alcoholism costs the United States about $50 billion annually in accidents, medical bills, lost production and other expenses. Half of traffic accident deaths, about 25,000 annually, are caused by drunken drivers. More Americans were killed by drunken drivers the last two years than were killed during the war in Vietnam. "About three Americans are killed and 80 are injured by drunk drivers every hour on every day."[16] One-quarter of a million Americans were killed over the past decade by drunk drivers. The National Highway Traffic Safety Administration (NHTSA) estimates that about 10 percent of all drivers on weekend nights are intoxicated. Unless there is a dramatic drop in the number of drunk drivers, "one out of every two Americans will be victimized by a drunk driver in his lifetime."[17] Alcohol is involved in one-fourth of all other accidental deaths, and in one-half of all the murders that are committed. About one-fifth of all divorces are related to alcohol.

Alcohol can permanently damage the liver, resulting in cirrhosis. It can also cause heart disease and brain damage. Alcohol, if taken by a pregnant woman, can adversely affect the health and normal development of the fetus.

LSD

LSD (lysergic acid diethylamide), mescaline (derived from peyote, a cactus plant), psilocybin, and phencyclidine or PCP (popularly called Angel Dust) belong to a group of drugs that sometimes are called *hallucinogens and psychedelic* (Greek word for mind-opening) *drugs*. LSD, strictly speaking, does not produce hallucinations, but it intensifies the sensory perceptions of present objects. Colors are seen more saturated. Synesthesia can be produced, i.e., sounds can be "seen" and colors can be "heard." Perceived objects have greater depth and clarity, ordinary objects appear tremendously beautiful and meaningful, immobile objects move, time stands still, mental activities, sensations and emotions are fused into one central point of the ego. The LSD "trip" transcends time and space and is sometimes compared to a mystical experience that cannot be described by ordinary language.

LSD was discovered accidentally in 1943 by Dr. Albert Hofman at Sandoz Laboratories in Basel, Switzerland. He synthesized a compound of lysergic acid when he accidentally ingested a small part of the compound, which then produced in him the strange effects of LSD. LSD and LSD-like drugs are not addictive. Their use, however, can cause serious personality disorders and, while under the influence of the drug, the user cannot function normally.

Marijuana

Marijuana is the popular name for the plant *hemp*, scientifically called *cannabis sativa*. The leaves and the flower of the plant are dried and then smoked or taken in food and drink. *Hashish* is the dried resin secreted by the marijuana plant. Hashish contains more cannabinol, the active chemical of marijuana, than the leaves of the plant.

Despite a legal ban, smoking "pot" is widespread in the United States and around the world and the number of users is growing. The National Institute of Drug Abuse estimated that by 1983, 57 million Americans had smoked marijuana. This means that 31.3 percent of Americans aged 12 or older had tried it. In 1982, 64 percent of adults aged 18 to 25 smoked pot. Only 4 percent of this age group smoked it in 1962.[18]

The effects of marijuana vary widely depending on the amount one takes. After smoking one "joint," a person experiences a feeling of well-being and occasionally a dreamy sensation. He begins to talk rapidly and loudly and has the impression that he is expressing his thoughts very profoundly. He is convinced that what he says is very witty. At "pot parties" there is a lot of laughter and giggling. As more marijuana is smoked, a person's perception of time and distance may become distorted and his ability to make quick decisions is weakened. Driving an automobile under the influence of marijuana can easily lead to fatal accidents. Taken in large amounts, marijuana or hashish can induce a state similar to alcohol intoxication and result in hallucinations.[19]

Marijuana is an illicit drug. The great number of regular users, however, is a sign that marijuana is easily available. Street sales of marijuana amount to more than $25 billion a year in the United States.

Smokers, growers and distributors of the plant obviously have a vested interest in removing all or some of the legal limitations. They argue that marijuana is less dangerous to one's health than tobacco or alcohol. The defenders and the opponents of marijuana point respectively to studies of its harmless or harmful effects as controversy about marijuana legislation continues. The National Organization to Revise Marijuana Laws (N.O.R.M.L.) is especially active in this regard.

As a result of various studies, it is safe to say that marijuana is not the most dangerous drug on the black market. Nevertheless, it is not as harmless as its defenders claim it to be. There is a consensus among experts that marijuana distorts perceptions and impedes psychomotor skills needed for operating machines and driving automobiles. In addition, there are definite health hazards connected with smoking pot.

Dr. Gabriel Nahas, research anesthesiologist at Columbia University and U.N. consultant on narcotics, and his research team have established that cannabinoids interfere with the ordinary formation of RNA and DNA and proteins; sperm cells, female germ cells and white blood cells, important for our immunological system, are also adversely affected. Cannabinoids have damaged such cells in prepared cultures. Marijuana may produce miscarriages and cause malformation of the fetus, as research with rats and monkeys has proved. Since the widespread use of marijuana among women is of recent date, we do not yet have the data of generations needed to prove by statistics that the same results are produced in human beings as well. In the Near East and Africa, where marijuana has been used for over a century, women were not accustomed to use it, so that no data can be collected there either. Animal tests, however, have shown that toxic cannabinoids pass through the placenta and affect the developing fetus. It has been proved that THC, the psychoactive agent of marijuana, is fat soluble and accumulates in the fat-laden tissues and in the nervous system of the body. It has been shown that half of the THC inhaled from smoking one joint is stored in the body a week after smoking it. Regular marijuana users accumulate so much THC in their body that it constantly acts on their system. In this regard, it is even more dangerous than alcohol because alcohol is water soluble and it is removed from the human system in a day after ingestion.[20]

Recently, a number of scientists and researchers in this field have reached a consensus that marijuana cannot be judged harmless and that some persons should definitely avoid using this drug. These persons are: teenagers, pregnant women, persons with heart and lung ailments, and those who have emotional problems.[21]

On February 26, 1982, a blue-ribbon panel of the National Academy of Science's Institute of Medicine released a comprehensive report of a long study on the health effects of marijuana. The report says that while there are no reliable data about long-term health hazards of marijuana smoking, scientific evidence published so far indicates that "marijuana has a broad range of psychological and biological effects, some of which . . . are harmful to human health."[22] Marijuana affects good perception and motor coordination. Pot slows learning and weakens short-term memory. It induces apathy and impairs school performance. The so-called "antimotivational syndrome" seems to be the result of marijuana smoking in many cases. Heavy use can produce chronic bronchitis and lung cancer. "Our major concern is," the report relates, "that what little we know for certain about the effects of marijuana on human health—and all that we have reason to suspect—justifies serious national concern."[23]

The Ethics of Using Drugs

There are two kinds of ethical problems relating to mood drugs. One problem is the individual's responsibility in using drugs. The other refers to the responsibility of civil society in regulating the use of these drugs.

1. Mood Drugs and the Individual

As we have seen in Chapter 1, the morally good act is that which is in conformity with human nature. According to his nature, man must be in charge of his own actions, and he must not turn over responsibility to others for his own life. He must retain his freedom of choice, the basis of responsibility and morality. In addition, man has the duty to use ordinary means to preserve his own health, which is necessary for him to lead a normal human life.

It follows from this that a person may use drugs to the extent they help his self-control. A cup of coffee or tea that helps him to be alert or a drink that dissipates tension and improves his self-mastery would be actions according to rational human nature. There are many objects and substances that are legitimately and ethically used by man to help him to act according to his rational nature. It is not ethical for him to use substances, however, which make him lose self-control. Some substances taken moderately may help a person's self-mastery. Their excessive or constant use, however, may lessen the ability of self-determination, and this makes a person less of the self-possessed rational being he is supposed to be in accordance with his nature.

Drug-Dependence, Alcoholism

As we have seen, the frequent use of certain drugs creates physical and psychological dependence and decreases self-control. Even excessive coffee drinking may produce dependence. Instead of helping a person to be alert and more independent, it may make him nervous and cause him to be controlled by a chemical substance without which he cannot function. Drinking alcohol to excess and getting intoxicated only occasionally is not so damaging as a real dependence on alcohol. Nevertheless, even single cases of intoxication are acts unworthy of rational human beings. The drunken individual loses his ability to think rationally and make even simple decisions necessary for normal human living. Few persons get drunk deliberately; they just drift into it as they continue drinking. A rational human being, however, has to plan his life. When he realizes later what has happened, he has the duty to take appropriate steps to prevent it from happening again.

As is well known, the frequent use of alcohol can produce a habit, a dependence on, and a craving for alcohol. The large number of alcoholics in America and in many other parts of the world indicates the complexity of the problem. It is not the task of this work to suggest remedies and forms of psychological help for the many unfortunate victims of alcoholism. We simply want to point to the ethical questions connected with alcoholism. A person may not be entirely responsible for becoming addicted to alcohol. Whether he is or is not responsible for becoming an alcoholic, once he realizes his state, he has the duty to try his best to overcome his habit. It is, however, a sad fact that some habits become so powerful that a person loses self-control almost totally and, despite his sincere determination, finds he simply cannot resist looking for and taking a specific substance like alcohol or heroin. It seems that a person can lose his freedom of choice. The duty of such a person is obvious: he must restore his self-control as soon as he can. He must seek help in this task because in most cases he cannot win this fight alone. Unfortunately, some persons can reach such a degree of addiction that they are incapable even of asking for help. Society will have to come to the help of these addicts, as well be discussed later.

Tranquilizers

Twenty million Americans take Valium and Librium regularly. Forty-four million prescriptions were filled in 1978 for Valium alone. Some 15 percent of adults use Valium on a regular basis. According to authorities, "overuse of tranquilizers ranks second only to alcoholism as the nation's major health problem."[24] After several months of constant use a dependence and physical addiction develops. Overuse of tranquilizers cannot be approved ethically. They do not solve the problems of the individual; they just make him feel dull and insensitive. The user gives up the conscious self-determination of his life by constantly fleeing into a tranquilized, dull state of mind. Tranquilizers may be used to help us regain self-control and thus enhance our humanity, but not to lessen it.

Smoking

Tobacco smokers, even heavy smokers, do not lose their ability to think rationally or make free choices. If they miss their usual quota of tobacco, they may become irritable and less self-controlled, but a few puffs usually will restore their composure. From the point of view of rational thinking, then, smoking does not render them less human. Perhaps one might argue that it is demeaning and dehumanizing to be so dependent on tobacco that one cannot function normally without it.

The real problem, however, with smoking is that it is a health hazard. It is a moral duty to maintain our health as much as we can and to avoid risks. Some smokers argue, however, that the relaxing effects of smoking counterbalance the risk of weakening their health. They deliberately and freely choose the risk of endangering their health in exchange for the good effects of smoking. This, they argue, is a morally justifiable choice. There would seem to be some flaws in this reasoning. The twelve-hundred page report of the Surgeon General, Dr. Julius B. Richmond, issued in 1964, and the 1982 report of the Surgeon General, Dr. C. Everett Koop, offer overwhelming evidence that smoking is dangerous to one's health. The risk from tobacco smoking is not speculation but fact. It is true that not every smoker develops lung cancer and other diseases mentioned in the report, but taking a definite risk is not a rational act when one can easily avoid the risk. One does not walk into the flow of traffic in the hope that he will not be hit. In addition, the smoker exposes non-smoking bystanders to risks. A pregnant woman who smokes blocks off the unborn baby's oxygen; the baby can be born addicted to nicotine and suffer withdrawal symptoms for several months. It is unethical to expose others to risks, whether adults or the unborn. The aim of our argument is not to prove smokers to be unethical persons, deliberately causing harm to themselves and others. Our intention is only to show that it is difficult to find good reasons for smoking. Many smokers, especially those trying to break their addiction, readily admit that smoking is a bad habit and that they would be much better off without it.

Why, then, do so many people smoke? Is it really a deliberate choice, as many affirm? According to statistics, 75 percent of the 54 million American smokers acquired the habit before the age of twenty. Many of them did not really deliberate about whether they should smoke or not. They were under the subtle but strong influence of the advertising of the tobacco industry and under the pressure of their smoking peers to start smoking. For most of them it was not an entirely free and deliberate choice. Once the habit is formed, most smokers remain addicted to it even if they would like to get rid of it. From the moral point of view, most smokers should be judged according to the degree of responsibility for starting and maintaining the habit.

2. The Use of Drugs and Public Policy

Civil society has a duty to create and maintain harmonious social conditions, in which citizens can easily lead a decent life, not being exposed to deception or to undue pressures to use substances that are harmful. It is not the obligation of civil society to educate every individual with respect to moral conduct. That duty belongs primarily to the family and to religious and other associations. Society, however, has a duty and a right to regulate the sale of poisonous and harmful substances in order to protect the members of society. Since the drugs we are discussing can be very harmful, it follows that the government has the right and duty to control them.

This argument, as is well known, led to the prohibition of the sale and use of alcohol in the United States from 1920 to 1933.

There is overwhelming evidence that alcohol is by far the most dangerous mind-affecting drug used in America and in many parts of the world. The Eighteenth (Prohibition) Amendment was repealed in 1933, however, because the thirteen years of American experience revealed that prohibition was not working. Alcohol remained widely available through the black market; "bootleg" and "moonshine" alcoholic beverages, not controlled by any authority, frequently contained poisonous material. There was a shift from light wines to hard liquor, which was less bulky and less risky to produce, transport and sell. An organized underworld dealing in alcohol developed and the rate of crime escalated.

There is a valid principle in social ethics that a law that does not achieve its purpose must be replaced by another that does achieve the goal for which the original legislation was passed. The government must see to it that citizens are protected in an appropriate and more practical way. Prohibition was replaced by other laws regulating the production and sale of alcoholic beverages. Do these laws work today? It seems they do not. Alcoholism has become an epidemic in America. Prohibition did not work; we should not go back to experimenting with it again. There are legitimate and ethical uses of alcohol and those uses should not be forbidden. Excessive consumption of alcoholic beverages, however, should be prevented by some measures that work. Advertisers of alcohol cannot maintain that it is morally neutral to promote the use of alcohol without adequate and clear warning that its excessive use is greatly harmful. Drinking is frequently glorified or, at least, presented as a good social pastime in TV plays and in advertisements. This practice should stop. Beer cans and liquor bottles should be labeled in large letters as indicating their contents are dangerous to one's health when used frequently or in excess. It seems that the country has gone from prohibition to almost unlimited permissiveness with respect to alcohol.

It is not the purpose of this work to suggest particular legislation. It must be emphasized, however, that civil society has a moral duty to regulate the use of alcohol by prudent and practical laws. The steadily increasing number of the victims of alcohol is a proof that civil society is not performing its duty in this regard.

U.S. laws regulating the advertising and sale of cigarettes are stricter than the laws referring to alcohol. Other countries, however, have passed even stricter laws than the United States to protect the health of their citizens from the use of tobacco. Although the per-capita tobacco consumption in Sweden is only about one-third and in Norway about one-fifth as high as in the United States, these two countries passed legislation in 1975 aimed at raising a new generation of non-smokers. The laws provide for antismoking education, ban cigarette vending machines, call for annual price increases and the gradual elimination of smoking in public places, the prohibition of sale of tobacco to persons under the age of sixteen, the outlawing of tobacco advertising, and a possible increase of insurance premiums for smokers. In the United States, controversy is developing about a number of laws prohibiting smoking at certain places and of separating smokers from non-smokers. Smokers insist on their right to smoke. Non-smokers, on the other hand, emphasize their right not to be exposed to tobacco fumes that have been proved to be as dangerous as smoking itself. One has to side with the non-smokers in this dispute: there is no right to cause harm to others. As for raising insurance premiums for smokers, it seems to be fair and equitable that non-smokers not be forced to pay for the higher incidence of illness among smokers.

The National Organization to Revise Marijuana Laws (N.O.R.M.L.) is very active in lobbying for some form of legalization of marijuana. In view of the well-documented harmful effects of marijuana on human beings, it would be ill advised to legalize "pot." What is needed is a prudent adjustment of marijuana laws so that they will be enforceable and will protect citizens, especially the younger generation, from being induced into using a harmful drug.

Despite strict laws prohibiting the sale and use of the so-called hard drugs, the number of addicts has not diminished in the United States. It is estimated that there are as many as six hundred thousand heroin addicts alone.

In 1982, a report to the Governor of New York State estimated that the number of heroin addicts in New York City had increased by 50 percent since 1978. There is one heroin addict for every 40 to 43 residents. Addicts can maintain their expensive habit only by turning to crime. A 1982 Rand Corporation study of crime by heroin addicts found that those inmates in California who were addicted to heroin averaged 167 crimes a year in contrast to 2.3 crimes a year by prisoners who were not addicts.[25] The United States has the dubious distinction that its illicit drug use per capita surpasses that of any other industrial nation.

It is very sad that authorities have not been able to prevent the well-organized underworld from continuing its unscrupulous and destructive trade. It seems that for various reasons, the present drug laws do not work. Civil society, however, has the obligation to see to it that effective laws are passed which work and protect innocent citizens. The driving force of the illicit drug trade is, of course, its high profitability. The "street price" of hard drugs is many times that of their cost of production.

Consumers Union suggested that the heroin black market can be abolished only "by eliminating the demand for black-market heroin."[26] In order to destroy the black market, new laws should insure that narcotic addicts need not get their drugs from the black market, but that they will be made available free under medical auspices. Both society and the addicts are better off if the addicts can receive free or low-cost drugs legally. The project should, of course, include vigorous education and programs for the rehabilitation of drug addicts.

This program, however, even if it could diminish the problem of heroin addicts, could not be applied to the many million users of other illicit drugs, who create an enormous problem for the physical, psychological and industrial health of the nation.

The British tried to eliminate or lessen heroin addiction by prescribing heroin for confirmed addicts. Although some promoters of the program initially hailed the experiment as a success, *The Lancet*, the prestigious British medical journal, judged the system as a failure.[27] The number of addicts and illegal street traffic have increased.

Making the drug available does not solve the problem of addiction and abuse. It seems that authorities will have to concentrate on stopping the flow of illicit drugs to the country and strengthen law enforcement. Law enforcement, however, becomes almost impossible when about 30 percent of the adult population uses or has used illicit drugs. One cannot put one-third of the nation in jail. If the abuse of alcohol, a legal drug, is added to the abuse of illicit drugs, the question of drug abuse can be seen as a menacing threat to the health and moral fiber of the nation. Only a better education toward healthy moral values, coupled with prudent enforcement of laws and the prevention of drugs from reaching the shores of America, can avert a national tragedy.

QUESTIONS FOR REVIEW AND DISCUSSION

1. Describe the difference between psychotherapeutic and mood drugs.

2. May society confine its mentally disturbed citizens?

3. Describe the main classes of mood drugs which are frequently used in America.

4. How does a person become an alcoholic? How do you explain addiction? Is it wrong to drink alcohol?

5. What are the effects of smoking marijuana? Is it wrong to smoke pot?

6. If smoking tobacco is harmful to a person's health, how can you ethically justify smoking, producing and selling this dangerous substance?

7. Are health insurance companies justified to charge smokers higher premiums than non-smokers?

8. Explain the ethical principle that governs the use of mood drugs.

9. If marijuana smoking cannot be stopped, would society be justified in legalizing it?

10. What kind of practical measures would you propose to control the use of harmful drugs?

Notes

1. Cf. Philip A. Berger, "Medical Treatment of Mental Illness." *Science*, Vol. 200, May 26, 1978, p. 975.
2. Cf. Thomas Szasz, *Law, Liberty, Psychiatry*. New York: Macmillan, 1963.
3. Cf. *Science News*, June 26, 1982, p. 420.
4. Cf. *The New York Times*, June 5, 1981, p. A 26.
5. Cf. George J. Annas, J.D., M.P.H., Leonard H. Glantz, J.D., and Barbara F. Katz, J.D., *Informed Consent to Human Experimentation: The Subject's Dilemma*. Cambridge: Ballinger Publishing Co., 1977, pp. 159–168.
6. Cf. Edward M. Brecher and the Editors of Consumer Reports, *Licit and Illicit Drugs*. Mount Vernon: Consumers Union, 1972.
7. *New York Post*, February 7, 1977.
8. Cf. "How Drugs Sap the Nation's Strength." *U.S. News & World Report*, May 16, 1983, p. 55.
9. *The New York Times*, April 27, 1979.
10. *Ibid.*, May 5, 1978.
11. *The Washington Star*, October 22, 1979.
12. Cf. "Surgeon General Report Broadens List of Cancers Linked to Smoking." *The New York Times*, February 23, 1982, p. A 1.
13. *Ibid.*
14. Cf. *The New York Times*, November 18, 1983, p. D 18.
15. Henry Post, "The Doctor's Report." *New York Cue*, October 26, 1979, p. 29.
16. Cf. "The War Against Drunk Drivers." *Newsweek*, September 13, 1982, p. 34.
17. *Ibid.*
18. Cf. "How Drugs Sap the Nation's Strength." *Op. cit.*, p. 55.
19. Giorgio Lolli, M.D., *Tuned In or Turned Off?* New York: The Lion Press, 1969, pp. 53–57.
20. Richard Hawley, "Science, Politics and Marijuana." *America*, September 22, 1979, pp. 133–134.
21. Harold M. Schmeck, Jr., "Research on Marijuana Finds Many Risks, Some Benefits." *The New York Times*, October 9, 1979.
22. "Excerpts from the Federal Report on Marijuana." *The New York Times*, February 27, 1982, p. 9.
23. *Ibid.*
24. *Time*, September 24, 1979, p. 78.
25. Peter Kihss, "50% Rise in Heroin Addicts Since '78 Reported for City." *The New York Times*, June 15, 1982, p. B 1.
26. Edward M. Brecher, *op. cit.*, p. 530.
27. *The Lancet*, January 9, 1982.

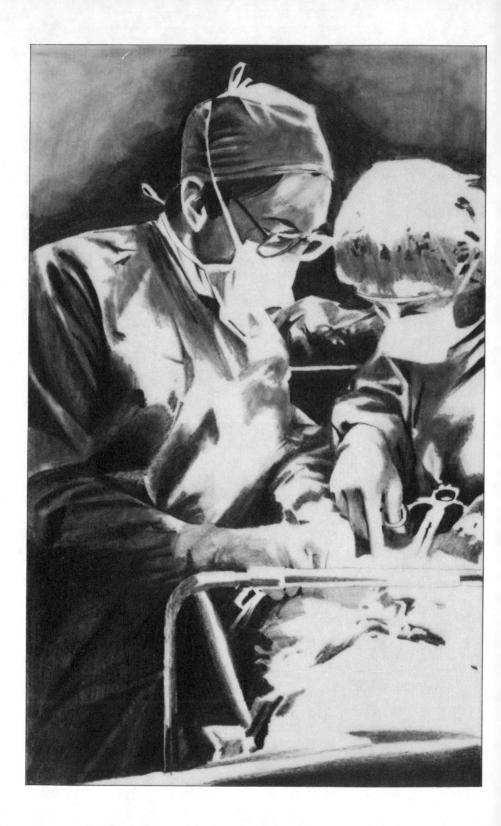

11 Organ
Transplantation

The idea of organ transplantation is as old as mythology and ancient literature. The possibility of replacing diseased organs or lost blood with healthy organs and blood taken from animals or from other human beings was an old dream whose time and realization did not come until the twentieth century. There are reports that skin grafts and transfusion of both human and animal blood were attempted in the past. Blood transfusion, however, became an accepted medical procedure only when the different blood types and their mutual compatibility or incompatibility were discovered and a method was developed to preserve blood. Blood transfusion was widely used during the First World War when blood banks were established to store blood.

Blood, however, is not an irreplaceable part of man; it regenerates itself. Blood transfusion, therefore, does not raise the ethical problems of transplantation of organs, which do not regenerate.

The most frequently transplanted organs are the kidney, the cornea and skin. Other organs less frequently transplanted are: the heart, the lung, the liver, the pancreas, bone marrow, ovaries and testicles. All of these organs have been transplanted successfully.

There are various kinds of transplantations. *Autograft* is the transplantation of an organ within the same individual—for example, transplantation of skin or bone from one part of one's body to another part. *Homograft* is the transplantation of an organ from one individual to another of the same species—for example, from one human being to another human being, or from a dog to another dog. *Heterograft*, on the other hand, is the transfer of organs between individuals of different species—for instance, from animals to man or

211

from dogs to monkeys. *Isograft* is transplantation between two genetically identical persons—for example, between identical twins.

The Immune System
and Rejection

The technique of suturing blood vessels, developed by Dr. Alexis Carrel and Dr. Charles C. Guthrie shortly after the turn of the century, gave an impetus to experiments with animal organ transplantation. Dr. Emmerich Ullmann, an Austrian surgeon, reported in 1902 that he had taken a kidney from a dog and transplanted it to the neck of another dog. The kidney functioned for a few days but then stopped producing urine. He thought for a while that the reason for the failure was his faulty suturing of the blood vessels. After a great number of experiments, however, it became clear that certain genetic factors were the cause of the phenomenon that today is called rejection. It was found that the closer the donor and the recipient were genetically related, the longer the transplanted organ functioned. Kidneys of dogs transplanted to dogs of the same parents functioned for some fourteen days. When the donor and the recipient were identical twins, the transplanted kidney worked as well as if it had been an original organ of the recipient dog.[1]

It was finally the Australian, Dr. Peter Medawar, who solved the enigma of rejection, for which he received the Nobel Prize in 1960. He and his team experimented with rabbits in the early 1940's and arrived at the conclusion that in the case of transplantation of organs, an immunization process begins to work in the body of the recipient against the tissues of the donor. The organism of man and of higher animals has an immune system. It consists in the ability of an organism to recognize foreign bodies that enter it, for example, bacteria, and to start a process of destroying or expelling the intruder. There are markers, or *antigens,* on the surfaces of cells that somehow enable the organism to recognize a foreign body which has different markers. Coming into contact with different tissues or different organisms, the antigens stimulate the production of *antibodies,* which play an important role in fighting infections or in developing the phenomenon of rejection in organ transplantations. The more genetically similar the tissues are, the fewer antibodies are produced, thus lessening the danger of rejection. Dr. Medawar's discovery opened the door to further progress in the technique or organ transplantation.

Tissue typing is based on the knowledge of the immunological phenomenon. Before an organ transplantation is attempted, the recipient's and the donor's tissues are examined with regard to their compatibility. The antigens of both tissues are analyzed to determine whether they are similar enough so that they do not recognize each other as alien bodies and do not excite the destructive immune response. Since it is difficult to find completely matching tissues, rejection remains one of the main causes of failures in organ transplantation.

New drugs lessen the ability of organisms to develop antibodies, thereby reducing the likelihood of rejection. At the same time, however, these drugs also weaken the recipient's immune system and increase the danger of infection.

On September 2, 1983, the Food and Drug Administration (FDA) approved cyclosporine, produced by Sandoz, a Swiss pharmaceutical company. This drug, which has been experimentally used the last three years, greatly eases the rejection problem. It selectively inhibits the functioning of white cells that cause the rejection of foreign tissues, and at the same time it does not damage their ability to combat viruses and bacteria. The recipient of an organ transplant must, however, take the drug for the rest of his life. The yearly supply of the drug costs between $5,000 and $8,000. Nevertheless, it is still less expensive to have a kidney transplant and use cyclosporine than to be on renal dialysis, which costs about $35,000 a year. The expenses of the surgery for kidney transplant were $25,000 to $35,000 in 1983.

Blood typing is equally important for the success of transplantation of organs. It is well known now what kinds of blood types are compatible or incompatible. Organs then must be selected not only according to tissue compatibility, but they must also be matched according to blood types.

History of Transplants

Skin grafts, the first human tissue transplantations in the late 1920's, also contributed to the understanding of the immune system.

It was found that skin grafts between identical twins could be performed without the problem of rejection.

The first *kidney transplantation* was performed by Dr. David Hume in Boston in 1951. He used a cadaver donor in his unsuccessful attempt to save the life of a patient whose kidney had failed. During the next four years, Dr. Hume and his colleague, Dr. Joseph E. Murray, performed ten kidney transplants using cadaver donors. Most patients died soon after the operation. One, however, survived six months. In 1954, Dr. Murray and Dr. John Merrill carried out the first living donor kidney transplantation, which is recognized in medical history as the first successful operation of this kind. Richard Herrick, aged twenty-three, received a kidney from his twin brother, Ronald. Richard recovered completely and lived for eight more years before he died of a heart attack.

Kidney transplantation has advanced greatly since the first successful transplant in 1954. Although new medicines against rejection have helped considerably, relatives are still the best donors. A worldwide survey of 222 centers where kidney transplantations are performed found in 1974 that 80 percent of the patients receiving kidneys from siblings were still alive two years after the operation, while 70 percent of those who received the organ from parents or children, and 50 percent from cadaver donors, survived. The past five years over 23,000 kidney transplants were performed in the United States alone. Cyclosporine has increased the success rate of kidney transplants to 90 percent. The patient can, however, survive on dialysis if the kidney graft fails.

There are many well-trained transplant surgeons today in many countries, so that kidney transplantation is considered a routine operation. The problem is that there are not enough kidneys available. Less than one percent of Americans die under circumstances and at ages that leave their organs suitable for transplant, and only a limited number of these organs are used because of the lack of organization for bringing recipients and donors together. Legislators in Congress are now trying to set up a national clearing house to coordinate the donations of organs. There is also a private computerized network in the United States for speedy matching of donors and recipients.

A particular incident occurred at the end of June 1979. A fourteen year old girl died in a hospital in Norfolk, Virginia, from injuries received in a traffic accident. Her two kidneys were removed, and a computer search began for a compatible recipient. One was found in Newark. For the other kidney, however, no American recipient was found among the many patients on the waiting list because the antigens of the girl's kidneys were an unusual combination. The search then extended to Italy, Kuwait and Moscow. A Russian patient with matching tissue and blood type was located, and the kidney was flown to Moscow, where it was successfully transplanted in the waiting patient.[2] Less than three weeks later, a pair of kidneys arrived from Russia under similar circumstances. An excised kidney cannot be preserved for more than about seventy-two hours. Hence it is understandable that there is a great deal of pressure to find compatible recipients within such a short period of time. International arrangements, however, are informal and often based only on the personal contacts of the surgeons involved.

The *cornea* is the transparent cover that protects the lens and the pupil of the eye. When the cornea becomes damaged or grows opaque, vision becomes blurred or completely destroyed. If blindness is caused by a damaged cornea, vision can be restored by a corneal transplant. About 90 percent of corneal transplants are successful today.

The first successful cornea transplant was performed by Edward Zirm, an Austrian surgeon, in 1905. Nevertheless, it did not become an accepted routine operation until the 1940's. Dr. R. Townley Paton established the first Eye Bank for Sight Restoration in the Manhattan Eye, Ear, and Throat Hospital in 1944. People now can leave their eyes to an eye bank after their death. The cornea is preserved in the eye bank and used later when a patient needs it. There are more than eighty eye banks in the United States. Many nations of the world have similar institutions. About three thousand cornea transplants are performed annually in the United States alone. Many more blind persons could be helped, however, if there were more people leaving their eyes to eye banks. All fifty states and the District of Columbia now have anatomical gift acts or laws that make it easy and legal for a person to donate his body or specific organs for transplantation. Donation of one's eyes can be arranged by filling out a donor card, which can be obtained from any eye bank.

About 130,000 cornea transplants have been performed worldwide. The cost of the operation is about $2,500 to $5,000.

The first human *heart transplantation* was performed by Dr. Christiaan Barnard in Capetown, South Africa, on December 3, 1967. His patient, the 55 year old Louis Washkansky, lived only eighteen days. His second patient, the 58 year old Philip Blaiberg, however, survived eighty-four weeks. These successful operations were well publicized all over the world and prompted a great deal of controversy about the experimental nature and morality of such operations. Nevertheless, there was a rush to repeat the feat. In 1968, 101 heart transplant operations were performed by sixty-four teams in twenty-four countries.

Human heart transplantation was preceded by experimentation on dogs. Dr. Norman E. Shumway and Dr. Richard R. Lower, of Stanford University, began a major project of dog heart transplants and developed the technique now used in human transplantation.[3]

The first heterograft, or animal-human, heart transplant was performed by Dr. James Hardy and his team at the University of Mississippi Medical Center. They transplanted the heart of a chimpanzee into a 68 year old man who had only about an hour to live. Dr. Hardy had hoped to use the heart of a young man who was dying of brain damage, but he was still alive when time for the life-saving operation began to run out. The chimpanzee heart functioned for ninety minutes, then stopped, and the recipient died.[4]

The relatively short survival rate discouraged many surgeons from performing heart-transplant operations. Dr. Shumway, however, continued, and by the middle of 1983 he had done 275 heart transplants with 114 survivals.[5] He and his team perform an average of one heart transplant a month. Recently there has been a renewed interest in heart transplants since progress has been made in controlling the rejection phenomenon. The world's longest case of survival is that of Emmanuel Vitria who received a transplant in 1968 in Marseilles, France, and is still alive at the time of this writing. The survival rate now is about 78 percent at the end of one year with a 5 percent annual death rate the following year.[6] Dr. Norman Shumway recently told a congressional hearing that there has not been a single rejection of a transplanted heart since he began to use cyclosporine in 1980.

There have been over 500 heart transplants in the United States and Western Europe up to the end of 1983. The cost of heart transplant surgery is between $57,000 and $110,000.

Liver transplants, after initial failures, have become more successful as new drugs have been used to prevent rejection. There have been over 540 liver transplants in the United States and Western Europe, with a 39 percent survival rate of non-cancerous patients after one year. The use of the new immunosuppressant drug has raised the successful liver grafts to 70 percent. The first successful liver transplant was performed in 1963 by Drs. William R. Waddell and Thomas E. Starzl at Denver's Veterans Administration Hospital. The 17 year old William Grigsby, who received the transplant, lived only 22 days after the operation. His death was caused by blood clots in his lung that resulted from surgical complications.

Pancreas transplantation is done in an attempt to prevent complications arising from diabetes. Instead of transplanting the whole organ, Dr. Paul E. Lacy and his research team transplanted insulin-producing cells in rats who survived 100 days. The aim of the experiment was to develop a technique of transplanting pancreatic cells to a diabetic person. It is hoped that such a transplant in human beings would produce enough insulin hormone to cure a diabetic person. Animal studies are encouraging, but experiments with human beings are still years away.[7]

The first pancreas transplant was performed in 1966 by Dr. Richard C. Lillehei at the University of Minnesota Medical School. The patient, however, died of pneumonia 114 days later. Since then over 300 pancreas transplants have been performed, and 25 percent of the grafts function so that the pancreas recipients can live without insulin. If the transplant fails, the patient can still survive on insulin. Mary Ellen Baran, a 35 year old woman, received a pancreas transplant in 1978 at the University of Minnesota Medical School and she has been doing well ever since, cured of diabetes. Her surgeon, Dr. David Sutherland, and his team performed 80 pancreas transplants before the middle of 1983 and 24 of their patients are now able to live without insulin injection.

The first *lung* transplant was performed by Dr. James D. Hardy in 1963. The graft took but the patient died 18 days later of failure of other organs. Since then only 38 lung transplants have been performed but the longest survivor lived only 10 months.

It seems that the combined *heart-lung* transplant has a better chance of succeeding than a single lung transplant. In 1981, Drs. Norman E. Shumway and Bruce Reitz transplanted a heart-lung into Mary Gohlke, a 45 year old woman. Today, more than two years after the surgery, she is well and back at her job. Of the 22 heart-lung transplant receivers, 13 patients are still alive.

Bone-marrow is transplanted in persons who are unable to produce the white blood cells necessary for destroying infectious bacteria and other organisms entering the body. This operation has been performed in several countries in more than 2,000 cases; 60 percent of children and 40 percent of adults were cured of acute leukemia after the transplants.

According to an Associated Press report, Dr. Paul Blanco, head of an Argentine surgical team, gave an account at the Brazil-Israeli Congress of Fertility and Sterility of his having performed an *ovary transplant* in March 1971 in Buenos Aires. The young Argentine woman who was the recipient became pregnant and was expecting a child. While ovarian transplantations had been done before, this was the first case in which a woman had become pregnant after the operation. The genetic characteristics of the baby obviously are those of the woman who donated the ovary and not of the mother.

A *testicle transplant*, another first, was reported by UPI on August 29, 1978. Dr. Sherman J. Silber and his team transplanted the organ to a man who was born without testicles. The operation was performed in 1977 but was kept secret until the doctors could be certain that the recipient's body would not reject the testicle. The recipient and the donor were twins and genetically identical, except that one was born with two testicles and his brother with none. Dr. Silber reported that the transplanted testicle functions normally and that the man is now capable of fathering children.

It is not entirely fictional that a *head or brain* could be transplanted. Dr. Robert J. White, neurosurgeon at the Western Reserve University in Cleveland, Ohio, isolated brains of rhesus monkeys and kept them alive for hours. He also excised the brains of dogs and transplanted them into other dogs.[8] In 1970 he and his team transplanted the head of a monkey to the body of another. In subsequent experiments he succeeded in keeping alive two transplanted monkey heads for a week. The transplanted heads, however, could not control their bodies. It is impossible to connect 100 to 200 million severed nerve ends. According to Dr. White, "transplanting an entire (human) head from one body to another is possible now." The situation would resemble a quadriplegic person "who lost all movement and sensation below the neck, but who still can see, hear and, with some adaptation, speak." Such people are living now and even enjoy life with the aid of mechanical devices.[9] Dr. White has been invited to Russia several times, and recent talks with Soviet neurosurgeons made him suspect that the Russians are planning to transplant the head of a man onto another's body. He himself has no plans to transplant human heads. His experiments with animals are useful for human brain surgery and for the study of the human brain.

The Ethics of Organ Transplantation

The ethical problems of transplantation of organs can be grouped around the donor (cadaver or living), the recipient and the social costs.

Cadaver Donor

It is a morally praiseworthy act to donate one's organs or body after death to help the living. In the United States the Uniform Anatomical Gift Act helps people to make the donation without much red tape. Many other countries have similar legislation.

Moral problems may arise, however, in relation to determining the time of the donor's death. Organs become useless for transplantation if they are not removed promptly after death. It has become a medical practice to hook up the newly dead to a heart-lung machine to keep the circulation going until the specific organ can be excised. It is now a generally accepted policy in medical circles that the transplant team be different from the medical team that cares for the dying person in order to avoid conflicts of interest. Nevertheless, conflicts may arise because the two teams must be in constant contact with each other about the timing of the planned transplant. It would be regrettable if the dying patient were not given all the competent care in the last hours of his life to which he is entitled as a human being. The medical team caring for the dying person must establish the fact of death before the body can be turned over to the transplant team.

Brain Death

When does a person die? Death is often called "passing" because it is deemed that the soul, the spiritual component of the person, passes into the spiritual realm. By this fact the human composite is broken up, disorganized. In the past, the cessation of breathing and heartbeat was assumed as the end of life and the presence of the fact of death. Recently, however, techniques have been developed to restart the heart and breathing of a person, to "resuscitate" him. In addition, respiration and heartbeat can artificially be maintained for a long period of time when, without the "life support machines," all this would spontaneously cease. These facts raised questions about the definition of death.

It has been suggested that a flat electroencephalogram (EEG) reading, that is, the cessation of brain functioning, be accepted as the criterion of death.

The Ad Hoc Committee to Examine the Definition of Brain Death of Harvard Medical School, however, has stated that a flat EEG reading is "of great confirmatory value" but that it should not be the only criterion. Three other criteria should also be present: irreceptivity and unresponsivity; no movements or breathing; no reflexes.[10]

Some persons object to the criterion of brain death, maintaining that perhaps we will learn how to restart the functioning of the brain just as we learned to restart the heart. They maintain that we cannot ascertain the fact of death until there is scientific evidence of the disintegration of individual organs and tissue. The President's Ethics Commission rejected this position as being against common sense and proposed the following *Uniform Determination of Death Act.*

An individual who has sustained either (1) irreversible cessation of circulatory or respiratory functions, or (2) irreversible cessation of all functions of the entire brain, including the brain stem, is dead. A determination of death must be made in accordance with accepted medical standards.[11]

It seems that this definition of death is satisfactory both scientifically and philosophically. Death means the irreversible cessation of all individual vital functions. By the end of 1983, 37 states and the District of Columbia as well as 13 foreign nations had adopted this or similar statutes. The acceptance of this criterion would ease the procedure for transplantation of organs and would remove the threat of a homicide or malpractice suit against the physicians involved in the case. In addition, the acceptance of brain death would exonerate the physician who turns off or removes the instruments providing artificial respiration and circulation for a patient who is in irreversible coma and has lost all brain function.

Nevertheless, the pragmatic aspects of transplantation are of secondary importance. They must yield to the primary right of the patient and the problems must be solved by working out appropriate techniques of transplantation that respect the primary right to life of the dying person.

Another ethical problem is the question of authority over the body of the newly dead who did not bequeath his organs to others during his lifetime. This question usually emerges in the case of accidental deaths. The accident victim is rushed to a hospital where a transplant team is waiting for suitable organ donors. Since many accident victims are healthy persons, their organs are in good condition for transplantation. Would it be ethical to take the undamaged organs of an accident victim when he dies and the next of kin does not object?

In April 1978 a new law came into force in France dealing with this problem. It became legal to transplant organs from the recently dead unless in his lifetime he signed a special hospital register forbidding the use of his organs for transplantation after his death. The new law abolished the previous requirement of authorization by the donor in his lifetime. It also abolished the right of relatives of the dead person to forbid the use of his organs for transplantation.[12] Finland, Greece, Italy, Norway, Spain and Sweden have laws of presumed consent of the deceased person to use his organs for transplants, but physicians still consult with the families of the deceased. In Austria, Czechoslovakia, Denmark, France, Israel, Poland and Switzerland, physicians proceed without asking the next of kin unless a prior objection has been raised by the family of the deceased. In the English speaking countries, a donor card of explicit family consent is required.[13]

In America the practice is to require the permission of the next of kin before steps can be taken for the transplantation of an accident victim's organs. It is debated, however, whether there should be legislation accepting presumed consent as justification for using the organs of an accident victim. There are some good reasons for the proposal. The present practice, however, seems to be ethically preferable to the taking of anybody's organs unless he has forbidden it in his lifetime. How many persons would take the trouble to register their objection? It would seem that a person would practically be reduced to being a means for the welfare of others. An action to help our fellow human being, however, should be a conscious and deliberate decision, as befits rational and free human beings. It should not just be imposed on us.

On the other hand, it would be advisable to educate the public about the possibility of becoming an organ donor. A well-organized education in this regard may be an adequate response to the growing need of suitable organs for transplant. In the absence of a "donor card," the permission of family members should be obtained. They can best interpret the wishes and attitudes of the newly dead. The request for permission, however, brings up another ethical problem. Family members are obviously in a state of shock when they are notified of the sudden death of a family member. Every effort should be made to respect the emotional, psychological and religious needs of the family when the question of transplantation of the deceased relative's organ is discussed with them.

Living Donor

For obvious reasons, the use of living donors is limited to paired organs, e.g., kidneys, and to parts of the human organism that regenerate, e.g., blood, bone marrow, skin. No one has proposed to use the liver or lungs of a living donor, so that the question of non-regenerating organs is mostly centered around the transplantation of kidneys *inter vivos*.

As we have seen, the success rate of kidney transplants is higher if the donor is a living person, especially if he is a family member, than it is in the case of a cadaver donor. The living donor, a healthy person, is asked to undergo a mutilation to help a sick person regain his health.

Two moral questions are involved here:

1. Is the healthy person allowed to mutilate himself for the sake of another?
2. Is he obliged to do this in order to save the life of a fellow human being?

1. The Principle of Totality

The principle of totality has been an accepted natural-law doctrine for centuries. It states that a diseased organ may be amputated or excised for the good of the whole organism. An infected leg or arm or any other organ that is beyond the hope of cure and threatens the whole organism may be removed to save the life of the person. Healthy organs, however, may not be amputated, for it would be an act of weakening a person's health, which he is obliged to maintain as much as he can. The principle of totality, then, would forbid the donation of a healthy organ.

The center of the problem is the interpretation of totality. If the idea of humanhood is taken in a biological sense, one can arrive at a conclusion that it is inhuman, that is, ethically wrong, to diminish one's humanity by truncating a part of it. Man is, however, more than just a biologically functioning organism. Man is essentially a social being. His most basic needs, even biological ones, cannot be satisfied without the cooperation of others. It is very much in accordance with a human being's rational and social nature, i.e., with the "totality" of man's humanness, for him to come to the help of his fellow human beings, as long as he does not expose himself to the grave danger of destroying himself, or of weakening himself so much that he could not function normally. This kind of understanding of the principle of totality does permit transplantation of organs *inter vivos*. The surgical removal of one's kidney is a service, voluntarily undertaken, to help others. Ordinarily it does not weaken the health of the donor. He can survive and function quite well with one kidney. Nevertheless, rational human nature urges us to develop or improve artificial organs that will enable us to eliminate the necessity of donating living organs. As we shall see in the following chapter, medical technology is moving in this direction.

2. Duty To Donate Organs?

Does it follow from the previous reasoning that a person, especially a family member, is morally obliged to become a donor? There is a difference between what is permissible and what is obligatory. While we can justify the donation of a live organ by pointing out that it is in accordance with the reality of true humanness, we cannot find sufficient reasons or prove that it is obligatory. There is a general duty to help our fellow human beings, but it cannot be proved that we have to go beyond ordinary means to come to the aid of others. Donation of a kidney is a very generous act, but it certainly goes beyond the ordinary human means to help others. In addition the alleged duty to donate a kidney is so vague that it would be impossible to carry it out. Who would be obliged—which one of the family members or relatives, who among the many biologically compatible strangers? Could the patient equally benefit from a cadaver transplant? An *affirmative* duty cannot be vague; it must be correctly defined to acquire obligatory force for a particular person. (Negative duty, on the other hand, for example, "You must not kill an innocent person," has to be fulfilled by any person because it is quite definite and concrete in its application.)

It follows from our previous reasoning that the donation of organs *inter vivos* must be an entirely free act. According to an Associated Press report on July 26, 1978 the principle of freedom with respect to organ donation was tested and upheld by the Allegheny Common Pleas Court. Robert McFall, a 39 year old former asbestos worker, filed suit to compel his cousin, David Shimp, to donate to him his bone marrow if tests found that they were biologically compatible. McFall had only a 25 percent chance of living one year without a marrow transfusion. Chemical treatment was available but not recommended. A marrow transplant would increase McFall's survival chance to 60 percent. The first test Mr. Shimp underwent indicated compatibility but he refused to take more tests. Other relatives and unrelated volunteers were unfortunately found biologically incompatible. It was argued that bone marrow regenerates itself and so Mr. Shimp would not suffer any weakening of his health.

It would take between 100 and 150 punctures of a pelvic bone to extract enough bone marrow, but it would be done painlessly under general anesthesia. Nevertheless, Mr. Shimp refused the transfusion of his bone marrow in the hope that his cousin would pull through in some other way. Judge John P. Flaherty upheld the transplant denial because forcible extraction of bodily tissues "would defeat the sanctity of the individual."

Voluntary donations of organs should be restricted to adults who can evaluate all the medical and ethical problems involved and make a free and informed decision. It is not unusual, however, that relatives are under subtle pressure to "volunteer" to donate a kidney to another relative. Pressure may build up not only by veiled suggestions and tendentious remarks but also by the very existence of family ties. To neutralize this kind of pressure, the practice has developed of having donor candidates interviewed privately by the transplant staff, and if any reluctance is discovered on the part of a candidate to go through with the donation he is pronounced "incompatible" for the transplant.

Minors should not be offered by their parents to be donors. "Proxy consent" in the case could not be justified as it can be with regard to no-risk experimentation when it is necessary to do testing with children. A child cannot evaluate the risk and inconvenience of living all his life with one kidney. Nobody should be forced into such a situation without making an informed, voluntary consent. Other ways than transplantation from a child donor can be found to help a sick brother or sister.

Donation of blood is an accepted practice in almost all nations of the world. Blood regenerates itself and usually there is no risk connected with the procedure involved. Some religious groups, for example, the Jehovah's Witnesses, object to blood transfusion on religious grounds. No ethical arguments can be raised, however, against blood donation and blood transfusion if the donors are not forced to give their blood and are not exploited commercially.

The Choice of Recipients

This ethical problem arises from the fact that generally there are far more would-be recipients than there are organs available.

Who shall live when not all can be saved? What principle should govern the selection of recipients? There is a consensus that patients who would not really benefit by a transplantation should be dropped from the list of potential recipients. This selection by a committee, however, is not always easy. There are many uncertain elements involved in evaluating this condition. Money and wealth certainly should not be a deciding factor. Kidneys should not be sold and purchased. Not long ago, a Detroit man on the waiting list for a kidney transplant placed an ad in a newspaper offering $3,000 for the organ. He received over a hundred calls from people willing to sell one. The hospital, however, rightly refused to transplant a kidney that was bought.[14] Soliciting the sale of body organs should be avoided, for it could lead to many abuses and even to a black market dealing in organs. Many nations now cover the medical expenses of kidney transplants by various kinds of health insurance, but there is no provision for financial remuneration for donated organs.

After eliminating patients who, for various reasons, would least benefit by an organ transplant, a just selection is still so difficult that some have suggested that selection by lot or by the principle of "first come, first served" would be the most equitable method. All other criteria, for instance, social worth and social usefulness, could be so subjective that they inevitably would lead to unfair discrimination. Drawing lots has at least the advantage that everybody has an equal chance, based only on his need for the organ and on nothing else.

The Social Cost

In addition to the donor and the recipient, society is also involved in programs of organ transplantation by providing the financial means. The total cost of a kidney transplant was estimated to be about $35,000 in 1983, and that of a heart transplant about $100,000 for the operation and $5,000 to $8,000 yearly maintenance after the surgery. In 1972 the U.S. federal government created the End Stage Renal Disease Program (ESRD) and extended Medicare coverage to persons of any age who need a kidney transplant or regular periodic treatment with kidney machines, i.e., dialysis. According to recent government estimates, about 60,000 kidney patients were helped in 1983 at the cost of $2 billion. At present, there is no Medicare coverage for the more expensive heart and liver transplants. Those who need such transplants and their families obviously want society to cover the expenses because individual families of average income are not capable of financing them. Medical and financial resources, however, are limited. It must be investigated, therefore, whether distributive justice is being observed by spending so much on organ transplants. Are all sick people treated equitably or is the relatively small group of kidney patients favored at the expense of others? Would it be better to spend more resources on preventing disease or trying to cure a greater number of people having less debilitating illnesses? It is difficult to give satisfactory answers to these questions. A comprehensive national health-insurance program has to face this problem of distributive justice by weighing the available medical and financial resources and the most equitable way of distributing them.

QUESTIONS FOR REVIEW AND DISCUSSION

1. Explain the immune system and the phenomenon of rejection.

2. Review the history of failure and success of organ transplantation.

3. What are the ethical problems arising in connection with cadaver donors?

4. Is brain death an ethically acceptable criterion of death?

5. Who owns the body of a deceased individual? Who may ethically decide on the use of organs of a newly dead individual?

6. Explain the principle of totality. Does it forbid the transplantation of organs *inter vivos*?

7. Is a family member obliged to donate his organ to another member of the family to save his life?

8. Whose life should be saved by transplantation when not every-body's life can be saved?

9. Should society cover the costs of organ transplantation or should the patients and their families pay for it?

Notes

1. Dr. Hans Jorg Bohmig, "Organtransplantationen," in *Kunstlich le-ben-gesteuert sterben?* Wien: Veritas Verlag, 1974, pp. 7–11.

2. *The New York Times*, July 1, 1979.

3. Gerald Leach, *The Biocrats*. Middlesex: Penguin Books, Ltd., 1970, p. 298.

4. Leach, *op. cit.*, p. 297.

5. *Newsweek*, August 29, 1983, pp. 41–42.

6. *Ibid.*

7. Paul E. Lacy, Joseph M. Davie, and Edward H. Finke, "Prolonga-tion of Islet Allograft Survival Following *in vitro* Culture (24°C) and Single Injection of ALS." *Science*, Vol. 204, April 20, 1979, pp. 312–313.

8. Robert J. White, Maurice S. Albin, and Javier Verdura, "Isolation of the Monkey Brain: In Vitro Preparation and Maintenance." *Science*, Vol. 141, September 13, 1963, p. 1060.

9. Edythe Westenhaver, "Robert White Is a Catholic Neurosurgeon Who Has Attracted the Notice of Two Popes." *Religious News Service*, No-vember 10, 1982, p. 5.

10. "Refinements in Criteria for the Determination of Death: An Ap-praisal." *Journal of American Medical Association*, Vol. 221, July 3, 1972, pp. 48–53. Reprint: "Readings" by Institute of Society, Ethics and the Life Sciences.

11. President's Commission for the Study of Ethical Problems in Med-icine and Biomedical and Behavioral Research, *Defining Death*. Washing-ton: U.S. Government Printing Office, 1981, p. 73.

12. "France Widens Authority for Transplants from Dead." *The New York Times*, April 16, 1978.

13. J.B. "How Other Countries Handle Consent." *The Hastings Center Report*, December, 1983, p. 30.

14. David Dempsey, "Transplants Are Common; Now It's the Organs That Have Become Rare." *The New York Times Magazine*, October 13, 1974, p. 59.

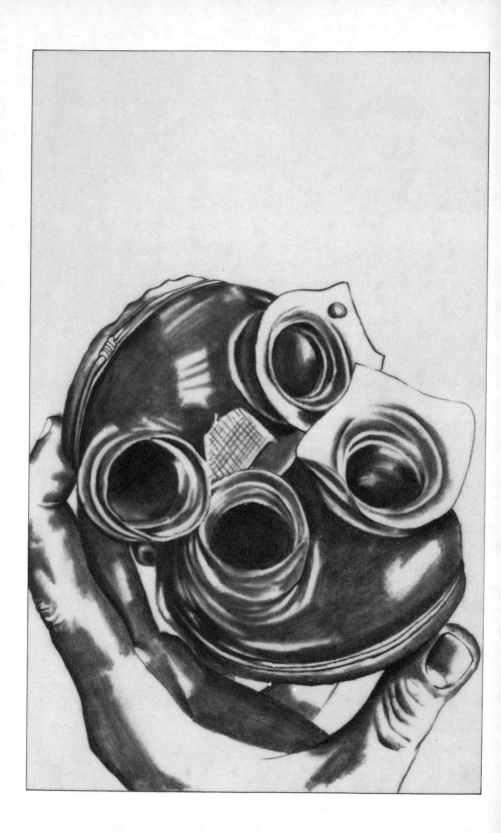

12   Artificial Organs

Primitive man who lost his leg and was fortunate enough to survive had to use a stick to keep his balance and to be able to move around. The crutch was later supplanted by wooden legs. Hooks were attached to the arm to substitute for a severed hand. Partial or total dentures, that is, artificial teeth, have been used since the emergence of dentistry. These objects, however, are only externally attached to the human body. Modern technology has created other types of artificial organs, which are in closer symbiosis with the living man than a wooden leg can be. The new prostheses can be connected with the muscles in such a way that they can bend and perform many functions of natural limbs. Artificial arms use a system of receivers on the skin and microtransmitters under the skin to convey information from the nerves to the mechanical controls of the artificial arm that is powered by batteries. The sophistication of artificial limbs is increasing as modern technology constantly improves their functioning and enables them to perform a variety of movements.

Other artificial organs go even further. They can be surgically implanted and replace natural organs. Television's *The Six-Million Dollar Man* and *The Bionic Woman* are science-fiction fantasies but they express a desire and trend to replace any natural part of the human body by artificial "spare parts" when an original organ is damaged. When certain parts of a machine wear out, we replace them with spare parts.

There are two questions concerning human spare parts:

1. What is possible technically today?
2. Are there any ethical problems involved in using artificial organs to replace natural ones?

231

1. The Development of Technology

According to an article in *Forbes* magazine[1] the "human spare parts industry was a $700 million business worldwide" in 1978, and it was growing by 15 percent yearly.

Today there are more than 200 companies involved in a great variety of sophisticated products that can replace human organs. As an executive in the multi-billion dollar human spare parts industry put it: "We are trying to copy what God did."[2] A great number of small laboratories are working to produce custom-made products and to further improve this already sophisticated technology. The commercial market for artificial organs has grown by leaps and bounds. The sales of heart pacemakers alone amounted to about $500 million in 1983.

Prostheses

Some examples of artificial organs are prostheses to replace severed limbs. *Artificial arms and hands* can be controlled by remaining arm muscles or by pneumatic springs and electric devices. Modern *leg prostheses* can enable a person to walk securely. Knee and ankle articulation is achieved by a pneumatic or hydraulic piston-cylinder system. The price of these prostheses varies from $300 to $40,000. In 1975, scientists at Northwestern University and engineers at the medical products division of General Atomic developed an eight-pound experimental myoelectric (*myos* is Greek for muscle) arm at the cost of $40,000. The prosthesis was prepared for Reid Hilton, a karate expert who lost his right arm in an accident. The controls of this experimental arm are directly connected to the nerves in the stump of his arm. A battery power pack is located inside the prosthesis, which also includes a feedback device that enables him to have a sense of touch.[3]

Richard B. Stein, of the University of Alberta, Canada, and his colleagues fashioned a sophisticated prosthetic device that enabled a saxophone player who lost his hand to play the saxophone again.[4] Larry Leifer, a mechanical engineer at Stanford University, developed a one-armed robot that responds to voice commands. The robot can prepare meals and perform other housekeeping chores for quadriplegics and elderly people. It is an expensive device but it will cost less than human care for the handicapped.[5] With the advance of computerized technology, a great variety of devices have been developed to aid the handicapped or to replace their limbs.

Implantable Organs

Other artificial parts are not simply attached to the body but are permanently implanted. There are a number of substances the human body does not reject. Among these are stainless steel, special alloys, silicone elastomers, Teflon, and Dacron. Many artificial parts become covered with a lining of living tissue within months of their implantation. *Artificial heart valves* are made of metal and plastic; their price is about $2,000. Presently, a combination of pig heart valve and artificial material is being used to repair damaged hearts. The pig valves are first treated with chemicals making them inert. They are then sewn into a flexible frame and covered with Dacron. Arthritic *hips, elbows, shoulders, knees, ankles, finger and toe joints* are routinely replaced by artificial ones. A total hip costs about $1,000 to $2,000, an elbow about $1,200. The cost of surgery and hospitalization, of course, has to be added to the price of the parts. A surgeon's fee for implanting a new hip was about $5,000 in 1983. *Heart pacemakers*, which regulate heartbeat, are manufactured by a number of well-known companies, such as Atlantic Richfield Co., Fiat, and Siemens. Breast implants are made of silicone and cost about $300 a pair. They are used after cancer surgery or for cosmetic reasons. More than 100,000 silicone implants are performed a year. The market for artificial limbs, mostly legs, is about 100,000 a year.

Intraocular lenses are implanted after cataract operations. Intraocular lenses that are permanently implanted replace the thick eyeglasses or contact lenses that formerly had to be worn by patients after a cataract operation.

Work is being done on *artificial eyes* or *"electronic vision"* for the blind. The plan is to implant a small TV camera in an artificial eye or in eyeglasses. Light impulses are then transmitted to a miniature computer that sends them through electrodes implanted in the head to the brain's visual cortex. The electronic stimulation of this part of the brain enables the blind to perceive spots of light. Dr. William Dobelle, director of the Division of Artificial Organs in the Department of Surgery at the College of Physicians and Surgeons at Columbia University, has already developed a device that has produced some limited vision in volunteer blind persons.[6]

In 1982, at the University of Western Ontario Hospital Dr. John Girvin and his team used a Dobelle device on a Vietnam veteran who was blinded in 1966 when a Vietcong land mind exploded in front of him. Sixty-four platinum electrodes were connected with the visual center of his brain. He expressed his excitement when he saw white points of light for the first time in seven years as an electric current was passed through the electrodes.[7]

The device is far from being perfect or practical but fast development in electronic technology and miniaturization may make it practical within the foreseeable future. The principle applied to artificial vision was tried with some success to elicit hearing in the totally deaf.[8]

In 1975, Dr. Louis R. Head and his colleagues at Northwestern Memorial Hospital in Chicago began testing a totally *implantable artificial lung* in dogs and sheep. They hope to perfect the artificial lung for human use as well.[9]

Artificial Kidney, Hemodialysis

The first *artificial kidney* was designed by Dr. Willem J. Kolff, a Dutch surgeon, in 1944. He is now working with Dr. Dobelle's team at the University of Utah on the development of "electric vision." The kidney machine takes over the functions of the natural kidneys of purifying the blood of the patient. The hemodialysis machine, as it now is called, has been considerably improved since the first model. It can be installed in the home of the patient. Yearly treatment, nevertheless, is still expensive; at a dialysis center it costs about $35,000 a year, while it costs about $20,000 if it is done at home. Plastic tubes are permanently implanted in an artery and vein in the forearm or the leg where the machine's tubes are plugged in. As the patient is hooked to the machine, he begins a four to five hour session that he has to repeat three times a week. The blood of the patient is taken out through one of the tubes and conducted through sheets of very fine synthetic membrane surrounded by a specially prepared purifying solution. The patient's blood is thus cleansed, the accumulated impurities eliminated. When the patient is not on the machine, the permanently implanted plastic tubes are connected outside of the body by a shunt so that his blood can circulate normally and the formation of clots is prevented. In addition to this periodic blood-cleaning process, the patient has to keep to a very rigid diet and his liquid intake must be regulated very carefully.

Portable experimental models of the kidney machine were developed by Dr. Kolff and his team of engineers and physicians in 1975.[10] When perfected, it could be mass-produced. The portable machine would simplify dialysis treatment, but the basic difficulties connected with it would remain. Another group of researchers, however, demonstrated a new version of the kidney machine in 1978. The conventional kidney machine applies gallons of specially treated wash water to remove impurities from the blood. The new model works without water, using a filter system that collects the impurities, which are then chemically treated before being returned to the body. Since no cleaning liquid is needed, the kidney machine is much lighter and can be worn as a backpack. The machine has been successfully tried on animals but not yet on human beings.[11]

A further improvement of the kidney machine is the *Continuous Ambulatory Peritoneal Dialysis (CAPD)* developed by Dr. Robert Popovich, professor of biomedical engineering at the University of Texas, and Dr. Jack Moncrief, nephrologist. CAPD is the device closest to an internal artificial kidney. Instead of a man-made membrane, CAPD uses the thin membrane lining the abdominal, or peritoneal, cavity to cleanse the blood of poisonous waste. A small, permanent opening is cut below the navel and a permanent tube is inserted, which leads through the peritoneal membrane into the abdominal cavity. A small plastic bag, containing two liters of dialysate fluid, is hooked up to the permanent tube. The patient then hangs up the bag to let the liquid flow into the cavity. When this is done, he clamps the tube, folds it and tucks it into a pouch he can wear on a belt. The peritoneal membrane contains many small blood vessels, which are bathed in the blood-cleansing fluid for some five hours. In the meantime the patient can continue working, walking and engaging in even strenuous physical labor. After some five hours, the patient lowers the bag, removes the clamp from the tube, and lets the solution flow out from his abdominal cavity into the bag. He disconnects the bag, replaces it with a new one filled with a fresh blood-cleansing solution and repeats the previous procedure. He has to do this four times a day. He need not get up at night to change the bag, however, because he can keep the fluid in his abdominal cavity for eight hours before changing it. It is a great deal less expensive and less inconvenient than the conventional kidney-machine treatment.[12] Several thousand patients were already using it in 1983.

Artificial Heart

The *heart-lung machine* was developed in the early 1950's. This device is not intended as a permanent replacement for the natural organs. It only temporarily takes over the functions of the heart and lungs during a surgical intervention in the heart. The arteries and veins leading into and out of the heart are clamped and tubes are introduced into them so that the blood flow by-passes the heart and is drawn out into the machine. Here the deoxygenated blood is mixed with oxygen and forced back into the circulatory system. Thus the functions of both the heart and lungs are replaced by the heart-lung machine while the surgery takes place.

The idea of a totally implantable artificial heart (TIAH) emerged in 1964. The National Heart Institute drew up a master plan for the construction of a prototype and obtained the financial support of Congress for the project. The plan called for a mass production and mass implantation of artificial hearts in patients by February 1970.[13] However, at the end of 1983, no artificial heart is still beating in any human being.

Nevertheless, some remarkable progress has been made. Calves lived for several months with artificial hearts implanted in them. They died only when they outgrew the human-size heart. There is Russian-American cooperation, agreed upon in 1974, in developing a functioning artificial heart. A Russian team visited the United States in March 1976 and watched American surgeons implant an American-made artificial heart into a six week old calf. Then the Russian team implanted a Soviet-made heart into another calf. The purpose of the performance was to acquaint each side with the techniques of the other.

The pump of the artificial heart is operated by a motor that can be driven by rechargeable batteries or a nuclear engine powered by plutonium. It is thought that the motor could possibly also be powered by a biological fuel cell. In 1968, the National Heart and Lung Institute, successor to the National Heart Institute, concluded a contract with three companies to develop artificial hearts powered by a nuclear engine. The plan was to produce the totally implantable artificial heart that would operate for ten years without refueling and without external support.[14] The Institute announced on March 2, 1972 that a nuclear-powered heart pump was implanted for the first time in a calf on February 14, 1972 at Boston City Hospital.[15] The device, however, supported the calf for only two days.

Dr. Denton A. Cooley, of the Texas Heart Institute in Houston, was the first to implant an artificial heart into a dying patient, Haskell Karp. The patient lived sixty-five hours with the artificial heart, after which it was replaced by a human heart. He died, however, soon after the human heart transplant. In 1977, a surgical team at Zurich Hospital in Switzerland used a newly developed total artificial heart in a woman patient for two days, which enabled her to survive a severe heart failure she had suffered after cardiac surgery.[16]

The media gave extensive coverage to the story of a more recent and more successful artificial heart implant. On December 2, 1982, Dr. Barney B. Clark's heart was removed and a Jarvik-7 artificial heart was implanted in him. The device was made of polyurethane and named after its principal designer, Dr. Robert Koffler Jarvik. The operation was performed at the University of Utah Medical Center by Dr. William C. DeVries and his team. The motor driving the heart, however, was too bulky to be implanted. It was placed on a cart which the patient was able to push around. Dr. Clark, a retired dentist, died 112 days later on March 23, 1983. His death was caused, however, by the failure of most of his organs and not by the failure of the artificial heart, which continued to pump even after his death.

These cases represent only limited successes. The original plan is much behind schedule, and the initial optimism about mass production of a functioning artificial heart within a short time has been replaced by a more realistic appraisal that it cannot be expected before 1990. It is estimated that some fifty thousand patients annually might benefit in the United States alone from an artificial heart. In 1983, the price of one heart was estimated to be between $50,000 and $80,000. The expenses of the "installation" of the artificial heart by a team of specialized surgeons must be added to the price of the device.

While a group of scientists has been working on a totally implantable artificial heart, partial hearts, called left-ventricular-assist devices (LVAD), have been successfully developed and used as temporary life-support machines. Some scientists derive encouragement from this achievement. They hope that a total artificial heart is not an impossible dream.

2. The Ethics of Artificial Organs

The development of artificial organs could eliminate many *ethical problems* associated with the transplantation of organs *inter vivos*. It is "good medicine" to restore the functioning of an organ or part of the human anatomy without endangering the health of a live donor.

The ethical questions of *experimentation with human beings* are fairly easily solved with respect to artificial organs. Animal experiments are a reliable indication in most cases as to whether an artificial organ will help or harm human beings.

The social costs of the development of artificial organs, however, may create an ethical dilemma. How should scarce medical and financial resources be distributed?

This is a moral problem of *distributive justice*. Financial and scientific investment in the development of artificial organs diverts scientists, medical personnel and funds from other much needed areas of application. As was previously pointed out, hemodialysis costs between $20,000 and $35,000 a year for one patient in the United States, depending on where the dialysis is performed. In America about 60,000 kidney patients were helped in 1983 at a cost of about $2 billion. Could the money and scientific resources be distributed more fairly?

Distributive justice demands an *equitable* distribution of goods society can dispose of. It has to be pointed out, however, that initial investments in the development of any scientific innovation are disproportionately high if one considers only the first specimens that are produced. The prototype of a new machine may cost many millions of dollars, but the investment pays off when it is mass produced later. Scientific and technical progress can be achieved only by investment of scientific and financial resources.

Distributive justice demands the careful consideration of whether fairness and equity in distributing the goods of society are being observed in the investment of these resources. Mathematical calculation, however, is impossible in this regard. It has to be kept in mind, nevertheless, that the beneficial results of scientific progress supported by public funds should not be available only to the rich, but to all who are in need of them. The great advantage of artificial organs consists exactly in the possibility of mass production so that the painful selection of a restricted number of recipients can be avoided.

In addition to the question of experimentation and distributive justice, the *totally implantable artificial heart raises some other ethical problems.* One is derived from the psychological fact that we have been conditioned by a popular belief that the heart is the center of human emotions, the organ of love. Having a mechanical heart, instead of a live organ, may produce psychological difficulties for the users of artificial hearts and others who live with them. This difficulty, however, should not be insurmountable. One can understand and psychologically become adjusted to the fact that the heart is a vital organic pump, and that it is not the inner core of the "self."

Another problem that can be foreseen will be the question of supply and demand when artificial hearts begin to come off the assembly line. The *choice of recipients* will be just as problematic as is today the selection of kidney transplants. Wealth or "social worth" should not be the factors for deciding who shall live and who shall die. The guiding principle suggested for the choice of recipients in Chapter 11 could be applied here, too.[17]

There is another ethical problem that pertains in a specific way to the totally implantable artificial heart. The mechanical pump replacing a live heart can function for a great number of years. It may keep pumping even at an age when other organs have already deteriorated. Should the artificial heart be stopped the way one turns off the motor of a car when one arrives at a destination? Who would do it? What principles would be used to determine that a person has lived long enough or has already arrived at the end of his earthly pilgrimage and that the motor of the artificial heart should be stopped?

Several sources of energy have been suggested for the motor of the artificial heart. Each of them involves the problem of deciding the termination of a person's life. Scientists, at least initially, favored the selection of a nuclear engine that would be powered by fifty-three grams of plutonium 238. This nuclear fuel was chosen because its half life is 87.8 years and thus it would give continuous service for more than ten years. The pump would be run by a thermal engine powered by a pellet of plutonium. The engine would be implanted in the abdominal cavity and the pump in the chest. It is foreseen that, with improvements in miniaturization, the combined size of both the engine and the pump will not be larger than the size of an adult human heart. Supposing that an artificial heart fueled by plutonium 238 is implanted in a person at the age of forty, would he be denied the refueling of his heart when the fuel runs out and he is already more than 100? Or would his heart be stopped before he reaches that age? We would face the same problem with rechargeable batteries, too, with the exception that the problem would come up more often because batteries do not last very long without recharging. For how many years should they be recharged? Would the family of the patient or the medical personnel be permitted to allow the battery to become exhausted? Would the omission of refueling be equivalent to suicide or murder?

Recently great concern has arisen about the use of atomic power even for peaceful purposes. This concern extends also to the nuclear engine of the artificial heart. Can radiation sufficiently be suppressed so that the user and the people around him are not harmed? A person with an artificial heart could become involved in an accident and the nuclear engine could be crushed, thus releasing radioactive material. In another scenario, the danger is foreseen that terrorists could kidnap and kill a number of persons with plutonium-fueled hearts and thus get enough material for an atom bomb.

No matter what kind of power source is used in the artificial heart, the question of the definition of death still has to be satisfactorily answered. A person with an artificial heart will continue to have circulation and respiration when his vital functions would have stopped without the help of the mechanical heart. The problem is, however, that one cannot be certain whether the vital functions would have really stopped without the assistance of the artificial heart. Is stopping the motor, then, equivalent to killing the person? Accepting the cessation of brain functions as the criterion of death in this case may offer a solution. A person whose EEG reading is flat but whose circulation is maintained by an artificial heart could be compared to the newly dead who is put on the respirator and whose blood circulation is maintained by machines. It would be advisable to discuss this problem and come to a consensus before we begin to implant artificial hearts in human beings. Experiments with animals should also be conducted to see how death comes about when an artificial heart is still beating but other organs have already failed.

QUESTIONS FOR REVIEW AND DISCUSSION

1. Describe the technical developments of prostheses.

2. What are the most frequently implanted artificial organs?

3. What is meant by a totally implantable artificial heart?

4. Is it ethically justifiable to replace human organs with artificial ones? Is "playing God" in this case wrong?

5. Who should bear the cost of the implantation of artificial organs? Is distributive justice violated if a small group's extraordinary medical expenses are paid by the whole society?

6. When should the refueling of the totally implantable artificial heart be stopped? Who should decide it? Is it suicide or murder not to refuel the artificial heart of an old, senile person whose other organs are failing?

Notes

1. Steven Solomon, "Spare Parts for Humans." *Forbes*, May 29, 1978, pp. 52–54.
2. N.R. Kleinfield, "Companies in Search of Bionic Man." *The New York Times*, November 20, 1983, Section 3, p. 1.
3. *Time*, December 1, 1975, p. 63.

4. *Science News*, December 3, 1983, p. 361.

5. Cf. *The New York Times*, May 31, 1983, p. C 3.

6. Douglas Colligan, "Artificial Organs: Replacing the Irreplaceable." *New York*, October 22, 1979, pp. 53–61.

7. Stephen Solomon, "Spare-Parts Medicine." *The New York Times Magazine*, November 28, 1982, p. 120.

8. Patricia E. Weil, "Computers Work Toward Eyes For the Blind, Ears For the Deaf." *The New York Times*, July 29, 1979.

9. George B. Ryan, "Future Shock: The Body's New Frontiers." *New York*, February 10, 1975, p. 45.

10. "Inventor of Artificial Kidney Demonstrates an Experimental Portable Model." *The New York Times*, November 5, 1975.

11. "Artificial Kidney Hailed as Dialysis Replacement." *The New York Times*, April 29, 1979.

12. Douglas Colligan, *op. cit.*, p. 61.

13. Cf. Lee Edson, "The Search For a 'Bionic' Heart." *The New York Times Magazine*, October 21, 1979, p. 36.

14. Robert K. Jarvik, "The Total Artificial Heart." *Scientific American*, January 1981, p. 78.

15. Harold M. Schmeck, Jr., "Nuclear Energy Drives Heart-Aid Pump in California." *The New York Times*, March 3, 1972.

16. AP, December 14, 1977.

17. Albert R. Jonsen, "The Totally Implantable Artificial Heart." *The Hastings Center Report*, November 1977, p. 3.

13 Sex Preselection and Sex Change

Various methods of determining the sex of children to be conceived are described in ancient literature and are found in the folklore of almost every nation. Scientific understanding of how nature selects the sex of children, however, is only of recent date. In the 1890's, researchers studying chromosomes noticed that male and female animals have chromosomal differences. One pair of chromosomes in the male differs from the pair of chromosomes in the female. These are known as the *sex chromosomes*. All the other chromosomes, which are called *autosomes*, are the same whether they are in the male or the female. The sex chromosome that is the same in either the male or the female is called the X chromosome. The sex chromosome that is different in the male is called the Y chromosome. Thus the combination of the pair of sex chromosomes is XX in the female and XY in the male.

Human beings have twenty-three pairs of choromosomes; twenty-two of these are autosomes, that is, structurally the same in both sexes. The structure of the twenty-third pair of chromosomes is different in the two sexes, and it is this pair of chromosomes that determines the sex of a human being. The female germ cell, that is, the ovum, always carries an X chromosome. The male germ cell, that is, the sperm, carries either an X or a Y chromosome. If a spermatozoon carrying an X chromosome fertilizes the egg, the fetus develops as a girl (XX); if, on the other hand, a Y chromosome carrying sperm fertilizes the egg, the fetus will be a boy (XY).

Balance of Sexes

Further studies have found that the Y-carrying spermatozoa outnumber the X-carrying spermatozoa by about 160 to 100. According to this finding, baby boys should outnumber baby girls by the same ratio. It was further found, however, that the X spermatozoa are more resistant to the acid environment of the vagina prior to ovulation than the Y spermatozoa. Although Y sperms swim faster toward the egg than X sperms, more Y spermatozoa are destroyed on the way toward meeting the egg. As a result of these combined factors, the ratio of boys and girls at birth is 51.4 percent to 48.6 percent. The mortality of boys, however, is higher than that of girls, and by age twenty the ratio is 1:1. Thus the number of men and women of marriageable age is about equal. After this age, however, at least in the United States, the ratio changes in favor of women, and by age sixty-five females outnumber males by ten to seven. In the United States the life span of women is longer than that of men. In rapid-growth countries, for example, in Mexico, the male life span is longer, and in a no-growth country, for instance, in Sweden, the life expectancy of both men and women is almost equal.[1] In rapid-growth countries there is usually a high rate of material mortality that accounts for the slight imbalance in the population ratio in favor of men. In addition, certain ethnic groups, especially in developing countries, neglect girls in favor of boys, and this factor, too, increases the imbalance in the ratio of the sexes.

Techniques of Sex Preselection

The knowledge of how nature determines the sex of children opens the way to a scientific method of preselecting the sex of babies. In order to control the sex of offspring, spermatozoa carrying Y and X chromosomes must be separated in some way and, depending on one's choice, only one kind of sperm must be allowed to reach the egg to fertilize it. Separation of the two kinds of spermatozoa can be achieved in different ways. One method is to reduce the acidity of the vagina and consequently let the male spermatozoa survive in greater number. Since these swim faster than female spermatozoa, they have a better chance of reaching the egg first and of producing an XY combination, that is, a boy. This method has achieved some limited results, but it cannot be considered reliable.

The fact that female (X) sperms are larger and heavier than male (Y) sperms is the basis of another method, namely, that of using centrifugation for separating them. Once they are divided, artificial insemination with one or the other kind of sperm would provide a reliable method of choosing the sex of children. Centrifugation, however, has not proven practical because the delicate structure of sperm gets easily damaged in the process, losing its fertility.

In 1973, Drs. Ronald J. Ericsson, C.N. Langevin and M. Nishino, working at the Schering Company laboratory in Berlin, after two years of research developed a technique that shows more promise than the previously mentioned methods. They relied on the differences in the speed of mobility of the two kinds of spermatozoa. They suspended sperm in a tube of dense albumin concentrate. A certain percentage of sperm swam down to the bottom of the tube. The sperm remaining on the top was removed and the separation process was repeated three times. It was found that the spermatozoa separated by this method were carrying Y chromosomes up to 85 percent.[2] Dr. Ericsson has patents or patents pending for his sperm-separation technique in some twenty countries. The method, if it is successfully applied in animal breeding, might be financially rewarding.[3]

Dr. Ericsson is now president of Gametrics Company. The method he invented is being used there and in more than a dozen fertility centers around the world. His method so far is the most successful approach to sex preselection but it is far from being perfect. According to statistics given by Dr. Ericsson, out of 84 children born to parents who wanted boys, 65 were boys and 19 girls.[4]

The Ethics of Sex Preselection

All the methods developed so far are cumbersome, expensive and unreliable. No simple and sure method has yet been invented. Nevertheless, the question must be asked as to whether it would be ethical to determine the sex of children artificially and whether the technique should be permitted universal application when it becomes so simple and inexpensive that everybody can employ it.

Why would parents choose a certain sex for their child? There may be various reasons depending on the circumstances. Parents may wish to have a male heir to carry on the name of the father or a family enterprise. Or they may think that a boy has a better chance to succeed in a male-oriented society and to be able to support his parents in their old age, or they may simply want to balance the number of boys and girls in the family.

Should children be brought into the world to *fulfill parental wishes*? Artificial preselection carries with it the danger of the children becoming simply means for certain goals of the parents. What reaction will the children have when they learn that their sex was determined by their parents for certain purposes? It would seem that procreating children without sex preselection is ethically preferable to choosing the baby's sex.

In addition, all sex preselection methods must go through a period of *experimentation* before they can be perfected. During this period, a number of fetuses may be exposed to the danger of genetic malformation because of the tampering with the sperm.

One reason favoring sex preselection is the possibility of thus avoiding *sex-linked genetic diseases*. One has to consider, however, that there are few such serious diseases that cannot be treated. One also has to weigh the danger of other disorders that may be caused by the uncertain methods of sex predetermination.

Would an effective and inexpensive sex preselection method upset the ratio of the sexes? As we have previously seen, the number of men and women, at least around the marriageable age of twenty, is now more or less equal. A significant imbalance in this ratio might have serious ethical consequences. The institution of monogamous marriage is based on a balanced ratio of the two sexes. If there are more men than women or vice versa, many persons will be unable to find marriage partners unless some form of polygamy is introduced. The incidence of homosexuality might increase as well. The struggle for the equality of the sexes, too, might suffer a setback.

Various polls seem to lend support to the concern that the sex ratio might be upset if a simple sex-preselection technique is universally available. The Division of Vital Statistics of the Department of Health, Education and Welfare's National Center for Health Statistics conducted a survey in 1973 concerning the preferred sex of progeny. A scientific random sample of wives aged fifteen to forty-four were questioned. It was found that 49 percent had a preference for sons, 22 percent for daughters and 19 percent wanted an equal number of each sex.[5] The worldwide situation is the same. In some cultures the desire to have boys is even stronger than in America.[6]

Roberta Steinbacher, a sociologist at Cleveland State University, offers some recent statistics. If parents were able to choose their children's sex, there would be 140 boys born for every 100 girls in the United States.[7]

According to another survey of American university students, both men and women strongly prefer a boy as their first child.[8] First-born children are usually preferred by parents with respect to education, employment in the family business and certain other social and economic aspects of life. This might lead to a secondary position for girls in the family and society. In addition, the growing trend to have only one child might further increase the imbalance of the sex ratio. Westoff and Rindfuss are of the opinion, however, that the imbalance of the sex ratio would be only temporary. The first surplus of male births would be followed by a surplus of female births to restore the balance. This phenomenon, however, may be projected in the United States according to the findings of the survey, but it may not be true in other cultures where boys are more strongly preferred to girls for various economic and social reasons.

Another problem connected with sex preselection is the tension in the family that might be caused when the spouses cannot agree upon the sex of their children.

A simple, inexpensive and universally applicable sex-preselection technique is not yet available. Its general use would be fraught with several ethical dilemmas. It would seem better, then, to prevent society from being burdened with new ethical problems by simply not making the new technique available for human beings. Scarce medical and financial resources might be better spent on other more useful projects.

Sex Change Operations

Every human being is born either male or female. Human hermaphrodites, who have both male and female external sexual organs at birth, biologically belong to one of the two sexes. They cannot both father and bear children. Hermaphroditism is a very rare occur-

rence, and surgical intervention can sometimes help the herma-
phrodite to live and function according to his or her chromosomal
sex.

Transsexuals are persons who are either male or female but
have a strong psychological desire to belong to the opposite sex. Various theories have been proposed to explain this phenomenon. Strong
arguments, however, have been advanced for the opinion that the
main cause of this disturbance is psychological in origin.

It was first suggested around 1930 in Europe that transsexual
persons could be helped by surgical intervention transforming them,
at least externally, into the desired sex, thus enabling them to live
either as female or male.

The first transsexual operation was performed in Europe in
1931. The first sex-change surgery, however, was made public only
in 1952. This was the case of the American George Jorgensen, a 26
year old man, who was transformed into a woman in a hospital in
Denmark. There was great publicity surrounding the event when he
returned to New York as Christine Jorgensen. Later, a film was produced about the transformation, *The Christine Jorgensen Story*.

Transsexual operations did not take place in America until
1966, when the Johns Hopkins Gender Identity Clinic was established. There are some forty gender-identity clinics now functioning
in America. About five thousand transsexual operations have been
performed in the United States during the past seventeen years.
Eight out of ten transsexual operations are from male to female, and
two out of ten from female to male. Recently, however, the number of
female to male operations has been increasing.[9]

The surgery is radical and complex. In the male it involves the
removal of the testicles, the amputation of the penis and the construction of an artificial vagina using parts of the penis. The Adam's
apple is reduced in size, and the breasts are enlarged by silicone implants. In the female to male operation the uterus and ovaries are removed, the breasts are reduced in size and an artificial penis is
constructed. At the present time, surgeons implant a small hydraulic
system in the artificial phallus that makes it capable of mimicking
erection. Both males and females receive sex hormones of their new
gender to develop the appropriate secondary sex characteristics. The
sex change is, of course, only external. The true biological sex is not

changed by the surgery. Neither the new "woman" can bear nor the new "man" father children.

Arguments for Sex Change Operations

Psychiatrists and operating surgeons justify the transsexual operations or "sex reassignments," as they are called in the profession, by pointing out that surgery is the only therapy available for certain transsexuals to help them lead an adjusted life. Surgery is chosen only when psychiatry fails to cure these persons. Nobody is accepted for sex-change surgery without a very thorough screening procedure aiming at determining whether or not a certain transsexual would benefit by the operation. Until it discontinued the operations, Johns Hopkins had been getting about 100 applications a year for the surgery. Of these, only five or six were accepted for the operation.

The Ethics of Sex Change Surgery

Is the argument for transsexual operations *ethically* valid? Is surgery a good "therapy" for psychological disorder? Are the patients really cured by the operation? It does not seem so. The chromosomal sex is not changed; only the genitals are transformed to resemble those of the opposite sex. The persons who undergo the operation are just fake females or fake males.[10] It is just in the patients' minds that their genders have changed. They live in a dream world that can hardly be called a good psychological adjustment to reality. Nevertheless, a number of moralists have agreed with the psychiatrists that transsexual operations are good therapy.[11]

Recently, however, persons involved in transsexual surgery have begun to dispute the benefits of these operations. As a result of certain studies on the therapeutic effects of sex-change operation, Johns Hopkins Hospital, the pioneer of sex-change operations, has stopped doing them.

The psychiatrist Jon K. Meyer, head of Johns Hopkins Sexual Behaviors Consultation Unit, published a study on the subject in the August 1979 issue of the *Archives of General Psychiatry*. He began collecting data on 100 individuals in 1971. He was able to follow the lives of fifty persons, fifteen of whom had sex-change surgery and thirty-five of whom had only psychiatric counseling therapy. Examining their life adjustment, he found that those who had received psychiatric therapy have had a better life adjustment than those who had the operation. Many of the severe psychological problems of the patients did not go away following surgery. Dr. Meyer and some of his colleagues are skeptical that anyone would benefit by the operation. Most of the applicants are young and going through certain developmental changes and crises. They seek a sex change as a "compromise formation," that is, they attempt to deal with their psychological problem by changing their sex. Another group of people apply for the operation in late middle age. These people, too, are going through developmental crises relating to the problems of death, retirement and other stress situations of late middle age. Psychiatry is more effective in dealing with all these problems than sex reassignment.[12] A drastic surgery that has only cosmetic value cannot be morally justified.

Johns Hopkins has stopped sex-change operations but other gender-identity centers are continuing the surgery.

Another ethical problem concerns the marriage of persons who have had transsexual surgery. They legally belong to their newly assigned sex and many of them marry persons who are actually of the same biological sex. Legally, these are not homosexual marriages, but in reality they are marriages between persons belonging to the same sex. A true marriage, however, is a union of opposite sexes. This has been the understanding of marriage in all ages among all nations. Transsexual marriages conflict with this universal acceptance of one of the main requirements of marriage, as well as with the natural law idea of the marriage union. Ethically they cannot be justified.

QUESTIONS FOR REVIEW AND DISCUSSION

1. How does nature select the sex of children? What are sex chromosomes, Y chromosomes and X chromosomes?

2. What is the ratio of the sexes at birth? How does nature keep the balance of sexes?

3. What methods are used to choose the sex of animal and human off-spring?

4. What is the ethics of sex preselection? What should public policy be if a simple and inexpensive method of sex preselection is invented?

5. Is it possible to change the sex of a person by surgery?

6. What reasons are proposed for the justification of sex change operations?

7. Does sex change surgery solve the psychological problems of transsexuals?

8. What is the morality of marriages concluded by persons whose sex was changed by surgery?

Notes

1. Cf. Population Reference Bureau, Inc., "Age-Sex Population Pyramids."

2. *The New York Times*, December 3, 1973.

3. "Delivering the Male: Sperm Separation Method Expected to Produce Higher Ratio of Boys." *Intercom*, September 1976, pp. 1, 6.

4. Ed Edelson, "The Sex Selection Game." *The Daily News*, June 27, 1982, p. 5.

5. "Study Says Women Show a Preference for Bearing Sons." *The New York Times*, November 25, 1977.

6. "World's Parents Prefer Boys, But Preselection for Sex Remains Elusive." *Intercom, The International Newsletter on Population*, January 1978, pp. 1, 6.

7. "Study of Sex Selection Gains." *The New York Times*, May 28, 1983, p. A 6.

8. Charles Westoff and Ronald R. Rindfuss, "Sex Preselection in the

THE MAIN ISSUES IN BIOETHICS

United States: Some Implications." *Science*, Vol. 184, May 10, 1974, pp. 633–636.

9. Jane E. Brody, "Benefits of Transsexual Surgery Disputed as Leading Hospital Halts the Procedure." *The New York Times*, October 2, 1979.

10. Thomas Szasz, "Male and Female Created He Them." *The New York Times Book Review*, June 6, 1979.

11. Cf. John F. Dedek, *Contemporary Medical Ethics*. New York: Sheed and Ward, 1975, p. 80.

12. "Sex Change Operations of Dubious Value." *Science*, Vol. 205, September 21, 1979, p. 1235.

14 Life and Death

Health is necessary for any person to lead a normal life and to be able to fulfill the duties derived from the universal existential goals of man and from one's particular circumstances in life. It follows from this necessity that man has a duty to take care of his health as well as is humanly possible. Where there is a duty, there is a corresponding right to the means by which one can fulfill one's duty. One of the main reasons for the establishment of civil society is the providing of the means, through social cooperation, by which one can fulfill his duties and assure his rights.

The Right to Health Care

No one can adequately care for his health alone. In ancient times the family looked after its sick members. With the advance of the science of medicine, however, the simple medical care a family can provide is not sufficient anymore. According to the *principle of subsidiarity* in social ethics, a larger social organization has to come to the help of an individual if the lesser group does not have the means to assist him. In our age, the lesser groups of charitable or voluntary associations are not adequately equipped anymore to care for the health of everybody. Consequently, the entire society has to do this in an appropriate way.

Insurance companies have been helpful in the past in providing health care for a fairly large segment of the population. Trade unions usually insist in their contract negotiations that their members be insured by the company for which they work. Nevertheless, there are 15 million to 18 million Americans who have no health insurance whatever, and 18 million more have only an adequate insurance that does not cover basic hospital bills, doctors' services and medical tests.

The United States spent $362 billion on health care in 1983. This was about 10.5 percent of the national gross product. The federal government is involved, at least partially, in the business of providing health care. In 1965, the government enacted the Medicare and Medicaid legislation as amendments to the Social Security Act. Medicare provides federal subsidy for the health care costs of Americans over the age of 65. The Medicaid program, on the other hand, is a joint federal-state program that pays the medical bills of needy persons. It is estimated that more than 25 million poor persons are helped annually by this program. As was mentioned previously, the Medicare program pays for kidney transplants and hemodialysis of persons of any age.

Since individuals alone can no longer carry the cost of health care when they become ill, the question emerges of how society should come to their aid. Should it be left to the individual to buy health care services on the free market with society just supervising that the rules of a free market are being observed, or should society provide equal access to health care delivery to every person in the nation?

Some countries have nationalized the health care delivery system; others, such as the United States, have a mixture of private insurance system and federal-state assistance programs. If health care distributions were left entirely to the dynamics of the free market, a great number of people would not be provided for adequately or at all. Society must, then, somehow get involved in the distribution of health care. First, it must be determined what kind of health care should be available to everybody when the need arises. Since health care costs are exorbitant, equal access to the most sophisticated and medically possible health care cannot financially be assured for everybody.

A certain consensus or policy decision must be reached concerning the allocation of medical and health resources. Recent terminology calls this policy decision *macroallocation* of scarce resources. It determines what portion of society's wealth ought to go into the treatment of what kinds of illnesses and into health care research. For instance, society now pays for kidney transplants in America. Should society pay for heart and liver transplants as well, for artificial hearts, etc.? Society must come to a prudent conclusion about what the basic minimum of decent health care is, care which everybody should have and which society can financially afford. This decision should be made by Congress or legally established institutions.

Once it has been decided that society, for instance, will pay for kidney transplants, further ethical questions must be faced. Not everybody who needs a kidney transplant can have it, because there are not enough kidneys available. This is the problem of *microallocation* of scarce medical resources. We have previously discussed this ethical dilemma in connection with organ transplants and artificial organs.

Macroallocation of Resources

We cannot examine or evaluate various plans for the macroallocation of health care delivery that are being proposed in America. That would go beyond the purpose of this work. It has to be pointed out, however, that there is no "free" health care. Society, that is, the taxpayer, has to pay for it. Today it is not the insurance companies who cover the expenses of health care; instead, they are covered by the premiums paid by the insured. It has to be decided, then, what the basic requirements of health care are that everybody should get and for which society is willing to pay. The available financial and medical resources must be taken into account lest an unrealistic goal be set that will bring disappointment and the breakdown of the system.

In addition, it has to be kept in mind that, in any system of insurance, costs tend to go up. This is explained by the fact that a "third" party covers the expenses. The auto mechanic or the physician tries to get as much for his services as he can. The car owner or the patient does not resist strongly enough to keep down the price because it is not he, but the "insurance company," that pays. People shortsightedly forget that it is they who ultimately must cover the expenses by the ever increasing automobile or health insurance premiums. Some control of the cost of health care must be built in, then, into any national health insurance plan. The interests of professional groups in a well-ordered society must be coordinated with the interests of the entire nation. Given the complexity of the problem and the opportunity for monetary gain by certain groups, it would be unrealistic to expect that social justice will prevail without proper legislation. Society has the right and the duty to regulate the work of professionals and of other groups when it becomes evident that the objective of the common good cannot be achieved without regulation.

Health care does not mean only looking after the sick; it involves the prevention of illness as well. It is a personal duty to develop a lifestyle that is sound and does not undermine one's health. As was discussed in Chapter 10, smoking, drinking to excess and using drugs can seriously harm one's health. Given the scientific data about the harmful effects of these practices, one cannot simply hold that no personal ethical questions are involved here. In addition to personal responsibility, civil society also has a duty to help citizens to stay away from these harmful substances. Governments have to see to it that their citizens are not exposed to the subtle but effective pressures of certain groups who are financially interested in inducing people to take up certain harmful habits.

Aging

No matter how well a person takes care of his health, inevitable *old age*, the decline of the vitality of his faculties, overtakes him almost imperceptibly. Although the human life span has increased considerably during the past decades, the problems and miseries of old age have not been eliminated. There are about 23 million people over sixty-five in the United States and their number is steadily growing. According to projections of demographers, 31 million people will be sixty-five or over by the year 2000. During the first three decades of the twenty-first century, their number will grow to 52 million. All developed countries are experiencing a similar increase in the life span of their citizens. There are two problems of old age that have special ethical relevance: the *care of the old*, and scientific research to further *prolong human life*.

Care of the Old

The presence of a proportionately large number of old people in society has been an incentive to the development of *gerontology*, a

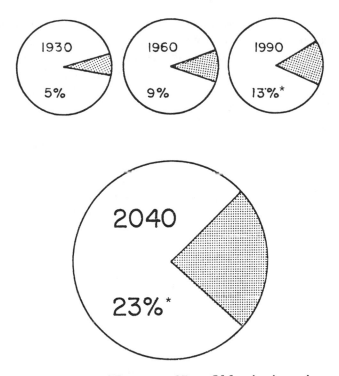

**Percentage of Persons 65 or Older in America
by Year**

The values marked with * are projections.

branch of science that deals with the social, psychological and medical problems of the aged, and which also investigates the causes and
mechanisms of aging. "Gray power," the large number of old voters,
was probably one of the reasons for the establishment of the National
Institute on Aging and for the initiating of many programs on aging
supported by government and private funds. One would hope, however, that the increasing interest in the welfare of the aged is not motivated only by "gray power" but is prompted much more by the
moral duty of helping our fellow human beings in their need.

In the past, in a predominantly agricultural society, old people
stayed with their children on the farm. Urbanization, however, has
created a special problem for the aged because many families, living
in cities, cannot adequately take care of them at home. The new en-

terprise of old-age homes and nursing homes purports to take over the responsibility of caring for the old. Some families, however, are perhaps too eager to transfer their responsibility to these agencies. There is undoubtedly a need for institutions to look after the old because many families, despite their best will, are incapable of giving adequate care to elderly parents. Unfortunately, many institutions have become an "industry," a money-making project, neglecting their assumed duty of giving loving and personal care to old people in their declining years.[1] Old people must be cared for either by their families or by institutions. There is no need to dwell on the duty of society to see to it that institutions do not exploit the helpless situation of the aged but that it force them to render the proper services they are pledged to.

Prolonging Life

People have always been interested in the secret of a long life. The Egyptians thought that eating garlic would help. Almost every age and every ethnic group has had some magic recipe. The alchemists were searching for the elixir of life, a substance or potion that would prolong life indefinitely.

Modern science, in a more sophisticated way, is trying to find the factor that controls the aging of human cells. An internal pacemaker or "clock of age" seems to stop growth in most animals at a certain age. Scientists think that cells have an intrinsic mechanism and program that limit their ability to divide.[2]

A number of theories have been proposed explaining the cause of senescence and the way of preventing the clock of aging from running down. For the time being, however, no breakthrough has been made in the understanding of the biological causes of aging or in the attempt to implant a biological pacemaker in man. Indefinite prolongation of life and physical immortality are not realistic ideas. Their time has not come. Nevertheless, a number of researchers, experimenting with animals, are making some progress in their attempt to discover the causes of aging.

No ethical objections can be brought against science trying to understand the process of aging. It would hardly be ethical, however, to prolong a man's life without maintaining his mental abilities so he can lead a fruitful life. The ethically acceptable elixir of life would be some low-cost, life-prolonging medicine that could keep old people in good health and active. While the social and economic consequences of substantial prolongation of human life cannot be overlooked, moral objections can be raised only against the extension of a life that would be useless.

A strange way of prolonging life or even of achieving immortality has been proposed by Robert C.W. Ettinger in his book, *The Prospect of Immortality.*[3] If sperm can be frozen and thawed without losing its fertility, why could not the whole human organism be frozen and brought back to life later? Ettinger believes that this can be done. The *cryonics movement* (*kryos* is Greek for icy cold), formed after the publication of his book, has a program for freezing human bodies immediately after death, to be thawed and revived when medicine will have found the cause of all illnesses, or at least of that disease of which a particular person to be revived had died. The Cryonics Society and its branches, which operate in many parts of the world, carry out the freezing-interment. The body is placed in liquid nitrogen and kept at the temperature of 196°C.

There is no scientific assurance, of course, that the idea of the Cryonics Society will ever work. It points, however, to a deep human problem, the reluctance to accept death as the end of our existence. The Egyptians embalmed their prominent dead to give them some form of immortality. All they could do was preserve the body in a mummified form for thousands of years. The cryonics movement promises to bring us back to life and give us physical immortality. Can modern man face death more realistically than by chasing after a worthless dream?

Care of the Dying

Man is the only living being who knows that he is going to die. There is nothing more certain in a person's life than *death*. Yet death is a fact of life he does not like to think or speak about. We may have conversations about business, sport, fashion, even sex, at a party, but death is a topic one must avoid in order not to upset the pleasant mood of a gathering. What we don't like to speak about we don't like to see either. In advanced societies, the critically ill and the dying are taken to hospitals, separated from the healthy, even from the family.

It is estimated that 80 percent of Americans die in institutions. The ratio was only 37 percent 30 years ago. Excepting the cases of sudden death, most people die in hospitals, in a strange environment. Machines are attached to them until the last moment; they become a case, a number for the doctor and hospital personnel. Relatives are allowed only short visits and they have to wait outside the hospital room to get information about their loved ones from a nurse. There seems to be a conspiracy not to tell the dying person that the end is approaching. The patient is fed false hope that everything will be all right. Most dying persons, however, know and feel that the end is at hand. They cannot talk to anybody about it, however, because nobody wants to speak about death. It is really cruel to abandon our loved ones this way just when they need us most.

The reality of death is an undeniable fact of life. It is a form of self-deception to avoid thinking or speaking about it. Our compassion and love demands that we improve our means of assistance to the dying, whether they are our relatives or members of our larger family of fellow human beings. Unrealistic and uncharitable ways of dealing with death and the dying seem to have reached their peak in the 1960's. Since then, more and more people have been coming to the realization that we have to change our attitude and do away with the "taboo" of death.

Centuries ago, in more simple times, death was not banished to a separated and closely guarded territory where only a few persons were allowed to see it. People died at home surrounded by the family, relatives and neighbors. Children saw their grandparents and parents die. As they were growing up, they became more and more familiar with the reality of death, their own death included. When their time came, they knew what to expect and what to do to get ready for the "big journey." Since most of the serious diseases were fatal, people were warned in time of their imminent death. It was the duty of the physician or of a friend to act as *nuntius mortis*, the messenger of death, to tell the patient that his earthly pilgrimage was coming to an end.[4] With the advent of modern medicine when people began to die in hospitals, physicians and relatives abandoned their role of telling the terminally ill that death was approaching. Instead of being frank with the dying, physicians and family members began to play a game of concealing the truth from their parents and loved ones. The insensitivity of the artificial and impersonal atmosphere surrounding the dying had grown to such a degree that a natural reaction to change the situation had to set in. Two decades ago, slowly but perceptibly, more and more persons began to speak and write about death and dying, first in Europe, then in America. Workshops on the problems of death and dying were organized and various movements and associations began to transform the impersonal and businesslike atmosphere surrounding the dying.

Hospitals originally were not established to assist the dying. They were instituted to cure diseases and return their patients to their usual surroundings. When the patient could not be cured, he was returned to the family to be taken care of at home in his final illness. It was a later development that saw terminally ill patients taken to hospitals to stay there until their death. Physicians and the hospital personnel were not well trained in assisting the dying. They don't seem to have sufficient preparation for this task even today. Not being able to restore a patient's health, the doctor can not do much beyond alleviating pain. He does not have the time and psychic energy to deal with the anxieties and fears of a dying person.

The Hospice Movement

A young British physician and former nurse, Dr. Cicely Saunders, pioneered an idea in the early 1960's to respond to the great need of caring for the terminally ill in a human, loving manner. She reached back to the Middle Ages for the idea of a *hospice. Hospes* is Latin for host, guest. Hence *hospitium*, a hospice, was a place where travelers were received as guests. The hospice was maintained by a community of people, usually a religious order, who cared for travelers and the sick. Dr. Saunders opened her modern hospice in 1966 in London and named it after St. Christopher, the patron saint of travelers. Here, she and her hospice community look after people whose earthly pilgrimage is nearing its end. It is not a hospital for curing people, but a home-like place where the terminally ill are cared for. Relatives, including children, are encouraged to come and stay with their loved ones as long as they can. Patients may walk around, chat with each other, eat their meals in the cafeteria if they prefer to and are able. The whole atmosphere is as home-like as possible. Even garden parties are held when the weather is suitable. Although staffed mostly by Catholic nuns and physicians, St. Christopher's Hospice is non-sectarian.[5]

St. Christopher's Hospice has become a model for the modern way of caring for the dying. The idea has spread to other countries and the movement is steadily growing. The first American hospice was established in New Haven, Connecticut in 1971. The volunteer program of Hospice, Inc., in New Haven, initially provided care for the dying at home with the support of the family and friends. This method was judged preferable to bringing the patient to a hospice building. In 1978, however, the New Haven hospice erected a forty-four-bed building as a backup for its home care.[6] It is estimated that there were 500 hospices in the United States in 1983 and many more were being planned. Some of these hospices are affiliated with hospitals; others are independent. A National Hospice Organization (N.H.O.) was formed in America that recognizes and guides groups in the establishment of hospices.

The clergy of all churches have always held that it was their special duty to minister to the dying. Most theological schools, however, failed to instruct the seminarians in the art of ministering to the dying. Fortunately, the situation has recently improved. Courses in death and dying are being offered on secular as well as theological campuses, and they are well attended. The popularity of workshops and seminars on this subject is an indication that they meet a genuine need to prepare people to deal with the human and religious aspects of death. As a result, a new discipline, *thanatology* (from the Greek word *thanatos*, meaning death), has come into existence. The Foundation of Thanatology, established in 1967 by four professors at Columbia University College of Physicians and Surgeons, is especially active organizing workshops and symposia as well as conducting research. It also publishes three journals dealing with the problems of death and dying. In addition, more and more scholarly books and articles on the philosophy and theology of death are being published.[7]

At the same time, the practical aspects of understanding and assisting the dying have been systematically explored. Dr. Elisabeth Kübler-Ross, a Swiss-born psychiatrist, now working in the United

States, has done universally acclaimed pioneering work in this field. In her book, *On Death and Dying*,[8] she identified five typical stages in the attitudes of the dying. They start with denial and isolation ("No, not me; it can't be true"), passing to anger ("Why me?"), bargaining ("God may be more favorable if I ask nicely"), depression, finally, and often then leading to acceptance. Understanding these typical phases, some or all of which the dying person may go through, helps us better to assist the dying.

Just observing a person die is an emotionally draining experience. All of us, but especially those who by their profession have to deal with the dying, need training to be able to help our fellow human beings in the last days of their life. Seminars and workshops on this subject are very helpful not only for professionals but for all of us, because sooner or later we all must go through the process of dying. The fear of death can be overcome only by facing it and preparing for it. This is not a "morbid" attitude; it does not destroy one's joy of living. On the contrary, the thought of death can have a healthy, balancing effect on one's life and value judgments. It can help us in choosing the priorities of life and in developing a genuine adjustment to the realities of a life in which the fact of death is a very important part.

Euthanasia

Modern hygiene and medicine have succeeded in prolonging man's life span, but finally all human beings must die. For many the length of the last illness may be stretched out. The dying process can even be expanded by the artificial sustaining of some of the vital functions. How long a terminal illness and the dying process should be drawn out or shortened by medical intervention is the subject of heated controversy in hospitals, the media and even the courts. The term euthanasia (Greek for "good death") is used in connection with this problem. Unfortunately, this term is often applied in a confusing way that only clouds the issue. It is important, then, that we clearly identify and evaluate the problems in this area.

Euthanasia, in general, means the causing of an easy or painless death to a patient who is dying of a terminal illness. Death can be induced by the patient himself without the knowledge and cooperation of any other persons. Or it can be effected by others at the request or with the consent of the patient. In all these cases it is called *voluntary euthanasia*. If death is induced against the will or without the knowledge of the patient, we speak of *involuntary euthanasia*.

This means by which death is brought about can be a positive intervention, for instance, an overdose of sleeping pills or other medication, or an injection of potassium chloride, that quickly causes death. Sometimes the term *mercy killing* is used for this kind of action. Usually, however, it is called *positive, or active, or active, or direct euthanasia*.

The omission of useless treatment, that is, not prolonging the dying process by life-sustaining machines, such as a respirator, is called *negative or passive or indirect euthanasia*.

Definitions may be helpful but they do not in themselves solve the moral problems involved. The question remains whether or not there is any difference, from the moral point of view, between the omission and the performance of an act. Can the omission of a treatment be equivalent to the killing of a patient? Does "pulling the plug" of the respirator directly kill the patient? Is the failure to put a patient on the machine, and letting him die, morally different from taking him off the machine? What is the moral difference here between omission and action, omission and commission? Is the patient or the doctor morally obliged to forestall death as long as possible? And by what means? All these questions must be examined.

The Ethics of Euthanasia

Involuntary positive or active euthanasia is the direct killing of a patient without his consent. May this ever be justified? An example of involuntary positive euthanasia was Hitler's eugenic euthanasia order that was issued in October 1939. (It was deceptively antedated September 1, 1939 as if it had been connected with the beginning of the military campaign against Poland.) More than eighty thousand German and Austrian mental patients, epileptics, feeble-minded and deformed persons were killed in gas chambers in 1940 and 1941. The law originally dealt only with small children but the age was raised later.[9] Another example is that of Napoleon. In 1799, Napoleon allegedly asked his military physican to administer euthanasia to soldiers infected with contagious diseases in order to stop their spread.

One would not expect that today any democratic country would order mass euthanasia of the unfit or the sick. What may occur today is the killing of deformed or abnormal babies soon after birth. Such a case attracted international attention in 1962. The Belgian, Mrs. Suzanne Coipel Van de Put, who had taken thalidomide during her pregnancy, gave birth to a daughter. The baby had no arms, only fingers coming out of her shoulders, her face was badly disfigured, and she had other abnormalities as well. Her mother and sister decided that the baby should not be allowed to live and Suzanne agreed with their decision. Soon after going home from the hospital, she mixed barbiturates with a honey-sweetened formula that killed the one week old baby. The police, tipped off by Mrs. Van de Put's suspicious pediatrician, arrested her and her accomplices. The defendants did not deny the fact of the killing. They argued only that it was a merciful act because it was better than letting the baby live. The prosecution argued for conviction on the charge of premeditated homicide but recommended leniency. The jury of twelve men reached a verdict in less than two hours of deliberation: not guilty. The fact that a public opinion survey ran ten to one in favor of the not guilty verdict indicates that a large number of people might agree with voluntary positive euthanasia, at least in circumstances similar to those of Mrs. Van de Put.[10]

The moral question is whether any individual or any public authority is allowed forcibly to take the life of an innocent person, whether that person is a baby, a crippled adult or someone who is old and senile. No valid argument can be offered to prove the position that an innocent person may be killed. Mrs. Van de Put, influenced by a very sad situation, may have been convinced in her conscience that she was doing the right thing in killing her baby. While we may sympathize with her plight, we cannot justify the deliberate killing of an innocent person. Many so-called thalidomide babies, incidentally, who were allowed to live and are now in their teens, cope fairly well with their handicaps and enjoy life. The fact that somebody is killed by painless means does not alter the basic injustice of his being forcibly deprived of the basic right to life. Executions, wherever the death penalty is retained, are becoming more "humane" in the way they are carried out. Nevertheless, the fact that life is taken does not change because of this. Several states in America have recently introduced lethal injection as the most "humane" method of executing condemned criminals.[11] It is not our concern here to discuss whether or not capital punishment can be justified. The point is that the method of killing does not change the basic fact of taking somebody's life. Whether a baby or an innocent old man is killed, and whether brutally or painlessly, does not alter the injustice of violating his or her basic right to life.

Courts in various countries, dealing with involuntary positive euthanasia, in most cases rightly maintain that it is equivalent to homicide. However, they take into account the mitigating circumstances and impose lenient sentences. In England, for example, Mrs. Elisabeth Wise admitted killing her nine month old blind and deaf daughter by mixing barbiturates with her milk. She was found guilty of manslaughter but was placed on only twelve months' probation.[12] In another case, the South African Dr. Alby D. Hartman admitted that he had given his 87 year old father a sodium pentathol injection to end his suffering caused by terminal cancer. Dr. Hartman was found guilty of homicide and was sentenced to one year's imprisonment, but the sentence was suspended.[13]

Voluntary positive euthanasia means that a patient procures for himself a painless death either without the cooperation of others or with the help of a physician or some other person. Death is not forced upon the patient but rather sought by him. In essence, this type of euthanasia is suicide or cooperation with others in committing suicide. It is a special case of suicide, however, because it is committed only to end unbearable pain or a "useless" life. This type of suicide was defended by certain philosophers in ancient times and was also practiced by certain nations. Socrates held that man was the property of the gods and that it would be unjust to destroy this property. A manifest necessity of dying, however, is a sign of the gods' permission to end one's life. Epicurus taught that the goal of life is to have pleasure, and that if life ceases to be pleasant, one is allowed to end it. Seneca argued that it is reasonable to end one's life to escape from the suffering and decay of old age and disease.[14] In ancient Greece and Rome hemlock was drunk by old people to put an end to their misery. Jewish and Christian tradition, on the other hand, has always been against any form of suicide. Nevertheless, there have been a number of writers and philosophers in the Christian era who have defended man's freedom to commit suicide—for example, David Hume in his *Essay on Suicide.*

In the United States and other countries various pro-euthanasia groups campaign for the legalization of voluntary active euthanasia under certain restricted conditions. In 1936, in Great Britain, the Voluntary Euthanasia Legislation Society sponsored the introduction of a bill in the House of Lords to legalize, in certain circumstances, voluntary active euthanasia of persons suffering from an incurable and painful disease. The bill, however, was defeated. Renewed attempts to pass a bill in Britain have failed so far. In 1950, over the signature of 2,513 prominent Britons and Americans, a petition was sent to the United Nations for an amendment of the Declaration of Human Rights to include the right of incurable sufferers to voluntary euthanasia. The amendment, however, was not accepted. In America, several state legislatures have discussed euthanasia bills but so far no voluntary positive euthanasia bill has been passed. Many nations, however, consider an incurably ill patient's request for euthanasia as a mitigating factor in a murder trial of those who comply with such a request. In Uruguay and Peru, the person who commits a homicide out of compassion and responding to the repeated request of an incurably ill patient is exempt from penalty.[15]

In the United States, the law forbids any person to help an incurably ill patient commit suicide. Any accomplice in such a suicide is charged with manslaughter. However, if he is found guilty, he usually receives a light sentence. An example is the case of Robert C. Waters, who gave in to his gravely ill wife's pleas and helped her commit suicide. He put his wife in the family car in their garage, kissed her good-bye, turned on the ignition key and let her die of carbon-monoxide poisoning. He pleaded *nolo contendere* to manslaughter charges and was sentenced to thirty months of probation and a fine of $3,750.[16]

In some cases the jury finds the defendant not guilty on the ground of temporary insanity. An example is the case of Lester Zygmaniak. His brother, George, who had been injured in a motorcycle accident and had become paralyzed from the neck down, begged him to put him out of his hopeless situation. Lester complied. He returned to the hospital with a sawed-off shotgun and killed his brother with one shot. The State of New Jersey pressed the charge of first degree, premeditated murder but the jury acquitted him on the ground of temporary insanity.[17]

Arguments for Voluntary Positive Euthanasia

The following arguments are usually proposed in favor of voluntary positive euthanasia.

1. The life of a person who is suffering from terminal illness has become useless to his family, to society and to himself. A healthy person may not commit suicide because he has many duties he is morally obliged to fulfill toward his family, society and his own development. A person suffering from a terminal illness, however, does not have any more duties to fulfill because he is simply incapable of doing anything for himself or others. Nobody gains anything by his continued life burdened as it is with suffering. It is reasonable, then, to hold that such a person is morally justified in terminating his own life either alone or with the help of others.

2. Faced with the conflict of two evils, one has to choose the lesser evil. The prolongation of useless suffering, however, is a greater evil than procuring immediate death that would come anyhow within a short time.

3. It is inhuman and unreasonable to keep a terminally ill patient alive when he does not want to live any longer and an injection could painlessly end his misery.

4. A person not believing in God can reasonably conclude that man is the master of his own life. Consequently, he may freely decide to terminate his own life either alone or with the help of others when he does not have any more duties to fulfill with regard to his family and society.

5. Man's freedom to act should not be restricted unless there are convincing arguments that his freedom to act comes into conflict with the rights of others. No such conflict can be shown, however, in the case of a terminally ill person. Consequently, such a man has the right to die as he chooses.

6. Voluntary positive euthanasia is an act of kindness toward one's family and society because the terminally ill person chooses not to burden them with his prolonged illness, expenses and all the work

of caring for a gravely ill patient. It is better to free scarce medical and financial resources to be employed in curing those who can lead a useful life.

7. Believers hold that God gave us our life. But it does not follow from this that we may not interfere in our lives, because God made us stewards of our lives. It is reasonable to assume, then, that God does not want us to suffer unnecessarily when we can easily terminate our misery.

Arguments Against Voluntary Positive Euthanasia

The following reasons are proposed against voluntary positive euthanasia.

1. Western tradition and theistic philosophy have been against the direct killing of oneself either alone or with the help of others. The main argument for this position is that God has direct dominion over human life. We are managers of our own lives but we do not own it; consequently, we may not destroy it. Just as we cannot decide the beginning of our own life, we may not determine its end either. Although this argument is valid on the basis of theistic philosophy, it will not convince everybody, possibly not even the believer. Can any other reason be adduced?

2. Throughout this work we used rational human nature as the criterion of morality. We have justified intervention in our nature when it was possible to prove that such an intervention is reasonable and serves to enhance our humanity. Is voluntary positive euthanasia a reasonable intervention in our nature? Is it a humanizing or a dehumanizing factor for the individual concerned and for society?

For what reason might a person ask his doctor to terminate his life? It is for the sake of liberation from pain, for man has a natural desire to live and to live without pain and misery. But it is not wise to stop pain by terminating life. It would be a more reasonable intervention to alleviate pain rather than to kill the patient. Modern medicine, fortunately, is quite effective in mitigating pain. Since it is possible to lighten pain, it seems to be more humanizing to do this rather than to administer a lethal injection.

3. When we speak of voluntary euthanasia, it is assumed that the patient freely asks for death. To avoid any misunderstanding or deception, the patient's request should be done in writing and signed in the presence of witnesses. Is a patient weakened by a terminal illness really in a position to evaluate his own situation and make a request with a clear mind? How can the witnesses testify that he made the request for his own death with sane and sound mind? Then there is the problem of freedom in making the decision. Can pressures be eliminated? The possibility of abuse is not imaginary but very real, given the conflicting financial and other interests of the patient's family and of society.

4. In addition, the exact time for the lethal injection must be determined. This looks very much like execution. Most countries did away with the death penalty because it is an inhuman form of punishment. It is cruel to tell a person the exact time of his death. Are we now willing to reintroduce execution by injection on a mass scale? As we previously mentioned, several American states have passed laws for execution by lethal injection. Granted there is a difference between the execution of a criminal and the killing of a patient, but the gruesome dehumanizing circumstances of the execution and of the killing are the same.

5. Further, who will administer the lethal injection? Will physicians accept the role of dispensing death instead of healing?[18] The person who injects the lethal substance need not be a physician, for the simple procedure can be easily learned by others. Will there be a new profession whose task it is to deliver death, just as there are professional executioners who are paid for their "service"?

6. Someone might object that this description of euthanasia is exaggerated or even sarcastic. I don't think so. The concrete performance of euthanasia must not be overlooked. Taking all the circumstances into account, voluntary positive euthanasia is dehumanizing; it is not "dying with dignity." The possibility of abuses connected with the legalization of euthanasia might increase old people's fear that a serious illness is an occasion for the family or authorities to dispatch them from this world. It is much more in conformity with human dignity to let nature take its course and to accept death when it comes through factors that are not in the power of man to control.

Passive Euthanasia, Letting People Die

Does it follow from the previous reasoning that everything possible must be done to prolong the life of a terminally ill patient? Are we allowed to omit or refuse useless treatment that does not cure a disease but only prolongs dying? The opponents of any form of euthanasia argue that we have the duty to keep terminally ill patients alive as long as modern medicine can because, from the moral point of view, omitting treatment is equivalent to killing a person. The generally accepted meaning of passive or negative euthanasia is the omission of a treatment. It means letting a person die of an incurable disease. It is the disease that terminates the patient's life and not a positive human intervention.

Passive euthanasia can be voluntary or involuntary.

Voluntary passive euthanasia is simply the refusal of treatment. The right of a competent patient to refuse treatment is generally recognized in the Western legal tradition. It is another question whether it is morally justifiable. As we have seen previously, we have a moral duty to take care of our health in order to be able to fulfill the obligations our state of life imposes upon us. Consequently, it would be wrong to refuse treatment that can restore our health. It would not be wrong, however, to refuse treatment that is useless, that cannot cure a terminal illness and that only prolongs the dying process.

Traditional moralists used to distinguish *ordinary* and *extraordinary means*. According to them, one is obliged to use ordinary means but not extraordinary ones in medical care. With the rapid advancement of medical technology, however, it is difficult to determine what ordinary and extraordinary therapies are. What was extraordinary a few years ago may be quite ordinary and customary today. Every well-equipped hospital has respirators and other machines to sustain life. Patients brought to a hospital in a critical condition are routinely put on these machines, which not long ago were not available. It seems that the terms *useless* and *useful means* better explain the moral duty of a sick person to apply them or not. It is not a rational procedure to employ useless therapies. A terminally ill and competent patient may morally refuse them. Sooner or later everybody must die; this is a fact of human existence that has to be integrated into our thinking and life. It is very much in accordance with human nature, the criterion of morality, not to try to forestall in vain what is inevitable, but rather to accept it.

Is there a natural right to die when our time comes? Rights are derived from natural needs and duties. People having a natural need for food, clothing and shelter are obliged to provide these necessities for themselves in cooperation with others. They have a moral claim, that is a natural right, to the means by which they can procure them. It follows from this that nobody is allowed to prevent them from pursuing this goal. Is death a duty? Can a right to die be derived from that duty? In a certain way, death is a part of human existence, as are the natural processes of birth, growth and mental development. These processes are imposed upon us by our nature; consequently, we have the right not to be prevented from fulfilling these natural duties. We do not like to speak about the obligation to die. Nevertheless, it is a necessity of human existence. Consequently, we have the right not to be subjected to futile therapies that try to forestall death when it is inevitably coming as a result of natural causes. In other words, *man has a right to accept death peacefully when the time for dying arrives.*

The Living Will

One of the practical difficulties of exercising the right to die is the fact that many patients are brought to a hospital in a critical condition that prevents them from revealing their will not to be placed on life-supporting machines which can prolong the dying process for a long time. The *living will* is intended to remedy this situation. The essence of the various forms of a living will is the request of a person directed to all who care for him to let him die and not be kept alive by artificial means when there is no reasonable expectation of recovery. The living will is signed in the presence of witnesses and copies of it are given to the intestate's family, physician, lawyer, clergyman and others who might get involved with the medical facility caring for him in a critical illness.[19]

California was the first state in America to pass a law giving legal force to the living will. Assembly Bill 3060, the so-called "Natural Death Act," was signed by Governor Edmund G. Brown, Jr., on

August 30, 1976 and came into force on January 1, 1977. By the end of 1983, following California's example, 14 other states had passed "natural death" legislation, assuring the right to die of terminally ill patients under carefully circumscribed legal conditions. Seventeen more states are considering such legislation.

The proposed aim of these laws is the defense of the patient's right to die. Do they achieve this goal? It seems that is true only in a limited way. The patient's right is restricted by the requirement to write a living will, which has to be renewed from time to time according to various stipulations (in California, for example, every five years) to remain valid. How many people will take the trouble to write and renew a living will to protect the natural right they already have without any legislation? In California, more than one hundred thousand right-to-die forms were distributed in 1978. But according to a California Medical Association report, they are not being used frequently. In late 1977, a sampling of 112 doctors, who ordered a total of more than eleven thousand copies, revealed that the right-to-die forms had been used only in sixty-seven cases.[20] Any critically ill patient brought to a hospital without a legally executed living will runs the risk of being subjected to useless treatment prolonging his dying. The attending physicians, being concerned about malpractice suits, will be reluctant not to start or to stop useless treatment in the absence of a legal document protecting them.

The main concern of any natural-death legislation should be to assure, in a practical way, the natural right of any person not to be subjected to useless treatment. The state does not grant this right to us. Rather, it is called upon to protect it, for we have it by our very nature. Richard A. McCormick and Andre E. Hellegers suggest that such a law should stipulate the duty of a physician to register a fatal disease with an appropriate hospital body, which would have the right to verify the fact. "A mentally competent patient could then request in writing that no extraordinary treatment be applied to him. When a patient was incompetent to act, by age or condition, the family could make a similar written request. Once the written request had been made, the legislation could stipulate that the treating physician was not subject to civil or criminal prosecution for omitting or ceasing treatment."[21]

In an article written in 1981,[22] McCormick softened his opposition to living-will legislation because "an overwhelming number of physicians. attorneys and legislators continue to believe an individual's statement has no legitimacy without a statutory enactment." I think that the major objections against living-will legislation are still valid. The aim of such legislation, to assure the natural right of a terminally ill patient to die in peace, is commendable and ethically justified. This goal, however, is not reached easily because the laws require a legal document, an executed will, before the decision of not applying life-supporting means has to be made. Future legislation should take into consideration this difficulty so that the commendable goal of living-will laws can be achieved easily. Robert M. Veatch drafted such a bill, which is based on the natural right of the terminally ill patient to refuse life-prolonging treatment.[23]

Involuntary passive euthanasia. Is it moral to let an incompetent terminally ill patient die by not starting or by stopping useless treatment? If a terminally ill and mentally competent patient may refuse useless therapy, the guardians of a mentally incompetent patient should have the same right. In the case of children, the right of parents to refuse useless treatment is recognized in medical practice. There have been a number of cases, however, where the hospital refused to accept the parents' decision and went to court to have treatment authorized.[24] The case of Karen Ann Quinlan attracted international attention. Miss Quinlan, twenty-one, collapsed and went into a coma on April 15, 1975. She did not recover consciousness and was being kept alive by a respirator and intravenous feeding for several months. Since there was no hope for her recovery, her parents asked the hospital to take her off the respirator. When the request was refused by her doctors, the parents went to court and asked the judge to be permitted to turn off the life-sustaining machine. New Jersey Superior Court Judge Robert Muir, Jr., on November 10, 1975 rejected the petition of Karen's father. The case was appealed to the New Jersey Supreme Court, which on April 1, 1976 ruled unanimously that the respirator could be removed. Karen was taken off the respirator but continued to breathe on her own without coming out of the coma. At the time of this writing, she is still in a comatose state in a New Jersey nursing home and is being kept alive only by feeding.

There are two questions with respect to involuntary negative euthanasia:

1. Is it morally right in the case of a terminally ill, mentally in-

competent patient not to start useless treatment or to stop such therapy by turning off the machine, or "pulling the plug" as it is popularly called?

2. Who is entitled to make such a decision?

It follows from our previous discussion that it is morally right to allow every such patient to die. It is contrary to rational human nature to apply useless means. In an address to a group of anesthesiologists, on November 24, 1957 Pope Pius XII emphasized man's right to die in dignity. He used the then customary terms, ordinary and extraodinary means, and said rightly that there is no obligation to use extraordinary means to preserve life.[25]

On May 5, 1980, the Vatican issued a document entitled *Declaration on Euthanasia*. It repeats the traditional Catholic doctrine explained by Pope Pius XII and then applies it to contemporary conditions. It declares:

> . . . one cannot impose on anyone the obligation to have recourse to a technique which is already in use but which carries a risk or is burdensome. Such a refusal is not the equivalent of suicide; on the contrary, it should be considered an acceptance of the human condition, or a wish to avoid the application of a medical procedure disproportionate to the results that can be expected, or a desire not to impose excessive expense on the family or the community. (See the full text of the document in Appendix IV.)

Who is entitled to decide to let terminally ill patients die without prolonging the dying process? According to the order of nature, such a right belongs to those who have the duty to care for the person. These are the immediate family, parents, spouses, children, close relatives. This right does not belong to public authorities, for citizens are not the wards of the state. According to the principle of subsidiarity, public authorities have such a duty and right only when there are no competent family members or relatives to exercise this right.

The rights of parents to withhold treatment in the case of minors is generally recognized in America. There does not seem to be a clear policy, however, concerning mentally incompetent adults. The Massachusetts Supreme Court, in its ruling on November 28, 1977, referring to the case of Joseph Saikewicz, stated that the Probate Court has this authority. Such a decree, if it were recognized nationwide, would deprive families and those directly caring for the patient of their natural right to make this decision. The court would arrogate the right it does not have, and in addition it would be incapable of exercising it. There are so many such cases every day that the courts would become hopelessly cluttered. In the meantime all dying patients would be subjected to the torture of being placed on life-sustaining machines.[26]

The Massachusetts Supreme Court clarified later that a court order is not required in all cases. But it insisted that, ultimately, the legal validity of a decision made on behalf of a terminally ill patient can only be judged by the courts. In order to avoid the necessity of going to the courts, carefully drafted "Natural Death" legislation should clearly protect the natural right of the family and of all those who are directly involved in care of the dying.

The Ethics of Action and Omission

The position that passive euthanasia, that is, the withholding or discontinuing of useless treatment, is morally justified comes under attack from two sides. The pro-euthanasia group argues that passive euthanasia does not differ from active euthanasia. It does not matter whether a person dies as a result of a lethal injection or by the turning off of a respirator. The result is death in both cases. If passive euthanasia is morally justified and legally allowed, the argument continues, active euthanasia is equally justified and should be legalized. Certain anti-euthanasia people, similarly equating the two kinds of euthanasia, hold the opposite position. Since there is no difference between passive and active euthanasia, both are immoral and both should be outlawed. Consequently, a dying person should be kept on life-supporting machines indefinitely.

The controversy here is about the moral difference between *action and omission*, commission and omission. According to sound ethical principles, we are never allowed to perform an act that directly violates the right of others, but we are not always obliged to perform an act that would save others from injury. Not every omission is excusable, of course. The policeman omitting to patrol a street bears responsibility, to a certain degree, for a burglary he could have prevented. An ordinary citizen, however, is not obliged to get up at night to patrol the streets. If we are duty-bound to perform an act we have omitted, the results may be imputed to us. As we have seen, there are good reasons to hold that we are not obliged to apply useless therapy. The omission of such a therapy, then, is at least morally indifferent. In active euthanasia, or mercy killing, it is the lethal injection or some other means that directly kills the patient. In passive euthanasia, on the other hand, it is the disease, that is, a natural cause, that terminates the life of the patient. The omission of therapy is not direct killing.

Some physicians do not have any particular difficulty about not starting a useless therapy, but they are reluctant to stop it once it has been started. However, it is not turning off the respirator that kills the patient but the disease. Pulling the plug is not equivalent to giving a lethal injection.

The Swiss Academy of Medical Sciences discussed this distinction between passive and active euthanasia. The guidelines of the Academy were drafted by a committee of seventeen experts, which included a jurist and Catholic and Protestant moralists. The committee's work was prompted by the case of Dr. Urs Peter Haemmerli, head physician of a hospital in Zurich, where several comatose old patients were given water instead of intravenous nourishment. The Academy stated that "renunciation of therapy or its limitation to alleviate suffering is medically justified if putting off death would mean for the dying an unreasonable prolongation of suffering and if the basic condition has taken an irreversible course." On this basis Dr. Haemmerli was acquitted of homicide charges. He remarked that according to these guidelines, the artificial feeding of Karen Ann Quinlan could be stopped.[27]

Truth-Telling and the Dying

Patients cannot make a well-informed decision about whether or not to refuse treatment unless doctors *tell them the truth about their illness*. It is an unpleasant task to tell a patient that his illness is terminal. One can understand why many doctors and nurses shirk this duty. They may inform the patient's family and then both the family and the doctors begin to play a game with the patient, concealing the truth and offering false hope. Is it morally obligatory to tell patients the truth or may the truth be concealed? According to solid ethical principles, everybody has a right to the truth unless he has forfeited his right to it or indicates that he does not want to hear the truth or does not want to be informed. A patient may indicate in some way that he does not want to hear the truth about his illness. In this case, the doctor has no moral obligation to inform him. Otherwise he owes the truth to his patient. The Patient's Bill of Rights, approved by the American Hospital Association's House of Delegates on February 6, 1973, affirms: "The patient has the right to obtain from his physician complete information concerning his diagnosis, treatment, and prognosis in terms the patient can be reasonably expected to understand. When it is not medically advisable to give such information to the patient, the information should be made available to an appropriate person in his behalf. He has the right to know by name the physician responsible for coordinating his care." It seems to me that the physician should not easily assume that truthful information would be harmful to his patient. Non-communication could be actually more harmful than the truth.

According to recent reports, there has been a major change in the attitude of doctors with respect to informing their patients of their illness. A questionnaire was submitted to doctors in 1961 to indicate their preference for telling their patients or keeping secret from them the fact that they had cancer. Ninety percent of the responding physicians expressed a preference for not telling their patients that they had cancer.[28] In 1977, a similar questionnaire was submitted by the University of Rochester Medical Center. Ninety-seven percent of the doctors who responded expressed a preference for truthfully informing their patients of a cancer diagnosis.[29] According to various surveys, the overwhelming majority of patients want to be informed about the nature of their illness, even if it is terminal.

We owe it to our fellow human beings to be truthful with them all the time, but especially when they are approaching the end of their earthly pilgrimage. We ourselves don't want less than compassionate sincerity in the last moments of our lives.

QUESTIONS FOR REVIEW AND DISCUSSION

1. What reasons can you propose to prove everybody's right to adequate health care? Whose duty is it to deliver health care? What is the principle of subsidiarity?

2. Explain the concepts of macroallocation and microallocation of scarce resources.

3. Is it feasible to guarantee everybody the best possible health care? What kind of health care should be given to everybody?

4. Who is obliged to take care of the elderly—their families or society? Why?

5. Describe the attitude of modern man toward death and dying. What are the causes of this attitude?

6. Describe the method and practices of hospices in caring for the dying.

7. Describe the concept and the different kinds of euthanasia.

8. Explain and evaluate the reasons advanced for and against the justification of voluntary positive euthanasia.

9. Evaluate the reasons given for the justification of voluntary passive euthanasia.

10. Is living-will legislation effective to guarantee the right of the terminally ill to die without uselessly prolonging the dying process?

11. In the case of a terminally ill incompetent patient, is it the next of kin or society who is entitled to make the decision to stop useless medical treatment?

12. Is the seriously ill person entitled to the truth, or may the concealment of the nature of his illness ethically be justified?

Notes

1. Robert L. Kane and Rosalie A. Kane, "Care of the Aged: Old Problems in Need of New Solutions." *Science*, May 26, 1978, p. 913.
2. Jean Marx, "Aging Research (II): Pace-makers for Aging?" *Science*, December 27, 1974, pp. 1196–1197.
3. Robert C.W. Ettinger, *The Prospect of Immortality*. New York: Doubleday, 1964.
4. Cf. Philippe Aries, "Death Inside Out." *The Hastings Center Studies*, May 1974, pp. 3–13.
5. Cf. David Dempsey, *The Way We Die*. New York: McGraw-Hill, 1975, pp. 233–237.
6. "A Better Way of Dying." *Time*, June 5, 1978, p. 66.
7. Cf. Ladislaus Boros, *The Mystery of Death*. New York: Herder and Herder, 1965.
8. Elisabeth Kübler-Ross, *On Death and Dying*. New York: Macmillan, 1969.
9. Paul Hoffman, "Jesuit Scans Origin of Hitler's Killings." *The New York Times*, March 25, 1975.
10. "Thalidomide Homicide." *Time*, November 16, 1962, p. 67.
11. Cf. Patrick Malone, "Death Row and the Medical Model." *The Hastings Center Report*. October 1979, pp. 5–6.
12. *Daily News*, October 26, 1974.
13. *The New York Times*, March 22, 1975.
14. Lucius Annaeus Seneca, *Ad Lucilium Epistolae Morales 2*, Epist. 70.
15. O. Ruth Russell, *Freedom to Die*. New York: Dell Publishing Co., 1975, p. 237.
16. UPI, January 13, 1975.
17. *The New York Times*, November 6, 1973.
18. Cf. Edith Summerskill, "On the Voluntary Euthanasia Bill of 1969," in Marvin Kohl, ed., *Beneficent Euthanasia*. Buffalo: Prometheus Books, 1975, pp. 204–208.
19. Cf. *A Living Will*, prepared by the Euthanasia Educational Council, 250 West 57th Street, New York, N.Y. 10019.
20. *The New York Times*, February 5, 1978.
21. Richard A. McCormick and Andre E. Hellegers, "Legislation and the Living Will." *America*, March 12, 1977, p. 213.
22. John J. Paris and Richard A. McCormick, "Living-Will Legislation, Reconsidered." *America*, September 5, 1981, p. 86.
23. Robert M. Veatch, *Death, Dying, and the Biological Revolution*. New Haven: Yale University Press, 1976, pp. 199–201.
24. Cf. Richard A. McCormick, "To Save or Let Die." *America*, July 13, 1974, pp. 6–10.
25. Acta Apostolicae Sedis, 49 (1957), pp. 1031–1032.
26. Cf. Richard A. McCormick and Andre E. Hellegers, "The Specter of

Joseph Saikewicz: Mental Incompetence and the Law." *America*, April 1, 1978, pp. 257–260.

27. "Swiss Issue Guidelines on 'Passive Euthanasia.'" *Intercom*, May 1977; "Swiss Medical Academy Issues Guidelines for Doctors to Discontinue Treatment for Dying Patients." AP, April 20, 1979.

28. Donald Oken, M.D., "What to Tell Cancer Patients." *The Journal of the American Medical Association*. Vol. 175, April 1, 1961, pp. 1120–1128.

29. *The New York Times*, February 26, 1979.

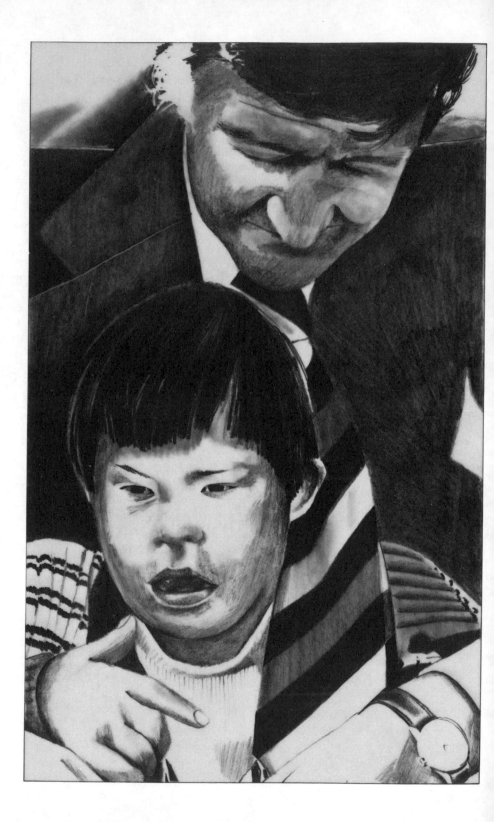

15   The Ethics
of Infant Euthanasia*

This chapter deals with infant euthanasia, a topic widely debated in America in recent years. Its purpose is to examine the *ethical* questions of:

(a)   letting defective newborns die by omitting or withdrawing their treatment;
(b)   terminating their life by direct intervention, that is, the passive and active euthanasia of defective newborns.

Although legal questions and court decisions will be referred to, the *legal* matters as such will not be the direct concern of this chapter.

Cases

On June 23, 1981 Dade County Circuit Judge Ralph Ferguson ruled that surgeons and other physicians should do what they could to assist Elin Daniels, a ten-day-old deformed baby, to survive. The parents opposed surgery because the baby was "a monstrosity whose death would be a benefit." Variety Children's Hospital, however, argued that surgery was necessary because without the operation the baby could fall victim to a fatal infection.[1] After the ruling, the par-

*This chapter originally appeared in *Thought* in a slightly different form. It is reprinted, by permission of the publisher, from *Thought*, Vol. 57, No. 227 (December 1982) pp. 438–448. Copyright 1982 by Fordham University Press.

ents signed a consent form allowing the operation. A three-hour operation was then performed on Elin on June 24.

Elin suffers from *spina bifida* or myclomeningocele. Spina bifida is a neural tube defect. The neural tube, which eventually forms the brain and spinal cord, in some rare instances does not close competely during the early stages of its formation. The hole in the spine leaves the spinal cord protruding from the back. The results of this defect are "Paralysis or weakness below the lesion. Incontinence of bowel and bladder. Hydrocephalus (in 65% to 75% of the patients)."[2] Hydrocephalus is caused by the accumulation of cerebrospinal fluid in the cavities of the brain and results in brain damage.

Neural tube defects affect about two out of every 1,000 Caucasian babies born, that is, about 6,000 of the three million babies born in the United States each year. Antibiotics and new techniques introduced in the 1950s have increased the survival of these babies to some 40%. Some researchers suggest that the survival rate can reach 90%. "Untreated, Elin had a 20% chance of survival during the next two years, according to Dr. Irwin Perlmutter, a neurosurgeon. With surgery . . . she might live six or eight years. Dr. Robert Lawson, another neurosurgeon, said that with treatment Elin is likely to live to adulthood."[3]

The severity of impairment of babies with spina bifida varies. Newly developed surgical and therapeutic procedures can save the life of these babies but the impairments remain life-long and in many cases, they are quite serious.

Spina bifida is often presented as a prototype of birth defects. It clearly points out the ethical dilemma of whether such defective newborns should be treated or rather should be allowed to die. Spina bifida, however, is by no means the only kind of birth defect that produces these ethical dilemmas for parents and physicians alike.

Some cases of defective infants reach the courts and gain wide publicity through the media. Such was the case of the son of Mr. and Mrs. Robert B. T. Houle, of Westbrook, Maine. He was born with many deformities and organic defects. He had no left eye, his entire left side was malformed, he could not be fed by mouth because of a tracheal esophageal fistula which necessitated intravenous feeding. In addition, air leaked into his stomach instead of going to his lungs. He developed pneumonia, had poor circulation and his condition was deteriorating rapidly. The parents requested that life-sustaining measures be halted and refused to give permission for surgery to remove the tracheal esophageal fistula that was the immediate threat to his survival. Officials of the Maine Medical Center, however, filed suit against the parents. Justice David Roberts appointed a Portland lawyer to be the guardian of the infant with power to consent to the operation. The subsequent surgery, however, could not save the life of the infant. He died on February 24, 1974 in the Maine Medical Center.[4] Appointing the guardian for Baby Houle, Justice Roberts said "the most basic right enjoyed by every human being is the right to life itself."[5]

Problems of Non-Treatment

The right to life is undoubtedly a basic human right. Nevertheless, it can be legitimately asked whether there is an affirmative duty to do everything humanly possible to protect human life or whether there are instances when non-treatment of severely defective newborns is ethically justified.

Richard S. Schweiker, Secretary of the Department of Health and Human Services, on May 18, 1982, warned hospitals that they could be denied federal funds if they withhold treatment from babies with birth defects or other handicaps. "In the aftermath of the recent death of a handicapped newborn child in Bloomington, Ind., there has been a great deal of justified public concern about the protection of newborn infants with birth defects and their right as human beings to receive appropriate medical treatment." he said.[6]

The case mentioned in the Secretary's statement referred to a newborn boy, identified in court records only as "Infant Doe." He was born with Down's syndrome and an incomplete esophagus which could be corrected by surgery to enable food to reach his stomach. The parents denied permission for the surgery and the Indiana Supreme Court refused to order the surgery. The Monroe County Deputy Prosecutor and a law professor, however, were going to fly to Washington to ask the Supreme Court for an emergency injunction on the boy's behalf. But the infant died before they were able to fly to Washington. In spite of the fact that two couples had offered to adopt "Infant Doe," the baby was starved to death.[7]

In 1973, the Supreme Court established an almost unrestricted

legal right to kill defective fetuses. It seems that the Indiana Supreme Court's decision was only an application and extension of this
legal right to the defective newborn. It is encouraging to see, however, that other courts have defended the right to life of the defective
newborn and that the Health and Human Services Secretary issued
a warning against denying "appropriate medical treatment" to infants with birth defects. The conflicting court rulings, nevertheless,
indicate the *confusion about the right to life of defective infants*, what
obligations this right imposes upon those who must care for these infants and what the ethically appropriate medical treatment is in
their case.

The ethical dilemma to treat or not to treat an infant with birth
defects is the result of medical progress. In the past, medicine could
not do much for a seriously defective newborn. Most of them died as
a result of their biological deficiencies. The history of infanticide suggests that many defective infants were abandoned or simply killed by
their parents. The killing of even healthy babies was condoned or legally accepted in several ancient civilizations. It was practiced even
in Rome where many human rights were otherwise protected by a
well-structured legal system. Toward the end of the 19th century pediatric medicine developed incubators and tube feeding techniques
that were instrumental in saving many premature and weak newborns.[8]

Contemporary medicine dramatically improved neonatal intensive care. It can save the life of many seriously defective infants.
Many premature babies survive now without physical and mental
damage. The same advanced techniques, however, save also the
lives of infants with serious birth defects who will then live with
physical and mental handicaps "often for many years without hope
of ever having an independent existence compatible with human
dignity."[9]

The possibility of saving the life of severely handicapped infants
caused ethical problems for physicians and parents alike. Should defective children be saved or may they be allowed to die? What practical and ethical principles should be applied for treatment or non-
treatment of these infants?

Dr. Raymond Duff testified before Senator Edward M. Kennedy's Health Subcommittee that in his opinion several thousand se-

verely handicapped babies were left to die each year in America. The infants were left to die after consideration by both doctors and parents because the "prognosis for meaningful life was extremely poor or hopeless."[10] Doctors and parents, however, do not always agree, and—as was seen in some of the previously quoted instances—some hospitals go to court to assure treatment of the newborn against the will of the parents. It is surmised that in many instances it is rather the fear of malpractice suits than ethical considerations that motivate the hospitals to initiate a lawsuit. My opinion would not be so negative in this regard, for most physicians consider it their duty to save lives and it is a challenge to their professional skill to succeed in their life-saving task.

Abortion of Defective Fetuses

Some persons would like to eliminate the ethical problem of choosing between treatment and non-treatment of defective infants by preventing their birth. Progress in the technique of screening for birth defects and liberal abortion laws have greatly reduced the number of defective newborns. Dr. Lorber recommends abortion in the case of spina bifida to prevent the difficult decision of choosing between treatment and non-treatment of infants born with this defect. "Already we can diagnose spina bifida in a large proportion of cases at an early enough stage of pregnancy so that the termination can be carried out. It is hoped that the routine use of . . . newer, yet unknown techniques will lead to a substantial reduction in spina bifida births and that in some ten years' time selection will be only of historical interest."[11]

The killing of fetuses with birth defects would be indeed a radical elimination of the hard choice whether or not to treat defective newborns. This procedure, however, does not eliminate the ethical question of directly killing the child before birth instead of letting it die after birth. In addition, mass screening of pregnancies could lead to coercion of abortion. In England already about 50 percent of pregnant women are screened.[12] There are no statistics as to how many of these women were carrying defective fetuses and how many of them opted for abortion or were persuaded to accept it. There are no statistics either as to how scrupulous medical and public authorities were in avoiding moral or financial pressures to choose abortion. One could conclude from Dr. Lorber's opinion that at least some doctors try to persuade the pregnant woman to opt for abortion.

According to studies of spontaneous abortion, a very high percentage of the fetuses are seriously defective. "For example, chromosomal defects are twenty times more frequent, and spina bifida (neural tube defects) is six to eight times more frequent in a population of spontaneous abortuses than in the live-born group . . . Thus nature discards most of the seriously defective fetuses."[13]

A certain number of defective fetuses, nevertheless, reach viability and those who care for them will have to make the decision of whether or not to save their lives in spite of their physical and mental handicaps.

Principles for Treatment or Non-Treatment

The moral law obliges us to perform actions that are clearly our duty to do under our specific circumstances, and to abstain from immoral actions. In ethics, these two kinds of duties are called *affirmative and negative duties*. Ethics considers the omission of a duty as an act even if the person does not do anything because it is the act of the will not to perform a certain act that is the subject matter of the ethical inquiry. *Omissions are imputed to us if we are bound to perform the act omitted.* A person who does not pay his taxes cannot excuse himself by saying that he did not do anything, because it was his duty to declare and pay his taxes.

Non-treatment, then, may be ethically wrong if there was a duty to treat the patient. It seems that some persons caring for defective newborns consider the omission of feeding or of corrective surgery, for instance, ethically less objectionable than the act of directly killing the infant. According to reports in the media the Siamese twins born a year ago in Danville, Ill., were not fed. "In the nursery, a terse message was placed on the twins' chart: 'Do not feed in accordance with parents' wishes.' "[14]

Dr. John M. Freeman mentions a practice of not properly feeding defective infants. The children are highly sedated and are fed only

"on demand." "With the gentle help of sedation and feeding on demand . . . children starve to death without making too much noise."[15]
Starving somebody to death when he could be fed can hardly be taken
as an innocent omission of an act. It is rather a deliberate termination of the life of a human being. It is puzzling that some persons are
unequivocally against the active killing of defective infants and do
not perceive the omission of feeding or of medically useful treatment
of the defective infant as equivalent to killing them. It was certainly
wrong to kill millions of Jews and Christians in gas chambers. But it
would not have been less wrong to starve them to death. Whether a
person is killed by active or passive means, it does not make any difference from the ethical point of view.[16]

*The crux of the question is, then, to determine when and under
what circumstances is the omission of an act ethically justifiable.*
When and under what circumstances is it not a duty to treat a defective or sick infant and let him die? Many defective newborns died in
the past because there was no effective treatment available. Since
about 1950, however, many of these children can be saved and can
live a good number of years notwithstanding some burdensome
handicaps they have to carry their entire life. Antibiotics and new
developments in infant surgery can save defective infants. The price
of survival can be enormous in suffering and inconvenience for the
patients themselves, for the families involved, and in medical expenses. In 1975, a pediatric surgeon estimated that the cost of spina
bifida treatment of one patient was $250,000 or $300,000.[17]

Would it be in the interest of the defective newborn and of the
family involved to let him die? When is it ethically justifiable to let
a newborn die and not to subject him to "heroic" and excessive treatment? The choice may be agonizing for those who have the responsibility to make the decision. As pediatric medicine improves
treatments for saving or prolonging the life of the defective infant,
the number of symposia, conferences, books and articles dealing with
this ethical dilemma is steadily increasing.[18] The main concern of
these writings is the establishment of guiding principles for helping
the selection of babies who may be allowed or should be allowed to
die, and of those who should be treated. As it happens in most controversial questions, there is no unanimity in the positions and responses given to this problem.

Useful and Useless Means

What are the basic ethical principles that can help us in this choice? In general, the purpose of medical intervention is to cure the patient or, at least, help him live with his impairment. Medical intervention in the case of defective babies must be a *useful means* for curing some of the baby's disorders or offer reasonable hope of benefit for strengthening the vital functions of the newborn so that further development and improvement will be possible. It is unreasonable to apply *useless means*. Nourishment is a basic necessity for maintaining and developing any vital functions. Consequently, corrective surgery that would restore the possibility of feeding the baby is an ethically mandatory medical intervention unless the infant is already dying of other impairments as well. Thus the esophagus of "Infant Doe," of Indiana, whose case was previously mentioned, should have been surgically corrected so that food could have reached his stomach. The fact that he had Down's Syndrome was not a justifying reason to terminate his life by starvation. A baby has the right to life and the parents have the duty to protect this right by means which are effective and are normally available to them.

It has to be pointed out here that we used the terms "useful" and "useless" means instead of the terms "ordinary" and "extraordinary" means. The reason for the former terminology is to avoid confusion and misunderstandings. For the average layman, the term "ordinary means" signifies what doctors customarily do. "Extraordinary means," on the other hand, signifies some unusual or experimental therapy not readily available in all hospitals. The popular opinion would hold, then, that the application of ordinary means is ethically obligatory and one may omit only the use of extraordinary means. The fact is, however, that sometimes the use of ordinary, that is, customary, means is useless and consequently, it is not reasonable or ethically obligatory to apply them.

Excessive Hardship

One has to consider also the *excessive hardship* that the application of the customary means would impose on the patient and on those who are involved in caring for the patient. Traditional natural-law ethics states that an affirmative duty admits of excuse because of impossibility or excessive hardship. No negative natural duty must be violated, however, in connection with the omission of an act that would involve excessive hardship. Thus no defective infant may be directly killed in order to avoid the excessive hardship of caring for him. It is a negative duty never to kill an innocent person. It follows from this that one may not kill a person to free him from suffering or inconvenience either.

Nevertheless, it may be difficult to apply the previous theoretical norm to concrete cases for judgments are based on conjectures of the efficacy of therapies and of the suffering and inconvenience caused by them. A subjective element may easily slip into the consideration of the application of the objective norm in concrete cases. When medical experts judge that the efforts to save the life of a defective infant are hopeless, the parents have nothing else to rely on in their decision than the opinion of competent physicians. In other cases, however, some doctors may be in doubt as to the effectiveness of a certain medical intervention and the excessive hardship this creates for the infant and the parents. In doubtful cases when the doubt is about a fact (*dubium facti*) and not about the existence of a duty (*dubium iuris*), one has to choose the safer course, that is, one has to make an attempt to save the infant's life.

Traditional Doctrine

Pope Pius XII in an address on November 24, 1957 stated that one is not obliged to use extraordinary means in medical interventions to save or prolong one's life. "But normally one is held to use only ordinary means—according to circumstances of persons, places, times and cultures—that is to say, means that do not involve any grave burden for oneself or another. A more strict obligation would be too burdensome for most men and would render the attainment of the higher, more important good too difficult. Life, health, all temporal activities are in fact subordinated to spiritual ends."[19] The Sacred Congregation for the Doctrine of the Faith on May 5, 1980 issued a document entitled *Declaration on Euthanasia*. The document states that in the past moralists held that " . . . one is never obliged to use 'extraordinary' means . . . which as a principle still holds good." Nevertheless, according to the document, this reply "is perhaps less clear today by reason of the impression of the term and the rapid progress made in the treatment of sickness. Thus some people prefer to speak of 'proportionate' and 'disproportionate' means."[20] One has to judge, then, whether the means is proportionate or is out of proportion as to the results that can be expected. In order to facilitate the application of this norm the *Declaration* adds the following qualifications: " . . . one cannot impose on anyone the obligation to have recourse to a technique which is already in use but which carries a risk or is burdensome. Such refusal is not the equivalent of suicide; on the contrary, it should be considered as an acceptance of the human condition, or a wish to avoid the application of a medical procedure disproportionate to the results that can be expected, or a desire not to impose excessive expense on the family or the community."[21]

The *Declaration* speaks of the decision of an adult patient. But the same principles can be applied to the persons who are entitled to make a decision in the care of an infant. A caution has to be added, however. The decision-makers must honestly strive to be as objective and sincere as humanly possible in their evaluation of the case. They must not be unduly motivated by their personal interests and comfort.

Excessive Expenses

The Vatican document includes *excessive expenses* in the category of disproportionate means that would be imposed upon the family or the community. Can the value of human life be measured by money? One frequently hears the objection that when it comes to saving a life, expenses should not be considered at all because human life is priceless. The question, however, is more involved than a simple monetary valuation of human life. Money pays for the scarce medical resources and scarce expert services. Expenses in many cases are so high that they can be paid only by the community. The principle of *distributive justice* must be invoked here to determine a certain *order of priorities* since not all medical or other kinds of needs can be satisfied. This is the reality of the human condition. Thus excessive expenses may become a practical and moral impossibility either for the family or for the whole community. A theoretical possibility of applying a great amount of scarce resources to one or another patient may exist but when all similar cases are considered together, it may become a burden that is beyond the means of the community. Nobody is obliged to do the impossible. Thus it is ethical to take into consideration excessive expenses when one decides whether or not a patient should be treated. Many sick people die because of lack of life-saving means. Health care, whether of infants or of adults, must take an important place among the priorities of a nation's economic planning. But it must be realized at the same time that there is a limit to the resources that can be spent on health care. *Human life is "priceless" but maintaining it has its price which sometimes may be impossible to pay.*

It is a great shock to expectant parents to learn that their newborn baby has Down's Syndrome or some other birth defect that will result in mental retardation or some other handicap. Is it ethically justified to take the inferior "quality of life" as a reason for not treating the baby for birth defects that immediately threaten his life and let him die? As pediatric medicine is increasingly capable of saving the life of such defective newborns, the ethical question of treatment or non-treatment weighs heavily on the conscience of those who must make the decision. The purpose of medical intervention in the case of defective newborns is not just the assurance of vegetative survival but also the assurance of at least some degree of rational and interrelational development. Many babies born with Down's Syndrome or spina bifida develop sufficiently well to reach satisfactory interrelationships. In many cases, families that care for them consider their presence in their families not a great burden but rather a blessing. It would be ethically wrong not to treat such babies if a surgical intervention or some other therapy can save lives.

Mere Biological Existence

Some newborn babies, however, suffer from defects that are so serious that there is little hope for their survival or their development beyond a simple vegetative life. Such is the case, for example, of the ancephalic newborn.[22] The seriousness of birth defects varies from child to child and it is not always easy to give a prognosis of the possible future development of the defective newborn. Specialists, nevertheless, can agree in a good number of cases that survival or development beyond a sheer biological existence is hopeless. It would not be sensible to make special efforts to prolong the biological life of such a child and consequently, non-treatment of such newborns is ethically justified. Non-treatment, however, does not mean that such a baby should not be fed or made comfortable as much as possible.

Dr. David Roy, Director of the Center for Bioethics, Clinical Research Institute of Montreal, Canada, clearly agrees with this opinion. "When biological damage is so extensive that curative, restorative, and corrective medical interventions cannot aid the patient's development but only succeed in perpetuating or prolonging a patient's fixation at a level of development which is not meant to be final and is far short of the variety of purposes and levels of life to which biological human life is ordained—when this obtains, then, . . . medical intervention has reached its limits, works contrary to its calling in perpetuating such fixations, and should not be employed."[23]

Infanticide

Defenders of active infant euthanasia argue that it is more humane to terminate the life of severely defective babies by direct intervention than let them die slowly once decision of non-treatment has been made. Richard B. Brandt, for instance, states, "It seems obvious . . . that once the basic decision is made that an infant is not to receive the treatment necessary to sustain life beyond a few days, it is mere stupid cruelty to allow it to waste away gradually in a hospital bed—for the child to suffer, and for everyone involved also to suffer watching the child suffer."[24] This kind of argument for active euthanasia is used also in the case of the terminally incompetent adult patient. The reasons for or against the validity of this argument can be applied to both infants and adults.

Killing or Letting Die

Is there a moral difference between killing a patient or letting him die? Some argue that the result is the same and furthermore, the mercy-killing of an infant is in the interest of all involved. It is better for the baby to die quickly without suffering and it is likewise better for the parents, the doctors, and the health-care personnel not to see the long, protracted suffering and dying of the infant. The defenders of this opinion, however, must demonstrate that human beings have the right to kill an innocent person whether he is dying or not. One of the basic human rights is the right to life. According to sound ethical principles, a right ceases to be in force if a stronger right prevails over it. An aggressor forfeits his right to his life if the assaulted person has no other way to defend his own life but by killing the aggressor. But the defective baby is not an aggressor and no one can justly claim the right to kill him. The fact that he will soon die does not change the ethical factors establishing his right. Would the closeness of death morally empower another human being to kill the patient? How close to death does one have to be to lose his right to life? We are all marching toward death since our birth. The length of time, its short or long duration that separates a person from death, does not create any justified claim in any of us to kill him. We are all mortal but this fact does not give a right to others to kill us. Mortality is a natural part of human existence but it does not follow from this that we have the right to impose death on an innocent person before his death comes naturally. Natural rights are not granted by governments, by parents or by a committee of experts. They cannot be taken away by these either.

Advocates of infanticide argue that it is prudent and ethical to stop the suffering of defective babies. There is a fallacy in this argument, however, because one stops the suffering by killing the patient. Modern medicine can stop suffering without killing the patient. The good end, that is, the elimination of suffering does not justify the application of bad means, that is, the violation of the patient's basic right to his life. One does not cut off the head of a patient to stop his headache.

Promoters of mercy-killing of defective newborns further argue that non-treatment in reality is a means to terminate life and consequently, it does not differ from a positive intervention of killing the infant. It was previously pointed out that the morality of non-treatment when there is no affirmative duty to treat the patient is not wrong ethically. In that case the intention is not directed to the violation of the patient's right. In the case of infanticide, however, the intention is directly to kill the infant which is the usurpation of dominion over another person's life. Some label this argument as hairsplitting casuistry. But its rejection would not only be logically and ethically wrong but would also have dire consequences, for it would justify the contention that a human being may have dominion over the life of another person. The advocates of infanticide maintain that dominion over another person's life would hold only in exceptional cases and would not be universally valid. Nevertheless, once the basic principle is broken, there is no reason why the "exceptions" could not be extended to other cases, to the old, the senile, the mentally deranged, the socially, racially or politically disturbing elements.

In conclusion, we can state that infant euthanasia must be basically judged by the same moral criteria as euthanasia of incompetent adults. The prognosis of the suffering and future development of a seriously defective newborn, however, is more difficult than that of an adult patient and this fact may create grave practical problems in the application of the criteria. In some cases, it will be difficult to abstract from personal and subjective considerations what will tip the scale in one or the other direction. In the case of well-founded doubt, however, one has to choose the treatment over the non-treatment of the defective infant.

QUESTIONS FOR REVIEW AND DISCUSSION

1. Explain the concepts of affirmative and negative duties.

2. Is non-treatment of an infant ever justifiable? Is non-feeding of an infant equivalent to killing him?

3. Explain the concepts of ordinary and extraordinary, useful and useless means.

4. Is it a duty to save and maintain mere vegetative life?

5. Can excessive expenses justify the non-treatment of defective infants? Can human life be measured by money?

Notes

1. *Daily News*, June 21, 1981, p. 3.
2. Chester A. Swinyard, M.D., Ph.D., et al. "Spina Bifida as a Prototype Defect for Decision Making: Nature of the Defect." in Chester A. Swinyard, M.D., Ph.D. ed. *Decision Making and the Defective Newborn.* Springfield, Ill.: Charles C. Thomas Publishers. 1978, p. 26.
3. *Daily News*, June 21, 1981, p. 3.
4. *New York Times*, February 17 and 25, 1974.
5. *New York Times*, February 17, 1974.
6. Frank Jackman, "Hospitals Get Baby Warning." in *Daily News*, May 19, 1982, p. 4.
7. *Daily News*, April 16, 1982. p. 4.
8. Cf. Maria W. Piers, *Infanticide, Past and Present.* New York: W.W. Norton & Co., 1978, and William B. Silverman, "Mismatched Attitudes about Neonatal Death." *The Hastings Center Report*, December 1981, pp. 12–16.
9. Dr. John Lorber, M.D., "The Doctor's Duty to Patients and Parents in Profoundly Handicapping Conditions." In Dr. David J. Roy, ed., *Medical Wisdom and Ethics in the Treatment of Severely Defective Newborn and Young Children.* Montreal: Eden Press, 1978, p. 11.
10. *New York Times*, June 12, 1974.
11. Dr. John Lorber, *op cit.* p. 22.
12. Gina Bari Kolata, "Mass Screening for Neural Tube Defect." *The Hastings Center Report*, December 1980, p. 8.
13. Swinyard, *op. cit.* p. 19.
14. *Newsweek*, August 31, 1981, p. 48.
15. Dr. John M. Freeman, "Ethics and the Decision Making Process for Defective Children." In Dr. David Roy, *op cit.*, p. 25.
16. Freeman, "Ethics," p. 25.
17. Samuel Gorovitz, et al., eds. *Moral Problems in Medicine.* Englewood Cliffs: Prentice-Hall, 1976, p. 341.
18. In addition to works cited in this article, cf. the following books: John A. Behnke and Sissela Bok, eds. *The Dilemmas of Euthanasia.* Garden City, New York: Doubleday, 1975; Donald G. McCarthy and Albert S. Moraczewski, eds. *Moral Responsibility in Prolonging Life Decisions.* St. Louis: Pope John XXIII Center, 1981; Paul Ramsey, *Ethics at the Edges of Life.* New Haven: Yale University Press, 1978; Bonnie Steinbock, ed., *Killing and Letting Die.* Englewood Cliffs: Prentice-Hall, 1980; Robert M. Veatch, *Death, Dying, and the Biological Revolution.* New Haven: Yale University Press, 1976.
19. Pius XII, *Acta Apostolicae Sedis* 49 (1957) 1031–1032.
20. Sacred Congregation for the Doctrine of the Faith, *Declaration on Euthanasia.* English translation in *Catholic Mind*, October 1980, p. 63.
21. *Ibid.*
22. Cf. Dr. David Roy, "Issues in Health Care Meriting Particular

Christian Concern—A Priority Issue: The Severely Defective Newborn."
Linacre Quarterly, February 1982, 68.

23. Roy, "Issues," 68.

24. Richard B. Brandt, "Defective Newborns and the Morality of Termination." In Marvin Kohl, *Infanticide and the Value of Life*. Buffalo: Prometheus Books, 1978, p. 56.

Appendix I
The Nuremberg Code

1. The voluntary consent of the human subject is absolutely essential. This means that the person involved should have legal capacity to give consent; should be so situated as to be able to exercise free power of choice, without the intervention of any element of force, fraud, deceit, duress, overreaching, or other ulterior form of constraint or coercion; and should have sufficient knowledge and comprehension of the elements of the subject matter involved as to enable him to make an understanding and enlightened decision. This latter element requires that before the acceptance of an affirmative decision by the experimental subject there should be made known to him the nature, duration, and purpose of the experiment; the method and means by which it is to be conducted; all inconveniences and hazards reasonably to be expected; and the effects upon his health or person which may possibly come from his participation in the experiments.

The duty and responsibility for ascertaining the quality of the consent rests upon each individual who initiates, directs or engages in the experiment. It is a personal duty and responsibility which may not be delegated to another with impunity.

2. The experiment should be such as to yield fruitful results for the good of society, unprocurable by other methods or means of study, and not random and unnecessary in nature.

3. The experiment should be so designed and based on the results of animal experimentation and a knowledge of the natural history of the disease or other problem under study that the anticipated results (will) justify the performance of the experiment.

4. The experiment should be so conducted as to avoid all unnecessary physical and mental suffering and injury.

5. No experiment should be conducted where there is an a priori reason to believe that death or disabling injury will occur; except, perhaps, in those experiments where the experimental physicians also serve as subjects.

6. The degree of risk to be taken should never exceed that determined by the humanitarian importance of the problem to be solved by the experiment.

7. Proper preparations should be made and adequate facilities provided to protect the experimental subject against even remote possibilities of injury, disability, or death.

8. The experiment should be conducted only by scientifically qualified persons. The highest degree of skill and care should be required through all stages of the experiment of those who conduct or engage in the experiment.

9. During the course of the experiment the human subject should be at liberty to bring the experiment to an end if he has reached the physical or mental state where continuation of the experiment seems to him to be impossible.

10. During the course of the experiment the scientist in charge must be prepared to terminate the experiment at any stage, if he has probable cause to believe, in the exercise of good faith, superior skill and careful judgment required of him that a continuation of the experiment is likely to result in injury, disability, or death to the experimental subject.

Of the ten principles which have been enumerated our judicial concern, of course, is with those requirements which are purely legal in nature—or which at least are so clearly related to matters legal that they assist us in determining criminal culpability and punishment. To go beyond that point would lead us into a field that would be beyond our sphere of competence. However, the point need not be labored. We find from the evidence that in the medical experiments which have been proved, these ten principles were much more frequently honored in their breach than in their observance. Many of the concentration camp inmates who were the victims of these atrocities were citizens of countries other than the German Reich. They were non-German nationals, including Jews and "asocial persons," both prisoners of war and civilians, who had been imprisoned and forced to submit to these tortures and barbarities without so much as a semblance of trial. In every single instance appearing in the record, subjects were used who did not consent to the experiments; indeed, as to some of the experiments, it is not even contended by the defendants that the subjects occupied the status of volunteers. In no case was the experimental subject at liberty of his own free choice to withdraw from any experiment. In many cases experiments were performed by unqualified persons; were conducted at random for no adequate scientific reason, and under revolting physical conditions. All of the experiments were conducted with unnecessary suffering and injury and but very little, if any, precautions, were taken to protect or safeguard the human subjects from the possibilities of injury, disability, or death. In every one of the experiments the subjects experienced extreme pain or torture, and in most of them they suffered permanent injury, mutilation, or death, either as a direct result of the experiments or because of lack of adequate follow-up care.

Obviously all of these experiments involving brutalities, tortures, disabling injury, and death were performed in complete disregard of international conventions, the laws and customs of war, the general principles of criminal law as derived from the criminal laws of all civilized nations, and Control Council Law No. 10. Manifestly human experiments under such conditions are contrary to "the principles of the law of nations as they result from the usages established among civilized peoples, from the laws of humanity, and from the dictates of public conscience."

United States v. Karl Brandt, et al., *Trials of War Criminals Before Nuremberg Military Tribunals Under Control Council Law No. 10* (October, 1946-April, 1949).

Appendix II
Declaration of Helsinki

(This Declaration was adopted in 1964 by the 18th World Medical Assembly in Helsinki, Finland, and revised by the 29th World Medical Assembly in Tokyo in 1975.)

Introduction

It is the mission of the medical doctor to safeguard the health of the people. His or her knowledge and conscience are dedicated to the fulfillment of this mission.

The Declaration of Geneva of The World Medical Association binds the doctor with the words "The health of my patient will be my first consideration," and the International Code of Medical Ethics declares that "Any act or advice which could weaken physical or mental resistance of a human being may be used only in his interest."

The purpose of biomedical research involving human subjects must be to improve diagnostic, therapeutic and prophylactic procedures and the understanding of the aetiology and pathogenesis of disease.

In current medical practice most diagnostic, therapeutic or prophylactic procedures involve hazards. This applies a fortiori to biomedical research.

Medical progress is based on research which ultimately must rest in part on experimentation involving human subjects.

In the field of biomedical research a fundamental distinction must be recognized between medical research in which the aim is essentially diagnostic or therapeutic for a patient, and medical research, the essential object of which is purely scientific and without

306

direct diagnostic or therapeutic value to the person subjected to the research.

Special caution must be exercised in the conduct of research which may affect the environment, and the welfare of animals used for research must be respected.

Because it is essential that the results of laboratory experiments be applied to human beings to further scientific knowledge and to help suffering humanity, The World Medical Association has prepared the following recommendations as a guide to every doctor in biomedical research involving human subjects. They should be kept under review in the future. It must be stressed that the standards as drafted are only a guide to physicians all over the world. Doctors are not relieved from criminal, civil and ethical responsibilities under the laws of their own countries.

I. Basic Principles

1. Biomedical research involving human subjects must conform to generally accepted scientific principles and should be based on adequately performed laboratory and animal experimentation and on a thorough knowledge of the scientific literature.

2. The design and performance of each experimental procedure involving human subjects should be clearly formulated in an experimental protocol which should be transmitted to a specially appointed independent committee for consideration, comment and guidance.

3. Biomedical research involving human subjects should be conducted only by scientifically qualified persons and under the supervision of a clinically competent medical person. The responsibility for the human subject must always rest with a medically qualified person and never rest on the subject of the research, even though the subject has given his or her consent.

4. Biomedical research involving human subjects cannot legitimately be carried out unless the importance of the objective is in proportion to the inherent risk to the subject.

5. Every biomedical research project involving human subjects should be preceded by careful assessment of predictable risks in

comparison with foreseeable benefits to the subject or to others. Concern for the interest of the subject must always prevail over the interests of science and society.

6. The right of the research subject to safeguard his or her integrity must always be respected. Every precaution should be taken to respect the privacy of the subject and to minimize the impact of the study on the subject's physical and mental integrity and on the personality of the subject.

7. Doctors should abstain from engaging in research projects involving human subjects unless they are satisfied that the hazards involved are believed to be predictable. Doctors should cease any investigation if the hazards are found to outweigh the potential benefits.

8. In publication of the results of his or her research, the doctor is obliged to preserve the accuracy of the results. Reports of experimentation not in accordance with the principles laid down in this Declaration should not be accepted for publication.

9. In any research on human beings, each potential subject must be adequately informed of the aims, methods, anticipated benefits and potential hazards of the study and the discomfort it may entail. He or she should be informed that he or she is at liberty to abstain from participation in the study and that he or she is free to withdraw his or her consent to participation at any time. The doctor should then obtain the subject's freely given informed consent, preferably in writing.

10. When obtaining informed consent for the research project the doctor should be particularly cautious if the subject is in a dependent relationship to him or her or may consent under duress. In that case the informed consent should be obtained by a doctor who is not engaged in the investigation and who is completely independent of this official relationship.

11. In the case of legal incompetence, informed consent should be obtained from the legal guardian in accordance with national legislation. Where physical or mental incapacity makes it impossible to obtain informed consent, or when the subject is a minor, permission from the responsible relative replaces that of the subject in accordance with national legislation.

12. The research protocol should always contain a statement of

the ethical considerations involved and should indicate that the principles enunciated in the present Declaration are complied with.

II. Medical Research Combined with Professional Care (Clinical Research)

1. In the treatment of the sick person, the doctor must be free to use a new diagnostic or therapeutic measure, if in his or her judgment it offers hope of saving life, reestablishing health or alleviating suffering.

2. The potential benefits, hazards and discomfort of a new method should be weighed against the advantages of the best current diagnostic and therapeutic methods.

3. In any medical study, every patient—including those of a control group, if any—should be assured of the best proven diagnostic and therapeutic method.

4. The refusal of the patient to participate in a study must never interfere with the doctor-patient relationship.

5. If the doctor considers it essential not to obtain informed consent, the specific reasons for this proposal should be stated in the experimental protocol for transmission to the independent committee (I,2).

6. The doctor can combine medical research with professional care, the objective being the acquisition of new medical knowledge, only to the extent that medical research is justified by its potential diagnostic or therapeutic value for the patient.

III. Non-Therapeutic Biomedical Research Involving Human Subjects (Non-Clinical Biomedical Research)

1. In the purely scientific application of medical research carried out on a human being, it is the duty of the doctor to remain the protector of the life and health of that person on whom biomedical research is being carried out.

2. The subjects should be volunteers—either healthy persons or

patients for whom the experimental design is not related to the patient's illness.

3. The investigator or the investigating team should discontinue the research if in his, her or their judgment it may, if continued, be harmful to the individual.

4. In research on man, the interest of science and society should never take precedence over considerations related to the well-being of the subject.

(Reprinted with the permission of The World Medical Association.)

Appendix III
AMA Ethical Guidelines for Clinical Investigation

(Adopted by House of Delegates, American Medical Association, Nov. 30, 1966)

1. A physician may participate in clinical investigation only to the extent that his activities are a part of a systematic program competently designed, under accepted standards of scientific research, to produce data which is scientifically valid and significant.

2. In conducting clinical investigation, the investigator should demonstrate the same concern and caution for the welfare, safety and comfort of the person involved as is required of a physician who is furnishing medical care to a patient independent of any clinical investigation.

3. In clinical investigation *primarily for treatment*:

A. The physician must recognize that the physician-patient relationship exists and that he is expected to exercise his professional judgment and skill in the best interest of the patient.

B. Voluntary consent must be obtained from the patient, or from his legally authorized representative if the patient lacks the capacity to consent, following:

   1. disclosure that the physician intends to use an investigational drug or experimental procedure,
   2. a reasonable explanation of the nature of the drug or procedure to be used, risks to be expected, and possible therapeutic benefits,

3. an offer to answer any inquiries concerning the drug or procedure, and

4. a disclosure of alternative drugs or procedures that may be available.

    i. In exceptional circumstances and to the extent that disclosure of information concerning the nature of the drug or experimental procedure or risks would be expected to materially affect the health of the patient and would be detrimental to his best interests, such information may be withheld from the patient. In such circumstances such information shall be disclosed to a responsible relative or friend of the patient where possible.

    ii. Ordinarily, consent should be in writing, except where the physician deems it necessary to rely upon consent in other than written form because of the physical or emotional state of the patient.

    iii. Where emergency treatment is necessary and the patient is incapable of giving consent and no one is available who has authority to act on his behalf, consent is assumed.

4. In clinical investigation *primarily for the accumulation of scientific knowledge*:

A. Adequate safeguards must be provided for the welfare, safety and comfort of the subject.

B. Consent, in writing, should be obtained from the subject, or from his legally authorized representative if the subject lacks the capacity to consent, following:

    1. a disclosure of the fact that an investigational drug or procedure is to be used,

    2. a reasonable explanation of the nature of the procedure to be used and risks to be expected, and

    3. an offer to answer any inquiries concerning the drug or procedure.

C. Minors or mentally incompetent persons may be used as subjects only if:

    1. The nature of the investigation is such that mentally competent adults would not be suitable subjects.

   2. Consent, in writing, is given by a legally authorized representative of the subject under circumstances in which an informed and prudent adult would reasonably be expected to volunteer himself or his child as a subject.

D. No person may be used as a subject against his will.

(Reprinted with the permission of the American Medical Association).

Appendix IV
Declaration on Euthanasia
Sacred Congregation for the Doctrine of the Faith

Introduction

The rights and values pertaining to the human person occupy an important place among the questions discussed today. In this regard, the Second Vatican Ecumenical Council solemnly reaffirmed the lofty dignity of the human person, and in a special way his or her right to life. The Council therefore condemned crimes against life "such as any type of murder, genocide, abortion, euthanasia or willful suicide" (Pastoral Constitution on the Church in the Modern World, *Gaudium et Spes*, n. 27).

More recently, the Sacred Congregation for the Doctrine of the Faith has reminded all the faithful of Catholic teaching on procured abortion.[1] The Congregation now considers it opportune to set forth the church's teaching on euthanasia.

It is indeed true that in this sphere of teaching, the recent Popes have explained the principles, and these retain their full force,[2] but the progress of medical science in recent years has brought to the fore new aspects of the question of euthanasia and these aspects call for further elucidation on the ethical level.

In modern society, in which even the fundamental values of human life are often called into question, cultural change exercises an influence upon the way of looking at suffering and death; moreover, medicine has increased its capacity to cure and to prolong life in particular circumstances which sometimes give rise to moral problems.

Thus, people living in this situation experience no little anxiety about the meaning of advanced old age and death. They also begin to wonder whether they have the right to obtain for themselves or their fellow men an "easy death," which would shorten suffering and which seems to them more in harmony with human dignity.

A number of episcopal conferences have raised questions on this subject with the Sacred Congregation for the Doctrine of the Faith. The Congregation, having sought the opinion of experts on the various aspects of euthanasia, now wishes to respond to the bishops' questions with the present declaration, in order to help them give correct teaching to the faithful entrusted to their care, and to offer elements for reflection that they can present to the civil authorities with regard to this very serious matter.

The considerations set forth in the present document concern in the first place all those who place their faith and hope in Christ, who, through His life, death and Resurrection, has given a new meaning to existence and especially to the death of the Christian. As St. Paul says, "If we live, we live to the Lord, and if we die, we die to the Lord" (Rom. 14:6, cf. Phil. 1:20).

As for those who profess other religions, many will agree with us that faith in God the Creator, Provider and Lord of life—if they share this belief—confers a lofty dignity upon every human person and guarantees respect for him or her.

It is hoped that this declaration will meet with the approval of many people of good will who, philosophical or ideological differences notwithstanding, have nevertheless a lively awareness of the rights of the human person. These rights have often, in fact, been proclaimed in recent years through declarations issued by international congresses; and since it is a question here of fundamental rights inherent in every human person, it is obviously wrong to have recourse to arguments from political pluralism or religious freedom in order to deny the universal value of these rights.[3]

The Value of Human Life

Human life is the basis of all goods, and is the necessary source and condition of every human activity and of all society. Most people regard life as something sacred and hold that no one may dispose of it at will, but believers see in life something greater, namely, a gift of God's love, which they are called upon to preserve and make fruitful. And it is this latter consideration that gives rise to the following consequences.

1. No one can make an attempt on the life of an innocent person without opposing God's love for that person, without violating a fundamental right and therefore without commiting a crime of the utmost gravity.[4]

2. Everyone has the duty to lead his or her life in accordance with God's plan. That life is entrusted to the individual as a good that must bear fruit already here on earth, but that finds its full perfection only in eternal life.

3. Intentionally causing one's own death, or suicide, is therefore equally as wrong as murder; such an action on the part of a person is to be considered as a rejection of God's sovereignty and loving plan. Furthermore, suicide is also often a refusal of love for self, the denial of the natural instinct to live, a flight from the duties of justice and charity owed to one's neighbor, to various communities or to the whole of society, although, as is generally recognized, at times there are psychological factors present that can diminish responsibility or even completely remove it.

However, one must clearly distinguish suicide from that sacrifice of one's life whereby for a higher cause, such as God's glory, the salvation of souls or the service of one's brethren, a person offers his or her own life or puts it in danger (cf. Jn. 13:14).

Euthanasia

In order that the question of euthanasia can be properly dealt with, it is first necessary to define the words used.

Etymologically speaking, in ancient times, "euthanasia" meant an easy death without severe suffering. Today one no longer thinks of this original meaning of the word, but rather of some intervention of medicine whereby the sufferings of sickness or of the final agony are reduced, sometimes also with the danger of suppressing life prematurely.

Ultimately, the word "euthanasia" is used in a more particular sense to mean "mercy killing," for the purpose of putting an end to extreme suffering, or saving abnormal babies, the mentally ill or the incurably sick from the prolongation, perhaps for many years, of a miserable life, which could impose too heavy a burden on their families or on society.

It is therefore necessary to state clearly in what sense the word is used in the present document.

By "euthanasia" is understood an action or an omission which of itself or by intention causes death, in order that all suffering may in this way be eliminated. Euthanasia's terms of reference, therefore, are to be found in the intention of the will and in the methods used.

It is necessary to state firmly once more that nothing and no one can in any way permit the killing of an innocent human being, whether a fetus or an embryo, an infant or an adult, an old person, or one suffering from an incurable disease, or a person who is dying. Furthermore, no one is permitted to ask for this act of killing, either for himself or herself or for another person entrusted to his or her care, nor can he or she consent to it, either explicitly or implicitly; nor can any authority legitimately recommend or permit such an action. For it is a question of the violation of the divine law, an offense against the dignity of the human person, a crime against life and an attack on humanity.

It may happen that, by reason of prolonged and barely tolerable pain, for deeply personal or other reasons, people may be led to believe that they can legitimately ask for death or obtain it for others. Although in these cases the guilt of the individual may be reduced or completely absent, nevertheless the error of judgment into which the conscience falls, perhaps in good faith, does not change the nature of this act of killing, which will always be in itself something to be rejected. The pleas of gravely ill people who sometimes ask for death are not to be understood as implying a true desire for euthanasia; in fact, it is almost always a case of an anguished plea for help and love. What a sick person needs, besides medical care, is love, the human and supernatural warmth with which the sick person can and ought to be surrounded by all those close to him or her, parents and children, doctors and nurses.

The Meaning of Suffering for
Christians and the Use of Painkillers

Death does not always come in dramatic circumstances after barely tolerable sufferings. Nor do we have to think only of extreme cases. Numerous testimonies which confirm one another lead to the conclusion that nature itself has made provision to render more bearable at the moment of death separations that would be terribly painful to a person in full health. Hence it is that a prolonged illness, advanced old age or a state of loneliness or neglect can bring about psychological conditions that facilitate the acceptance of death.

Nevertheless, the fact remains that death, often preceded or accompanied by severe and prolonged suffering, is something which naturally causes people anguish.

Physical suffering is certainly an unavoidable element of the human condition on the biological level. It constitutes a warning of which no one denies the usefulness, but, since it affects the human psychological makeup, it often exceeds its own biological usefulness and can become so severe as to cause the desire to remove it at any cost.

According to Christian teaching, however, suffering, especially suffering during the last moments of life, has a special place in God's saving plan. It is, in fact, a sharing in Christ's Passion and a union with the redeeming sacrifice which He offered in obedience to the Father's will. Therefore, one must not be surprised if some Christians prefer to moderate their use of painkillers, in order to accept voluntarily at least a part of their sufferings and thus associate themselves in a conscious way with the sufferings of Christ crucified (cf. Mt. 27:34).

Nevertheless, it would be imprudent to impose a heroic way of acting as a general rule. On the contrary, human and Christian prudence suggest for the majority of sick people the use of medicines capable of alleviating or suppressing pain, even though these may cause as a secondary effect semiconsciousness and reduced lucidity. As for those who are not in a state to express themselves, one can reasonably presume that they wish to take these painkillers, and have them administered according to the doctor's advice.

But the intensive use of painkillers is not without difficulties, because the phenomenon of habituation generally makes it necessary to increase their dosage in order to maintain their efficacy. At this point, it is fitting to recall a declaration by Pope Pius XII, which retains its full force. In answer to a group of doctors who had put the question, "Is the suppression of pain and consciousness by the use of narcotics permitted by religion and morality to the doctor and the patient (even at the approach of death and if one foresees that the use of narcotics will shorten life)?", the Pope said: "If no other means exist, and if, in the given circumstances, this does not prevent the carrying out of other religious and moral duties: Yes."⁵ In this case, of course, death is in no way intended or sought, even if the risk of it is reasonably taken; the intention is simply to relieve pain effectively, using for this purpose painkillers available to medicine.

However, painkillers that cause unconsciousness need special consideration. For a person not only has to be able to satisfy his or her moral duties and family obligations; he or she also has to prepare himself or herself with full consciousness for meeting Christ. Thus, Pius XII warns: "It is not right to deprive the dying person of consciousness without a serious reason."⁶

Due Proportion in
the Use of Remedies

Today it is very important to protect, at the moment of death, both the dignity of the human person and the Christian concept of life, against a technological attitude that threatens to become an abuse. Thus, some people speak of a "right to die," which is an expression that does not mean the right to procure death either by one's own hand or by means of someone else's as one pleases, but rather the right to die peacefully with human and Christian dignity. From this point of view, the use of therapeutic means can sometimes pose problems.

In numerous cases, the complexity of the situation can be such as to cause doubts about the way ethical principles should be applied. In the final analysis, it pertains to the conscience either of the sick person, or of those qualified to speak in the sick person's name, or of the doctors, to decide, in the light of moral obligations and of the various aspects of the case.

Everyone has the duty to care for his or her own health or to seek such care from others. Those whose task it is to care for the sick must do so conscientiously and administer the remedies that seem necessary or useful.

However, is it necessary in all circumstances to have recourse to all possible remedies?

In the past, moralists replied that one is never obliged to use "extraordinary" means. This reply, which as a principle still holds good, is perhaps less clear today, by reason of the imprecision of the term and the rapid progress made in the treatment of sickness. Thus, some people prefer to speak of "proportionate" and "disproportionate" means. In any case, it will be possible to make a correct judgment as to the means by studying the type of treatment to be used, its degree of complexity or risk, its cost and the possibilities of using it and comparing these elements with the result that can be expected, taking into account the state of the sick person and his or her physical and moral resources.

In order to facilitate the application of these general principles, the following clarifications can be added:

- If there are no other sufficient remedies, it is permitted, with the patient's consent, to have recourse to the means provided by the most advanced medical techniques, even if these means are still at the experimental stage and are not without a certain risk. By accepting them, the patient can even show generosity in the service of humanity.

- It is also permitted, with the patient's consent, to interrupt these means where the results fall short of expectations. But, for such a decision to be made, account will have to be taken of the reasonable wishes of the patient and the patient's family, as also of the advice of the doctors who are specially competent in the matter. The latter may in particular judge that the investment in instruments and personnel is disproportionate to the results foreseen; they may also judge that the techniques applied impose on the patient strain or suffering out of proportion with the benefits which he or she may gain from such techniques.

- It is also permissible to make do with the normal means that medicine can offer. Therefore, one cannot impose on anyone the obligation to have recourse to a technique which is already in use but which carries a risk or is burdensome. Such a refusal is not the equivalent of suicide; on the contrary, it should be considered as an acceptance of the human condition, or a wish to avoid the application of a medical procedure disproportionate to the results that can be expected, or a desire not to impose excessive expense on the family or the community.

When inevitable death is imminent in spite of the means used, it is permitted in conscience to take the decision to refuse forms of treatment that would only secure a precarious and burdensome prolongation of life, so long as the normal care due to the sick person in similar cases is not interrupted. In such circumstances, the doctor has no reason to reproach himself with failing to help the person in danger.

Conclusion

The norms contained in the present declaration are inspired by a profound desire to serve people in accordance with the plan of the Creator. Life is a gift of God and, on the other hand, death is unavoidable; it is necessary, therefore, that we, without in any way hastening the hour of death, should be able to accept it with full responsibility and dignity. It is true that death marks the end of our earthly experience, but at the same time it opens the door to immortal life. Therefore, all must prepare themselves for this event in the light of human values, and Christians even more so in the light of faith.

As for those who work in the medical profession, they ought to neglect no means of making all their skills available to the sick and the dying; but they should also remember how much more necessary it is to provide them with the comfort of their boundless kindness and heartfelt charity. Such service to people is also service to Christ the Lord, who said: "As you did it to one of the least of these my brethren, you did it to me" (Mt. 25:40).

At the audience granted to the undesigned Prefect, His Holiness Pope John Paul II approved this declaration, adopted at the ordinary meeting of the Sacred Congregation for the Doctrine of the Faith, and ordered its publication.

Rome, the Sacred Congregation for the Doctrine of the Faith, 5 May 1980.

Franjo Cardinal Seper
Prefect

Jerome Hamer, O.P.
Titular Archbishop of Lorium
Secretary

Notes

1. Declaration on Procured Abortion, Nov. 18, 1974, *A.A.S.* (*Acta Apostolicae Sedis*), 66 (1974), 730–47.

2. Pius XII, "Address to Those Attending the Congress of the International Union of Catholic Women's Leagues," Sept. 11, 1947, *A.A.S.* 39 (1947), 483; "Address to the Italian Catholic Union of Midwives," Oct. 29, 1951, *A.A.S.* 43 (1951) 835–54; "Speech to the Members of the International Office of Military Medicine Documentation," Oct. 19, 1953, *A.A.S.* 45 (1953), 744–54; "Address to Those Taking Part in the IX Congress of the Italian Anesthesiological Society," Feb 24, 1957, *A.A.S.* 49 (1957), 146; cf. "Address on 'Reanimation,' " Nov. 24, 1957, *A.A.S.* 49 (1957), 1027–33; Paul VI, "Address to the Members of the United Nations Special Committee on Apartheid," May 22, 1974, *A.A.S.* 66 (1974), 346; John Paul II, "Address to the Bishops of the United States of America," Oct. 5, 1979, *A.A.S.* 71 (1979), 1225.

3. One thinks particularly of Recommendation 979 (1976), "On the Rights of the Sick and Dying," of the Parliamentary Assembly of the Council of Europe in its XXVIIth Ordinary Session. Cf. Sipica, No. 1, March 1977, pp. 14–15.

4. We leave aside completely the problems of the death penalty and of war, which involve specific considerations that do not concern the present subject.

5. Pius XII, "Address of Feb. 24, 1957," op. cit., *A.A.S.* 49 (1957), 147.

6. Pius XII, "Address of Feb. 24, 1957," op. cit., *A.A.S.* 49 (1957), 143; "Address of Sept. 9, 1958," *A.A.S.* 50 (1958), 694.

Selected Bibliography

General Works on Bioethics

Abrams, Natalie, and Buckner, Michael D., eds., *Medical Ethics: A Clinical Textbook and Reference for the Health Care Professions*. Cambridge: The MIT Press, 1983.

Beauchamp, Tom L. and Childress, James F. *Principles of Biomedical Ethics*. 2nd edition. New York: Oxford University Press, 1983.

Brody, Howard. *Ethical Decisions in Medicine*. 2nd edition. Boston: Little, Brown and Company, 1981.

Cadbury, Henry J., *et al.*, *Who Shall Live? Man's Control over Birth and Death*. New York: Hill & Wang, 1970.

Culver, Charles M., and Gert, Bernard. *Philosophy in Medicine: Conceptual and Ethical Issues in Medicine and Psychiatry*. New York: Oxford University Press, 1982.

Dedek, John F., *Contemporary Medical Ethics*. New York: Sheed and Ward, 1975.

————, *Human Life*. New York: Sheed and Ward, 1972.

Gorovitz, Samuel, *et al.*, eds., *Moral Problems in Medicine*. 2nd edition. Englewood Cliffs, N.J.: Prentice-Hall, 1983.

Gorovitz, Samuel. *Doctors' Dilemmas: Moral Conflict in Medical Care*. New York: Macmillan, 1982.

Häring, Bernard. *Ethics of Manipulation: Issues in Medicine, Behavior Control and Genetics*. New York: The Seabury Press, 1975.

————, *Medical Ethics*. Notre Dame, Ind.: Fides Publishers, 1973.

Hunt, Robert, and Arras, John, eds., *Ethical Issues in Modern Medicine*. Palo Alto, Calif.: Mayfield Publishing Co., 1977.

Jonsen, Albert R., Siegler, Mark, and Winslade, William J., *Clinical Ethics: A Practical Approach to Ethical Decisions in Clinical Medicine*. New York: Macmillan Publishing Co., Inc., 1982.

Kelly, Gerald, *Medico-Moral Problems*. St. Louis: Catholic Hospital Association, 1958.

Leach, Gerald, *The Biocrats*. New York: Penguin Books, 1972.

McCormick, Richard A. *How Brave a New World? Dilemmas in Bioethics*. Garden City, N.Y.: Doubleday, 1981.

McFadden, Charles J., *Medical Ethics*. 6th edition. Philadelphia: F.A. Davis Co., 1967.

Nelson, James B., *Human Medicine: Ethical Perspectives on New Medical Issues*. Minneapolis: Augsburg Publishing Co., 1973.

Potter, Van Rensselaer, *Bioethics: Bridge to the Future*. Englewood Cliffs, N.J.: Prentice-Hall, 1971.

President's Commission for the Study of Ethical Problems in Medicine and Biomedical and Behavioral Research, *Summing Up: Final Report on Studies of Ethical and Legal Problems in Medicine and Biomedical and Behavioral Research*. Washington, D.C.: U.S. Government Printing Office, 1983.

Ramsey, Paul, *Ethics at the Edges of Life: Medical and Legal Intersections*. New Haven: Yale University Press, 1978.

————, *Fabricated Man: The Ethics of Genetic Control*. New Haven: Yale University Press, 1970.

————, *The Patient as Person*. New Haven: Yale University Press, 1970.

Reich, Warren T., ed., *Encyclopedia of Bioethics*. Four volumes. New York: The Free Press, 1978.

Reiser, Stanley Joel, *et al.*, eds., *Ethics in Medicine: Historical Perspectives and Contemporary Concerns*. Cambridge: The M.I.T. Press, 1977.

Restak, Richard M., *Premeditated Man: Bioethics and the Control of Future Human Life*. New York: The Viking Press, 1975.

Shannon, Thomas A., ed. *Bioethics: Basic Writings on the Key Ethical Questions That Surround the Major Modern Biological Possibilities and Problems*. Rev. edition. New York: Paulist Press, 1981.

Shannon, Thomas A., and Manfra, Jo Ann, eds. *Law and Bioethics: Texts with Commentary on Major U.S. Court Decisions*. New York: Paulist Press, 1982.

Smith, Harmon, *Ethics and the New Medicine*. Nashville, Abingdon Press, 1970.

Veatch, Robert M., *Case Studies in Medical Ethics*. Cambridge: Harvard University Press, 1977.

———, *A Theory of Medical Ethics*. New York: Basic Books, 1981.
Walters, LeRoy, ed. *Bibliography of Bioethics*, Vols. 1–. Detroit: Gale Research Co. Issued annually.

1 Moral Principles

Bourke, Vernon J., *History of Ethics*. Garden City, New York: Doubleday, 1968.
D'Arcy, Eric, *Conscience and Its Right to Freedom*. New York: Sheed and Ward, 1961.
D'Entreves, A.P., *Natural Law*. New York: Harper Torchbooks, 1965.
Fagothey, Austin, *Right and Reason*. 6th edition. St. Louis: The C.V. Mosby Co., 1976.
Frankena, William K., *Ethics*. 2nd edition. Englewood Cliffs, N.J.: Prentice-Hall, Inc., 1973.
Long, Edward LeRoy, *A Survey of Recent Christian Ethics*. New York: Oxford University Press, 1982.
Macquarrie, John, *Three Issues in Ethics*. London: SCM Press, Ltd., 1970.
Maritain, Jacques, *Moral Philosophy: An Historical and Critical Survey of the Great Systems*. New York: Charles Scribner's Sons, 1964.
McCormick, Richard and Ramsey, Paul, eds., *Doing Evil to Achieve Good: Moral Choice in Conflict Situations*. Chicago: Loyola University Press, 1979.
Messner, Johannes, *Social Ethics: Natural Law in the Western World*. Revised edition. St. Louis: B. Herder Book Co., 1965.
Ramsey, Paul, *Deeds and Rules in Christian Ethics*. New York: Charles Scribner's Sons, 1967.
Rommen, Heinrich, *The Natural Law*. St. Louis: B. Herder Book Co., 1948.
Ross, W.D., *Foundations of Ethics*. Oxford: The Clarendon Press, 1939.
Varga, Andrew C., *On Being Human: Principles of Ethics*. New York: Paulist Press, 1978.
Warnock, Mary, *Ethics Since 1900*. 2nd revised edition. London: Oxford University Press, 1966.

2   Population and Moral Responsibility

Brown, Lester R., *By Bread Alone*. New York. Praeger Publishers, 1974.

Brown, Lester R., McGrath, Patricia L., and Stokes, Bruce, "Twenty-Two Dimensions of the Population Problem." *Worldwatch Paper* 5 (March 1976).

Callahan, Daniel, ed., *The Catholic Case for Contraception*. New York: Macmillan, 1969.

Curran, Charles, ed., *Contraception: Authority and Dissent*. New York: Herder and Herder, 1969.

Grisez, Germain G., *Contraception and the Natural Law*. Milwaukee: Bruce Publishing Co., 1964.

Hardin, Garrett, *Exploring New Ethics for Survival: The Voyage of Spaceship Beagle*. New York: The Viking Press, 1973.

————, "The Tragedy of the Commons." *Science* 162 (December 13, 1968), 1243–48.

Lucas, George R., Jr., and Ogletree, Thomas W., eds., *Lifeboat Ethics: The Moral Dilemmas of World Hunger*. New York: Harper & Row, 1976.

Meadows, Donella H., *et al.*, *The Limits to Growth*. New York: Universe Books, 1972.

Mesarovic, Mihajilo, and Pestel, Eduard, *Mankind at the Turning Point: The Second Report to the Club of Rome*. New York: E.P. Dutton & Co., 1974.

Noonan, John T., Jr., *Contraception: A History of Its Treatment by the Catholic Theologians and Canonists*. Cambridge: Harvard University Press, 1966.

Pohlman, Edward, ed., *Population: A Clash of Prophets*. New York: New American Library, 1973.

Pope Paul VI, *Humanae Vitae: On the Regulation of Birth*. New York: Paulist Press, 1968.

Reed, James, *From Private Vice to Public Virtue: The Birth Control Movement and American Society Since 1830*. New York: Basic Books, 1977.

Warwick, Donald P., *Bitter Pills: Population Policies and Their Implementation in Eight Developing Countries*. Cambridge: Cambridge University Press, 1982.

Wojtyla, Karol, *Love and Responsibility*. New York: Farrar, Strauss & Giroux, 1981.

3 Abortion

Callahan, Daniel, *Abortion: Law, Choice and Morality*. New York: Macmillan, 1970.

Canavan, Francis, "The Theory of the Danforth Case." *Human Life Review* 2 (Fall 1976), 5–14.

Cox, Archibald, "The Supreme Court and Abortion." *Human Life Review* 2 (Fall 1976), 15–19.

Donceel, Joseph F. "Immediate Animation and Delayed Hominization." *Theological Studies*, Vol. 31, 1 March 1970, pp. 76–105.

Granfield, David, *The Abortion Decision*. Garden City, New York: Doubleday, 1971.

Grisez, Germain G., *Abortion: The Myth, the Realities and the Arguments*. New York: World Publishing Company, 1979.

McCormick, Richard A., "Moral Notes: Abortion Dossier." *Theological Studies* 35 (June 1974), 312–359.

Nathanson, Bernard N., M.D., *Aborting America*. Garden City: Doubleday & Co., 1979.

National Conference of Catholic Bishops, *Documentation on the Right to Life and Abortion*. Washington, D.C.: United States Catholic Conference, 1974.

Noonan, John T., Jr., *A Private Choice: Abortion in America in the Seventies*. New York: The Free Press, 1979.

———, "The American Consensus on Abortions." *Human Life Review* 4 (Winter 1978), 60–63.

———, ed., *The Morality of Abortion: Legal and Historical Perspectives*. Cambridge: Harvard University Press, 1970.

Perkins, Robert L., ed., *Abortion: Pro and Con*. Cambridge: Schenckman Publishing Co., 1974.

4 Eugenics and the Quality of Life

Bajema, Carl J., *Eugenics Then and Now*. New York: Halsted Press, 1976.

Creighton, Phyllis, *Artificial Insemination by Donor*. Toronto: The Anglican Book Center, 1977.

Culliton, Barbara J., "Genetic Screening: States May Be Writing the Wrong Kind of Laws." *Science* 191 (March 5, 1976), 926–929.

Davenport, Charles Benedict, *Heredity in Relation to Eugenics*. New York: Henry Holt & Co., 1911.

Ehrlich, Paul R., and Feldman, S. Shirley, *The Race Bomb: Skin Color, Prejudice and Intelligence*. New York: Quadrangle, The New York Times Book Co., 1977.

Fletcher, John C., *Coping with Genetic Disorders*. San Francisco: Harper & Row, 1982.

Galton, Francis, *Hereditary Genius: An Inquiry into Its Laws and Consequences*. London: Macmillan & Co. 1869. Reprint. Gloucester, Mass.: Smith Publisher, 1976.

Glass, Bentley, *Human Heredity and Ethical Problems*. Philadelphia: Society for Health and Human Values, 1975.

Grant, Madison, *The Passing of the Great Race: Or, the Racial Basis of European History*. New York: Charles Scribner's Sons, 1916.

Hamilton, Michael, ed., *The New Genetics and the Future of Man*. Grand Rapids, Mich.: Wm. B. Eerdmans Publishing Co., 1972.

Holmes, Helen B., ed., *The Custom-Made Child?* Clifton, N.J.: Humana Press, 1981.

Howard, Ted and Rifkin, Jeremy, *Who Should Play God?* New York: Dell Publishing Company, 1977.

Institute of Society, Ethics and the Life Sciences: Research Group on Ethical, Social and Legal Issues in Genetic Counseling and Genetic Engineering, "Ethical and Social Issues in Screening for Genetic Disease." *New England Journal of Medicine* 286 (May 25, 1972), 1129–1132.

Lipkin, Mack, Jr., and Rowley, Peter T., eds., *Genetic Responsibility: On Choosing Our Children's Genes*. New York: Plenum Publishing Corporation, 1974.

Ludmerer, Kenneth M., *Genetics and American Society: A Historical Appraisal*. Baltimore: Johns Hopkins University Press, 1972.

Milunsky, A. and Annas, G.J., eds., *Genetics and the Law*. New York: Plenum Publishing Corporation, 1976.

Murray, Robert F., Jr., "Problems Behind the Promise: Ethical Issues in Mass Genetic Screening." *Hastings Center Report* 2 (April 1972), 11–13.

President's Commission for the Study of Ethical Problems in Medicine and Biomedical and Behavioral Research, *Screening and Counseling for Genetic Conditions.* Washington: U.S. Government Printing Office, 1983.

Ramsey, Paul, *Fabricated Man: The Ethics of Genetic Control.* New Haven: Yale University Press, 1970.

Robtischer, Jonas, J.D., M.D., *Eugenic Sterilization.* Springfield, Ill.: Charles Thomas Publ., 1973.

Stevenson, Alan C., *et al., Genetic Counseling.* 2nd edition. Philadelphia. J.B. Lippincott Co., 1977.

5 In Vitro Fertilization and Embryo Transfer

Edwards, Robert G., "Fertilization of Human Eggs in Vitro: Morals, Ethics, and the Law." *Quarterly Review of Biology* 49 (March 1974), 3–26.

Francoeur, Robert T., *Utopian Motherhood.* New York: Doubleday, 1970.

Grobstein, Clifford. *From Chance to Purpose: An Appraisal of External Human Fertilization.* Reading, Mass.: Addison-Wesely, Advanced Book Program, 1981.

Kass, Leon R., "Babies by Means of In Vitro Fertilization: Unethical Experiments on the Unborn?" *New England Journal of Medicine* 285 (November 18, 1971), 1174–1179.

Marx, Jean L., "In Vitro Fertilization of Human Eggs: Bioethical and Legal Considerations." *Science* 182 (November 23, 1973), 811–814.

Ramsey, Paul, "Shall We 'Reproduce'?" *Journal of The American Medical Association* 220 (June 5, 1972), 1346–1350 and (June 12, 1972), 1480–1485.

Studdard, Albert, "The Morality of In Vitro Fertilization." *The Human Life Review* (Fall 1979), 41–55.

Walters, William, and Singer, Peter, eds., *Test-Tube Babies.* New York: Oxford University Press, 1982.

6   Anomalous Forms of Procreation

Etzioni, Amitai, *Genetic Fix: The Next Technological Revolution.*
New York: Harper & Row, 1973.
Francoeur, Robert T., *Utopian Motherhood.* New York: Doubleday,
1970.
Gaylin, Willard, "We Have the Awful Knowledge to Make Exact
Copies of Human Beings." *New York Times Magazine*, March 6,
1972, pp. 10ff.
Halacy, D.S., Jr., *Genetic Revolution: Shaping Life for Tomorrow.*
New York: New American Library, 1975.
Ramsey, Paul, *Fabricated Man: The Ethics of Genetic Control.* New
Haven: Yale University Press, 1970.
Rorvik, David, "The Embryo Sweepstakes." *New York Times Magazine*, September 15, 1974, pp. 16ff.
———, *In His Image: The Cloning of a Man.* Philadelphia: J.B. Lippincott Company, 1978.

7   Gene-Splicing, Genetic Engineering

Beers, Roland F., Jr., and Edward G. Bassett, eds., *Recombinant Molecules: Impact on Science and Society.* New York: Raven Press,
1977.
Berg, Paul, *et al.*, "Letter to the Editor—Potential Biohazards
of Recombinant DNA Molecules." *Science* 185 (July 26, 1974),
303.
———, Baltimore, David, Brenner, Sydney, Roblin, Richard O. III,
and Singer, Maxine F., "Asilomar Conference on Recombinant
DNA Molecules." *Science* 188 (June 6, 1975), 991–994.
Cohen, Stanley N., "Recombinant DNA: Fact and Fiction." *Science*
195 (February 18, 1977), 654–657.
Cooke, Robert, *Improving on Nature.* New York: Quadrangle, 1977.
Ellison, Craig, ed., *Modifying Man: Implications and Ethics.* Washington, D.C.: University Press of America, 1977.
English, Darrel S., ed., *Genetic and Reproductive Engineering.* New
York: MSS Information Corporation, 1974.
Goodfield, June, *Playing God: Genetic Engineering and the Manipulation of Life.* New York: Random House, 1977.

Griffin, Bryan, "Genetic Engineering: The Moral Challenge." *Human Life Review* 3 (Summer 1977), 30–39.

Hamilton, Michael P., ed., *The New Genetics and the Future of Man.* Grand Rapids, Mich.: Wm. B. Eerdmans Publishing Company, 1972.

Hanson, Earl D., ed., *Recombinant DNA Research and the Human Prospect.* Washington: American Chemical Society, 1983.

Howard, Ted, and Rifkin, Jeremy, *Who Should Play God?* New York: Dell Publishing Company, 1977.

Humber, James M., and Almeder, Robert F., eds., *Biomedical Ethics and the Law.* New York: Plenum Publishing Co., 1976.

Karp, L.E., *Genetic Engineering: Threat or Promise?* Chicago: Nelson-Hall Publishers, 1976.

Lappe, Marc, ed., *Ethical and Scientific Issues Posed by Human Uses of Molecular Genetics.* New York: The N.Y. Academy of Sciences, 1976.

Lipkin, Mack, Jr., and Rowley, Peter T., eds., *Genetic Responsibility.* New York: Plenum Press, 1974.

Mertens, Thomas R., *Human Genetics: Readings on the Implications of Genetic Engineering.* New York: John Wiley and Sons, 1975.

Milunsky, Aubrey, and Annas, George J., eds., *Genetics and the Law.* New York: Plenum Press, 1976.

Moraczewski, Albert S., ed., *Genetic Medicine and Engineering.* St. Louis: The Catholic Health Association of the United States, 1983.

Powledge, Tabitha M., "Recombinant DNA: The Argument Shifts." *Hastings Center Report* 7 (April 1977), 18–19.

President's Commission for the Study of Ethical Problems in Medicine and Biomedical and Behavioral Research, *Splicing Life.* Washington: U.S. Government Printing Office, 1982.

Reilly, Philip, *Genetics, Law, and Social Policy.* Cambridge: Harvard University Press, 1978.

Rogers, Michael, *Biohazard.* New York: Alfred A. Knopf, 1977.

Sills, Yole G., "Recombinant DNA: Debate Continues." *Hastings Center Report* 6 (August 1976), 9.

Smith, George, *Genetics, Ethics and the Law.* Gaithersberg, Md.: Associated Faculty Press, 1981.

Wade, Nicholas, *The Ultimate Experiment.* New York: Walker & Company, 1977.

8　Human Experimentation

Annas, George J., Glanz, Leonard H., and Katz, Barbara F., *Informed Consent to Human Experimentation: The Subject's Dilemma.* Cambridge, Mass.: The Ballinger Publishing Co., 1977.

Beecher, Henry K., *Research and the Individual: Human Studies.* Boston: Little, Brown & Company, 1970.

Berg, Kare and Tranoy, Knut Erik, eds., *Research Ethics.* New York: Alan R. Liss, Inc., 1983.

Bok, Sissela, "The Ethics of Giving Placebos." *Scientific American* 231 (November 1974), 17–23.

Cowles, Jane, *Informed Consent.* New York: Coward, McCann & Geoghegan, 1976.

Diener, Edward, and Crandall, Rick, *Ethics in Social and Behavioral Research.* Chicago: University of Chicago Press, 1978.

Experiments and Research with Humans: Values in Conflict. Washington, D.C.: National Academy of Sciences, 1975.

Gray, Bradford H. *Human Subjects in Medical Experimentation.* New York: John Wiley & Sons, 1975.

Hastings Center Report 5 (June 1975), 13–46. Special Issues on fetal research.

Hatfield, Frank, "Prison Research: The View from Inside." *Hastings Center Report* 7 (February 1977), 11–12.

Katz, Jay, ed. with Alexander M. Capron and Eleanor Swift Glass, *Experimentation with Human Beings.* New York: Russell Sage Foundation, 1972.

Levy, Charlotte L., *The Human Body and the Law: Legal and Ethical Considerations in Human Experimentation.* Dobbs Ferry, N.Y.: Oceana Publications, 1975.

McCormick, Richard A., "Fetal Research and Public Policy." *America* (June 21, 1975), 473–76.

Pappworth, M.H., *Human Guinea Pigs: Experimentation on Man.* Boston: Beacon Press, 1968.

President's Commission for the Study of Ethical Problems in Medicine and Biomedical and Behavioral Research, *Whistle-blowing in Biomedical Research.* Washington: U.S. Government Printing Office, 1981.

――――, *Implementing Human Research Regulations.* Washington: U.S. Government Printing Office, 1983.

Ramsey, Paul, *The Ethics of Fetal Research*. New Haven: Yale University Press, 1975.

Rosenthal, Robert, and Rosnow, Ralph L., *The Volunteer Subject*. New York: Wiley-Interscience, 1975.

9 Psychosurgery and Behavior Control

Annas, George J., "Psychosurgery: Procedural Safeguards." *Hastings Center Report* 7 (April 1977), 11–13.

Breggin, Peter Roger, *Electroshock: Its Brain-Disabling Effects*. New York: Springer, 1979.

Chorover, Stephen L., "Big Brother and Psychotechnology." *Psychology Today* 6 (October 1973), 43ff.

Delgado, Jose M.R., *Physical Control of the Mind: Toward a Psychocivilized Society*. New York: Harper & Row, 1969.

Gaylin, Willard, *Operating on the Mind*. New York: Basic Books, 1975.

———, "What's Normal?" *New York Times Magazine* (April 1, 1973), 14ff.

London, Perry, *Behavior Control*. 2nd edition. New York: The New American Library, 1977.

Macklin, Ruth, *Man, Mind, and Morality: The Ethics of Behavior Control*. Englewood Cliffs: Prentice-Hall, 1982.

Mark, Vernon H., and Ervin, Frank R., *Violence and the Brain*. New York: Harper & Row, 1970.

Menninger, Karl, *Whatever Became of Sin?* New York: Hawthorn Books, 1973.

National Commission for the Protection of Human Subjects of Biomedical and Behavioral Research. *Research Involving Psychosurgery—Report and Recommendation—With Appendix*. [Bethesda, Md.: USDHEW Publications No. (OS) 77–0001 and (OS) 77–0002; 14 March 1977].

Pines, Maya, *The Brain Changers: Scientists and the New Mind Control*. New York: Harcourt Brace Jovanovich, 1973.

Schrag, Peter, *Mind Control*. New York: Pantheon Books, 1978.

Schuman, Samuel I., *Psychosurgery and the Medical Control of Violence: Autonomy and Deviance*. Detroit: Wayne State University Press, 1977.

334   THE MAIN ISSUES IN BIOETHICS

Valenstein, Elliot S., *Brain Control: A Critical Examination of Brain Stimulation and Psychosurgery.* New York: Wiley-Interscience, 1973.
Valenstein, Elliot S., ed., *The Psychosurgery Debate: Scientific, Legal, and Ethical Perspectives.* San Francisco: W.H. Freeman, 1980.
Winter, Arthur, *Surgical Control of Behavior.* Springfield, Ill.: Charles C. Thomas Publisher, 1971.

10   Drugs and Behavior Control

Bloch, Sidney, and Chodoff, Paul, eds., *Psychiatric Ethics.* New York: Oxford University Press, 1981.
Brecher, Edward, ed., *The Consumers Union Report: Licit and Illicit Drugs.* Boston: Little, Brown & Company, 1972.
De Ropp, Robert S., *Drugs and the Mind.* Revised edition. New York: Delacorte Press, 1976.
Duster, Troy, *The Legislation of Morality: Law, Drugs and Moral Judgment.* New York: The Free Press, 1970.
Evans, Wayne, and Kline, Nathan S., *Psychotropic Drugs in the Year 2000: Use by Normal Humans.* Springfield, Ill.: Charles C. Thomas, Publisher, 1971.
Hyde, Margaret O., *Brainwashing and Other Forms of Mind Control.* New York: McGraw-Hill, 1977.
Klerman, Gerald L., "Psychotropic Drugs as Therapeutic Agents." *Hastings Center Studies* 2 (No. 1 for 1974), 81–93.
Lausch, Erwin, *Manipulation.* Glasgow: William Collins Sons and Company, 1974.
Musto, David, *The American Disease: Origins of Narcotic Control.* New Haven: Yale University Press, 1973.
Silverman, Milton, and Lee, Philip R., *Pills, Profits and Politics.* Berkeley: University of California Press, 1974.
Torrey, E. Fuller, *The Mind Game: Witchdoctors and Psychiatrists.* New York: Bantam Books, 1972.
United Nations Report, *Chemical and Bacteriological (Biological) Weapons and the Effects of Their Possible Use.* New York: Ballantine Books, 1970.

11 Organ Transplantation

Eastwood, R.T., *et al.*, *Cardiac Replacement: Medical, Ethical, Psychological and Economic Implications.* A Report by the Ad Hoc Task Force on Cardiac Replacement, National Heart Institute, National Institutes of Health. Washington, D.C.: U.S. Government Printing Office, 1969.

Jonsen, Albert R., "The Totally Implantable Artificial Heart." *Hastings Center Report* 3 (November 1973), 1–4.

Lyons, Catherine, *Organ Transplants: The Moral Issues.* Philadelphia: The Westminster Press, 1970.

Miller, George W., *Moral and Ethical Implications of Human Organ Transplants.* Springfield, Ill.: Charles C. Thomas, Publisher, 1971.

Moore, Francis D., *Give and Take: The Development of Tissue Transplantation.* Philadelphia: W.B. Saunders Company, 1964.

Sadler, Alfred M., Jr. and Sadler, Blair L., *Organ Transplantation: Current Medical and Medical-Legal Status: The Problems of an Opportunity.* Washington, D.C.: U.S. Government Printing Office, 1970.

Scott, Russel, *The Body as Property.* New York: Viking Press, 1981.

Simmons, Roberta G., *et al., Gift of Life: The Social and Psychological Impact of Organ Transplantation.* New York: John Wiley & Sons, 1977.

Wolstenholme, E.W., and O'Connor, Maeve, eds., *Ethics in Medical Progress: With Special Reference to Transplantation.* Boston: Little, Brown & Company, 1966.

12 Artificial Organs

American Heart Association Committee on Ethics, "Ethical Considerations of the Left Ventricular Assist Device." *Journal of the American Medical Association* 235 (February 23, 1976), 823–824.

Annas, George J., "Allocations of Artificial Hearts in the Year 2002: Minerva v. National Health Agency." *American Journal of Law and Medicine* 3 (Spring 1977), 59–76.

Foster, Lee, "Man and Machine: Life Without Kidneys." *Hastings Center Report* 6 (June 1976), 5–8.

Jarvik, Robert K., "The Total Artificial Heart." *Scientific American*, January, 1981.

Kaplan, Morris Bernard, "The Case of the Artificial Heart Panel." *Hastings Center Report* 5 (October 1975), 41–48.

Katz, Jay, and Capron, Alexander Morgan. *Catastrophic Diseases: Who Decides What? A Psychological and Legal Analysis of the Problems Posed by Hemodialysis and Organ Transplantation.* New York: Russell Sage Foundation, 1975.

Levy, Norman B., ed., *Living or Dying: Adaptation to Hemodialysis.* Springfield, Ill.: Charles C. Thomas, Publisher, 1974.

Schmeck, Harold M., Jr., *The Semi-Artificial Man: A Dawning Revolution in Medicine.* New York: Walker & Company, 1965.

"The Totally Implantable Artificial Heart." A Report by the Artificial Heart Assessment Panel, National Heart and Lung Institute, June 1973. National Heart and Lung Institute, National Institutes of Health, Bethesda, Maryland.

13   Sex Preselection and Sex Change

Dedek, John F., *Contemporary Medical Ethics.* New York: Sheed and Ward, 1975.

Etzioni, Amitai, *Genetic Fix: The Next Technological Revolution.* New York: Harper & Row, Publishers, 1973.

Gastonguay, Paul R. "Fetal Sex Determination." *America* (September 11, 1976), 123–124.

Greene, R., *Sexual Identity Conflict in Children and Adults.* New York: Basic Books, 1974.

Koranyi, Erwin, *Transsexuality in the Male.* Springfield: Thomas, 1980.

Lappe, Marc, "Choosing the Sex of Our Children." *Hastings Center Report* 4 (February 1974), 1–4.

Maccoby, Eleanor Emmons, and Jacklin, Carol Nagy, *The Psychology of Sex Differences.* Stanford: Stanford University Press, 1974.

"Marriage, Morality, & Sex-Change Surgery: Four Traditions in Case Ethics." *The Hastings Center Report,* August 1981, pp. 8–13.

Money, John, and Ehrhardt, Anke A., *Man and Woman, Boy and Girl: The Differentiation and Dimorphism of Gender Identity from Conception to Maturity.* Baltimore: Johns Hopkins University Press, 1972.

———, and Tucker, Patricia, *Sexual Signatures: On Being a Man or a Woman.* Boston: Little, Brown & Co., 1975.

Rorvik, David M. and Shettles, Landrum B., *Choose Your Baby's Sex.* Second edition. New York: Dodd, Mead and Company, 1977.

Westoff, Charles F. and Rindfuss, Ronald R., "Sex Preselection in the United States: Some Implications." *Science* 184 (May 10, 1974), 633–636.

Whelan, Elizabeth M., *Boy or Girl?* New York: Bobbs-Merrill, 1977.

14 Life and Death

A. *Aging and Health Care*

Barry, Vincent, *Moral Aspects of Health Care.* Belont, Cal.: Wadsworth Publishing Company, 1982.

Bier, William, ed., *Aging: Its Challenge to the Individual and to Society.* New York: Fordham University Press, 1974.

Binstock, Robert H., and Shanas, Ethel, *Handbook of Aging and the Social Services.* New York: Van Nostrand Reinhold Company, 1977.

Butler, Robert N., *Why Survive? Being Old in America.* New York: Harper & Row, 1975.

Fisher, D.H., *Growing Old in America.* New York: Oxford University Press, 1977.

Ginzberg, Eli, *The Limits of Health Reform: The Search for Realism.* New York: Basic Books, 1977.

Hayflick, Leonard, "The Biology of Human Aging." *American Journal of Medical Sciences* 265 (June 1973), 433–445.

Illich, Ivan, *Medical Nemesis.* New York: Pantheon Books, 1976.

Kart, Cary S., and Manard, Barbara B., *Aging in America: Readings in Social Gerontology.* Port Washington, N.Y.: Alfred Publishing Company, 1976.

Krause, Elliot A., *Power and Illness: The Political Sociology of Health and Medical Care.* New York: Elsevier, 1977.

Lewis, Charles E., *et al.*, *A Right to Health—The Problem of Access to Medical Care*. New York: John Wiley & Sons, 1976.

Neugarten, Bernice L., and Havighurst, Robert J., eds., *Extending the Human Life Span: Social Policy and Social Ethics*. Washington, D.C.: U.S. Government Printing Office, 1976.

President's Commission for the Study of Ethical Problems in Medicine and Biomedical and Behavioral Research, *Securing Access to Health Care*. Washington: U.S. Government Printing Office, 1983.

Rosenfeld, Albert, *Prolongevity*. New York: Alfred A. Knopf, 1976.

Schelp, Earl E., ed., *Justice and Health Care*. Dordrecht, Holland: D. Reidel Publishing Company, 1981.

Tancredi, Laurence, ed., *Ethics of Health Care*. Washington, D.C.: National Academy of Sciences, 1975.

B. *Care of the Dying, Death*

Annas, George J., *The Rights of Hospital Patients: The Basic ACLU Guide to a Hospital Patient's Rights*. New York: Avon Books, 1975.

Aries, Philippe, *Western Attitudes Toward Death: From the Middle Ages to the Present*. Trans. by Patricia M. Ranum. Baltimore: Johns Hopkins University Press, 1974.

Barton, David, ed., *Dying and Death: A Clinical Guide for Caregivers*. Baltimore: The Williams and Wilkins Company, 1977.

Becker, Ernest, *The Denial of Death*. New York: The Free Press, 1973.

Behnke, John A., and Bok, Sissela, *The Dilemmas of Euthanasia*. New York: Doubleday Anchor, 1975.

Bok, Sissela, *Lying: Moral Choices in Public and Private Life*. New York: Pantheon Books, 1978.

Boros, Ladislaus, *The Mystery of Death*. New York: Herder and Herder, 1965.

Cassell, Eric J., *The Healer's Art: A New Approach to the Doctor-Patient Relationship*. Philadelphia: J.B. Lippincott Company, 1976.

Choron, Jacques, *Death and Western Thought*. New York: Collier Books, 1973.

Corr, Charles A., and Corr, Donna M., eds., *Hospice Care: Principles and Practice*. New York: Springer Publishing Company, 1983.

Fletcher, John C., "Attitudes Towards Defective Newborns." *Hastings Center Studies* 2 (No. 1 for 1974), 21–32.

Harvard Medical School, Ad Hoc Committee of the Harvard Medical School to Examine the Definition of Brain Death, "A Definition of Irreversible Coma." *Journal of American Medical Association* 221 (July 3, 1972), 48–53.

Hendin, David, *Death as a Fact of Life*. New York: W.W. Norton & Co., 1973.

Horan, Dennis J., and Mall, David, eds., *Death, Dying and Euthanasia*. Washington, D.C.: University Publications of America, 1977.

Institute of Society, Ethics and the Life Sciences, Task Force on Death and Dying, "Refinements in Criteria for Determination of Death." *Journal of the American Medical Association* 221 (July 3, 1972), 48–53.

Jospe, Michael, *The Placebo Effect in Healing*. Lexington, Mass.: Lexington Books, 1978.

Kluge, Eike-Henner W., *The Ethics of Deliberate Death*. Port Washington, N.Y.: Kennikat Press, 1981.

Koff, Theodore H., *Hospice: A Caring Community*. Cambridge, Mass.: Winthrop Publ. Co., 1980.

Kohl, Marvin, ed., *Beneficent Euthanasia*. Buffalo: Prometheus Books, 1975.

Kübler-Ross, Elisabeth, *Death: The Final Stage of Growth*. Englewood Cliffs, N.J.: Prentice-Hall, 1975.

————, *On Death and Dying*. New York: Macmillan, 1969.

McCarthy, Donald G., and Moraczewski, Albert, eds., *Moral Responsibility in Prolonging Life Decisions*. St. Louis: Pope John XXIII Center, 1981.

McCormick, Richard, "The Quality of Life, the Sanctity of Life." *Hastings Center Report* 8 (February 1978), 30–36.

Maguire, Daniel C., *Death by Choice*. New York: Doubleday, 1974.

Morison, Robert, and Kass, Leon, "Death—Process or Event?" *Science* 173 (August 20, 1971), 694–702.

Oken, Donald, "What to Tell Cancer Patients?" *Journal of the American Medical Association* 175 (April 1, 1961), 1120–1128.

Pattison, E. Mansel, *The Experience of Dying*. Englewood Cliffs, N.J.: Prentice-Hall, 1977.

President's Commission for the Study of Ethical Problems in Medicine and Biomedical and Behavioral Research, *Defining Death*. Washington: Government Printing Office, 1981.

————, *Deciding to Forego Life-Sustaining Treatment*. Washington: Government Printing Office, 1983.

Russell, O. Ruth, *Freedom to Die: Moral and Legal Aspects of Euthanasia*. New York: Human Sciences Press, 1975.

Steinfels, Peter, and Veatch, Robert M., eds., *Death Inside Out*. New York: Harper & Row, 1975.

Standard, Samuel and Nathan, Helmuth, eds., *Should the Patient Know the Truth?* New York: Springer Publishing Co., 1955.

Stoddard, Sandol, *The Hospice Movement: A Better Way of Caring for the Dying*. New York: Stein & Day, 1978.

Veatch, Robert M., *Death, Dying and the Biological Revolution*. New Haven: Yale University Press, 1976.

Walton, Douglas N., *Brain Death: Ethical Considerations*. West Lafayette, Ind.: Purdue University Office of Publications, 1980.

Weber, Leonard J., *Who Shall Live? The Dilemma of Severely Handicapped Children and Its Meaning for Other Moral Questions*. New York: Paulist Press, 1976.

Weir, Robert F., ed., *Ethical Issues in Death and Dying*. New York: Columbia University Press.

Wilson, Jerry B., *Death By Decision: The Medical, Moral, and Legal Dimensions of Euthanasia*. Philadelphia: The Westminster Press, 1975.

15   The Ethics of Infant Euthanasia

Horan, Dennis J., and Delahoyde, Melinda, eds., *Infanticide and the Handicapped Newborn*. Provo, Utah: Brigham Young University Press, 1982.

Jonsen, Albert R., and Garland, Michael, eds., *Ethics of Newborn Intensive Care*. San Francisco and Berkeley: University of California School of Medicine and Institute of Governmental Studies, 1976.

Kohl, Marvin, ed., *Infanticide and the Value of Life*. Buffalo: Prometheus Books, 1979.

Roy, David, J., ed., *Medical Wisdom and Ethics in the Treatment of Severely Defective Newborn and Young Children*. St. Albans, Vt.: Eden Press, Inc., 1978.

Steinbock, Bonnie, ed., *Killing and Letting Die*. Englewood Cliffs, N.J.: Prentice-Hall, Inc., 1980.

Swinyard, Chester A., ed., *Decision Making and the Defective Newborn*. Springfield, Ill.: Charles C. Thomas, 1978.

Walton, Douglas N., *Ethics of Withdrawal of Life-Support Systems. Case Studies on Decision Making in Intensive Care*. Westport, Conn.: Greenwood Press, 1983.

Index